The
Fender
Telecaster
Handbook

For Brendan John Mark McCormack
1944–2009
Friend, teacher and 'Mind Scaffolding'

'Remember, it's just a plank of wood – **you** *have to find the music!'*

First published in 2009 by Voyageur Press, an imprint of MBI
Publishing Company, 400 First Avenue North, Suite 300,
Minneapolis, MN 55401 USA

Voyageur Press titles are also available at discounts in bulk
quantity for industrial or sales-promotional use. For details write
to Special Sales Manager at MBI Publishing Company, 400 First
Avenue North, Suite 300, Minneapolis, MN 55401 USA.

To find out more about our books, visit us online at
www.voyageurpress.com.

ISBN-13: 978-0-7603-3646-5

Printed and bound in England

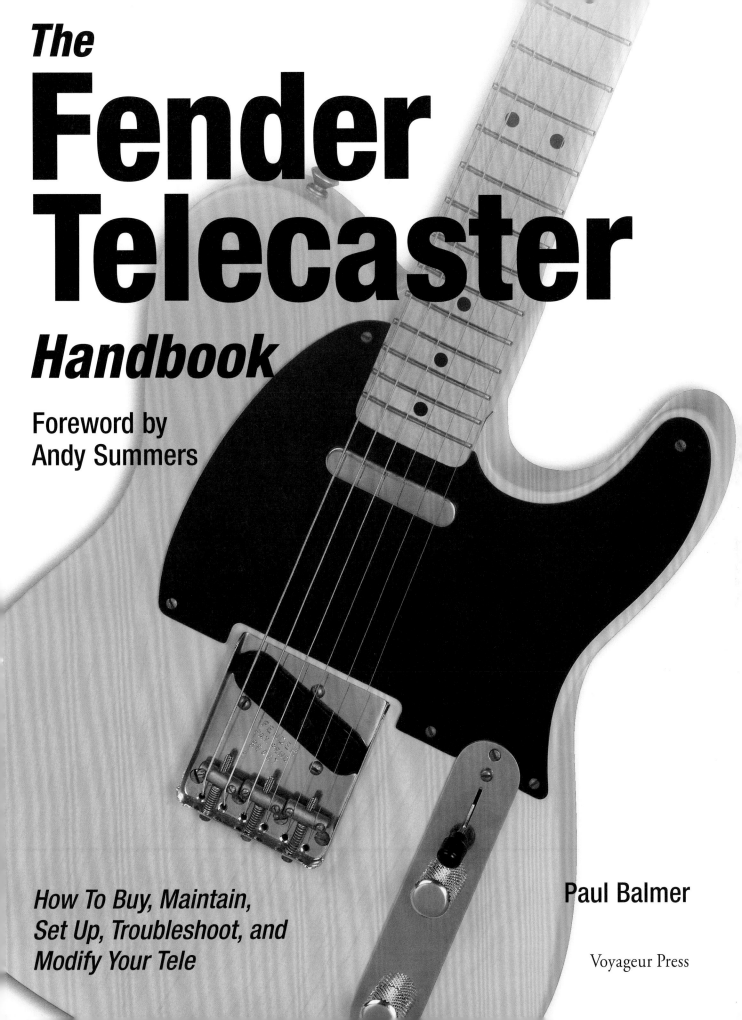

The Fender Telecaster
Handbook

Foreword by
Andy Summers

*How To Buy, Maintain,
Set Up, Troubleshoot, and
Modify Your Tele*

Paul Balmer

Voyageur Press

Contents

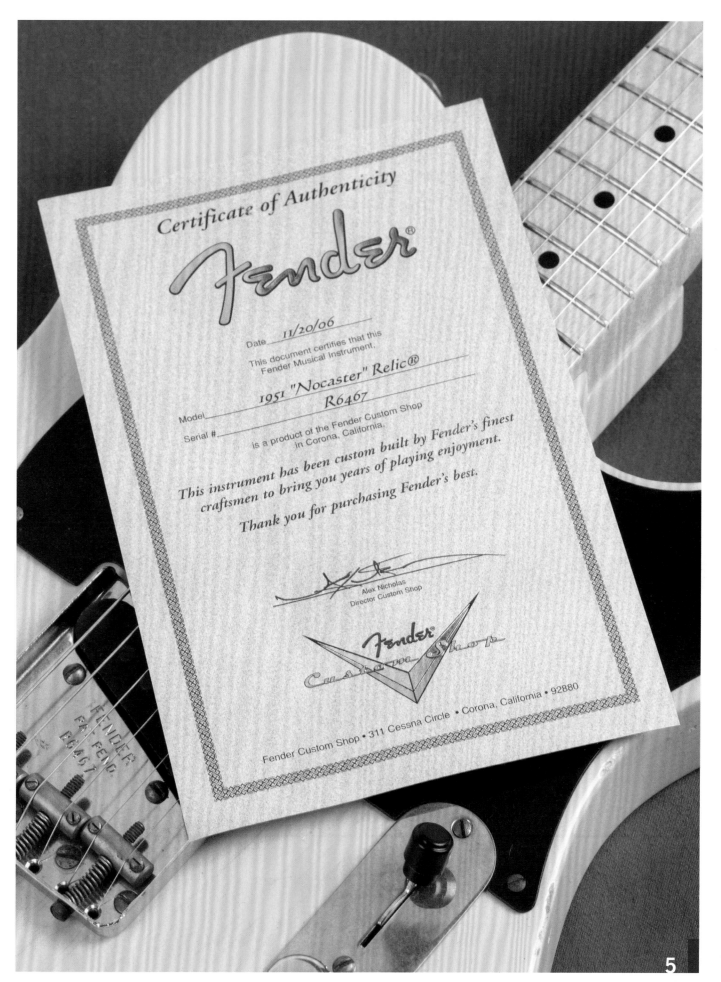

Foreword by Andy Summers

It was luck that early in my career, a period of impoverishment and nothing more than a bleak future, a battered old Telecaster came into my hands. Its outer appearance, beaten, scarred, and replete with artful modifications that would have shocked the purist, only made me love it more. It had soul.

As I started to play my old Telecaster, gig with it, practise on it, leave it in car trunks, jam with it, I began to feel that the arrow of life was pointing forward again. The guitar was bringing me luck... I realised I was entering a new phase, and it had something to do with this Telecaster. Like most players I had variously owned and tried other guitars, but somehow until this moment the magical bond hadn't happened, or put in a more prosaic way, I hadn't settled on one guitar.

Maybe it is overreaching to say that a few pieces of wood with metal strings can be a magnet for fortune, but with this guitar it suddenly seemed so. The point of this little love paean is to indicate that Leo Fender's Telecaster is one of the most perfect electric guitars ever devised; with its simple and to-the-point design, edgy silver sound and rudimentary controls, it is an instrument reduced to direct function, and therein lies its power.

Since its appearance on the commercial market in 1950, first as the Esquire, then the Broadcaster, the 'Nocaster' and finally, named after a new medium, the Telecaster, it has held its iconic position in the guitar world. Almost as if calling a spade a spade, Leo Fender simply sawed and routed his guitar bodies from slabs of wood, bolted them to the one-piece wood neck, added two electric pickups, overwound the bridge pick-up, and there you had it, a guitar for everyman. But despite its seemingly primitive construction, the Telecaster had a magic of its own. Guitarists were quick to identify its bridge pick-up tone, and the Telecaster sound was unleashed in 1950s America.

My own Telecaster, modified by a guitar nut, handy with electronics, was almost a forerunner of the way Fender themselves would play around with it in the years to come, so that in the end, rather than thinking of my own instrument as not being the real thing any more, it showed that its basic character held steadfast through everything.

Some years later, and after playing every conceivable gig with it, I still love this guitar that has proved its ability to sound right in just about every situation. The culmination of this love affair was a couple of years ago, when Fender gently asked me if I still had my original Tele. I bristled at the thought of being without it and replied in the affirmative. They asked if they might reproduce it in all its wounded glory. Naturally I felt honoured that this moment had arrived, and thinking of the inestimable service that this guitar had done, what it had brought into the world, it seemed justified. But, this being said, it was a rather strange moment when I actually saw the first reproduction. My guitar, which I had always thought of as a unique instrument, had been cloned, right down to the tiniest piece of scratched paint. It was as if my old friend had finally given birth.

...but maybe that is the power of the Telecaster.

Andy Summers
October 2009

Introduction

Clarence Leonidas Fender conceived the idea for his first solid electro-Spanish guitar whilst repairing a conventional but crudely amplified *acoustic* guitar. Such 'lash-ups' were common in the 1940s and usually consisted of a primitive magnetic or crystal microphone screwed or suspended in the sound hole of a standard guitar.

These 'Heath Robinson' concoctions were fraught with problems, the principal one being acoustic feedback: the pickup sound, amplified through a loudspeaker, is reheard by the pickup and reamplified in an exponential loop of disastrous squealing – a stage performer's nightmare.

Leo had seen solutions to this specific problem in the solid body of Adolph Rickenbacker and George Beauchamp's 1930s 'Frying Pan', as well as Les Paul's 'Log' and Paul Bigsby's 1948 'Merle Travis'. These all diverged from the resonating sound box concept of the 'Spanish' guitar. However, they were all too complex for factory production and, frankly, pig ugly. Still to be seen in the Roy Acuff Museum in Nashville Tennessee, Leo had in fact built his own ugly prototype Spanish 'oak log' guitar as early as 1943.

The genius of Leo would be to combine all the essential ingredients for a solid 'electric Spanish' in an easily maintained, playable, mass production model. All the prototypes mentioned above, including his own, had sort of worked, but in 1949 Leo simplified the concept and married it to a cool futuristic design.

But he was, in his own words, adapting 'a proven item'. His own 'Champion' Lap Steel – same colour, same controls same bridge and pickup relationship – is in fact the embryonic Telecaster!

By the late 1940s there was also a clear commercial opportunity, brought to Leo's attention by salesman Charlie Hayes: 'Western swing players *wanted* a louder guitar that would make it feasible for their instrument to take a solo alongside louder banjos and steel guitars. Leo Fender *always* listened to musicians and gave them what they wanted.'

Something Leo addressed in his first 'Tele'-shaped prototype was accurate intonation across six strings of varying thickness – less of an issue on an acoustic guitar, but amplified and heard loud

> " We wanted a standard guitar that had a little bit more of the sound of the steel guitar. "
>
> *Leo Fender*

Early Martin/Fender experimental guitar

Below: Fender Champion controls and bridge

Prototype Telecaster

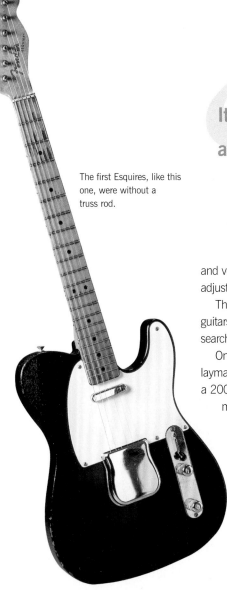

The first Esquires, like this one, were without a truss rod.

'It isn't a radically different thing that becomes a success; it is the thing that offers an improvement on an already proven item.'

Leo Fender

and very clear on his prototypes. Leo's solution adopted the now familiar three-saddle adjustable bridge.

The idea of a *combined* bridge and pickup also evolved from his 'Hawaiian' steel guitars and may have been born more from minimal assembly principles than the search for a new sound.

One of the most extraordinary aspects of the Tele is its immaculate conception – a layman might mistake the second 1949 prototype, with the now iconic headstock, for a 2009 '50s Vibe Squier Tele – all the key elements are there, and ironically both are made of pine. Cheap, simple to maintain, the guitar immediately had a distinctive voice of its own. Ash, maple, rosewood and alder would come later.

Though conceived and designed for the world of western swing, gingham frocks and cowboy hats, the Tele has found a home in every style of popular music. The familiar bite of that bridge pickup is just as at home in the diverse styles of early adopters Jimmy Bryant, Clarence Gatemouth Brown and Paul Burlison as well as the great blues of Roy Buchanan, the virtuoso country of Albert Lee, Jerry Donahue and Elvis's chosen guitar player James Burton.

The later addition of a humbucker pickup at the neck gave the Tele yet another voice, diversely gritty in the hands of Albert Collins, The Police's Andy Summers and Rolling Stone Keith Richards.

As if these solo uses were not enough, the Tele is THE electric rhythm guitar – Steve Cropper with Stax, Johnny Cash guitarist Luther Perkins, pop goddess Chrissie Hynde and Bruce Springsteen…the Telecaster's familiar offbeat percussive chime provides the 'chop' that has launched a thousand hits.

The Tele is simply one of the most versatile electric guitars ever. Consider the solos on *Hey Joe* and *Purple Haze*, classic Jimi Hendrix tones that send many a guitar player out in search of a late '60s 'upside-down' Strat – according to effects wizard Roger Mayer these solos were actually played on a Fender Telecaster borrowed from bandmate Noel Redding!

Champion lap steel guitar details.

A good investment

Wholesale price in 1950 $69 and 98 cents! Now changing hands for £15,000 plus. It's a great guitar and with a little maintenance will carry on rocking for another 50 years.

A classic Telecaster

This 'exploded' Tele – a '51 Nocaster Relic from 2008 – demonstrates that all the essential elements of Leo Fender's original conception have changed little in over half a century.

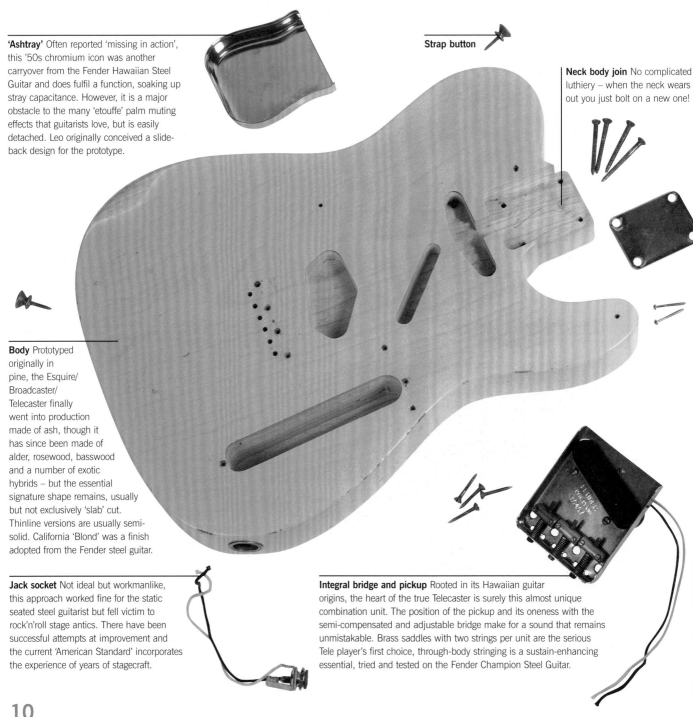

'Ashtray' Often reported 'missing in action', this '50s chromium icon was another carryover from the Fender Hawaiian Steel Guitar and does fulfil a function, soaking up stray capacitance. However, it is a major obstacle to the many 'etouffe' palm muting effects that guitarists love, but is easily detached. Leo originally conceived a slide-back design for the prototype.

Strap button

Neck body join No complicated luthiery – when the neck wears out you just bolt on a new one!

Body Prototyped originally in pine, the Esquire/Broadcaster/Telecaster finally went into production made of ash, though it has since been made of alder, rosewood, basswood and a number of exotic hybrids – but the essential signature shape remains, usually but not exclusively 'slab' cut. Thinline versions are usually semi-solid. California 'Blond' was a finish adopted from the Fender steel guitar.

Jack socket Not ideal but workmanlike, this approach worked fine for the static seated steel guitarist but fell victim to rock'n'roll stage antics. There have been successful attempts at improvement and the current 'American Standard' incorporates the experience of years of stagecraft.

Integral bridge and pickup Rooted in its Hawaiian guitar origins, the heart of the true Telecaster is surely this almost unique combination unit. The position of the pickup and its oneness with the semi-compensated and adjustable bridge make for a sound that remains unmistakable. Brass saddles with two strings per unit are the serious Tele player's first choice, through-body stringing is a sustain-enhancing essential, tried and tested on the Fender Champion Steel Guitar.

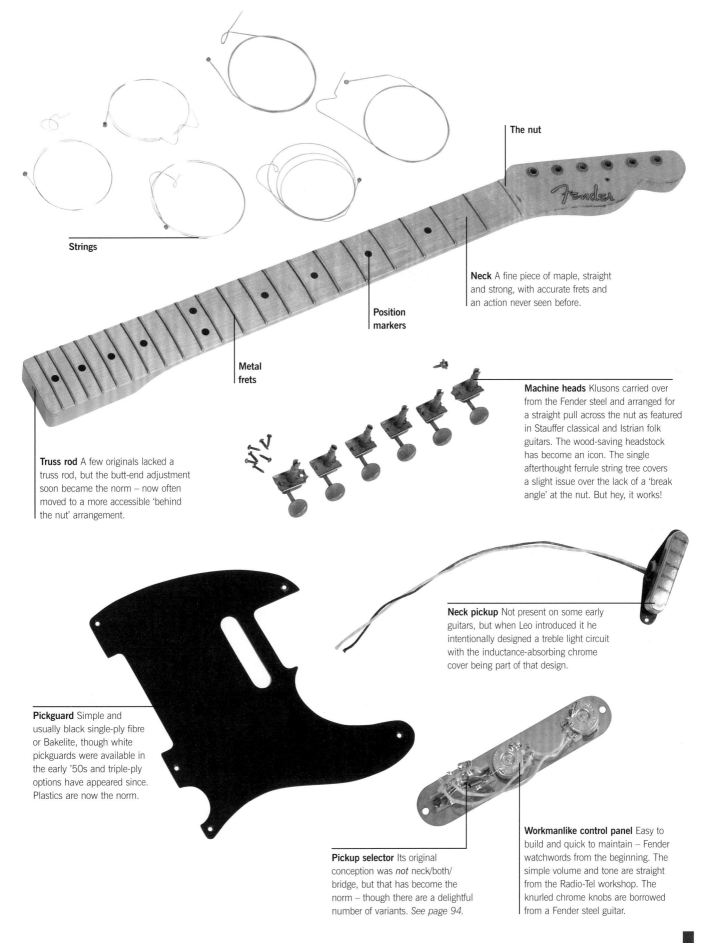

The nut

Strings

Neck A fine piece of maple, straight and strong, with accurate frets and an action never seen before.

Position markers

Metal frets

Truss rod A few originals lacked a truss rod, but the butt-end adjustment soon became the norm – now often moved to a more accessible 'behind the nut' arrangement.

Machine heads Klusons carried over from the Fender steel and arranged for a straight pull across the nut as featured in Stauffer classical and Istrian folk guitars. The wood-saving headstock has become an icon. The single afterthought ferrule string tree covers a slight issue over the lack of a 'break angle' at the nut. But hey, it works!

Neck pickup Not present on some early guitars, but when Leo introduced it he intentionally designed a treble light circuit with the inductance-absorbing chrome cover being part of that design.

Pickguard Simple and usually black single-ply fibre or Bakelite, though white pickguards were available in the early '50s and triple-ply options have appeared since. Plastics are now the norm.

Pickup selector Its original conception was *not* neck/both/ bridge, but that has become the norm – though there are a delightful number of variants. *See page 94.*

Workmanlike control panel Easy to build and quick to maintain – Fender watchwords from the beginning. The simple volume and tone are straight from the Radio-Tel workshop. The knurled chrome knobs are borrowed from a Fender steel guitar.

Buying a Fender Telecaster

1951 aside, there has never been a better time to buy a Telecaster. Whether your budget is limited to a Squier entry-level guitar or extends to a Custom Shop Relic, the classic shape remains the same, as do many of the details. The differences are largely in the timber, the component quality and the set-up. Generally the Custom Shop guitars are made from the finest woods and have a lot of handmade detail in their assembly. The USA 'Standards' have quite stringent quality control and you get a workmanlike instrument straight out of the box that may still benefit from a little fine tuning. The Squiers are fantastic value, invariably need a set-up and may benefit from a little hot-rodding before you commit to your first stadium gig.

LEFT 2008 American Standard.

RIGHT Squier '50s Vibe.

■ Fender Squier Telecasters

The current Squiers set a very high standard for entry-level guitars. Made in the Far East, they utilise a range of more economical and eco-friendly timbers including, ironically, the pine Leo Fender chose for his frugal prototypes. They come in a range of finishes to suit all tastes and include Vintage Vibe '50s-type guitars alongside celebrity Signature models. A little attention from a good luthier and the installation of a couple of high-grade pickups will produce a working professional instrument for a very small financial investment.

■ The American Standard

Subject to constant refinement this is the benchmark Tele, made in the USA and designed to be a workmanlike instrument for professional use. Finish options and left-handers are widely available. Leo Fender would likely have approved this no-nonsense 'refined' guitar. Though the details will change these are the basic specs:

1.The headstock end truss rod Modern behind-the-nut truss rod access, adjustable without removing or loosening the neck.

A '50s vibe Squier Telecaster   An American Standard Telecaster

2. Six saddles This is a controversial topic for the Tele, as many players prefer (with good reason) the original three-saddle arrangement. For more on this see the Jerry Donahue case study and interview. No 'ashtray' provision is available or possible on the redesigned bridge plate.

3. A conventional three-way selector Not Leo's original concept, but of the '50s, very simple and effective.

4. Modern polyurethane finishes There are good environmental and health arguments for the more durable polyurethane finishes – but purists won't settle for plastics.

5. Modern hardware including a modern low-friction string tree and Micro-Tilt neck adjustment – practical refinements on a classic concept.

6. 'Delta Tone' EQ options Many players like the straight-ahead sound that results from bypassing the EQ wiring – so here it is at the flip of a knurly knob!

Vintage reissues

American vintage '52s feature all the classic ash-bodied, maple-necked Tele Vibe with modern computer-assisted accuracy and consistency. The '62 Vintage offers a rosewood fingerboard, custom colours and a three-ply pickguard. Great affordable classics which are also available left-handed. They all come in matching period-correct tweed and vinyl cases – sumptuous.

American Deluxe

An update that includes 'S1 switching' for series/parallel options on the pickup routing. A modern polyurethane finish, more chrome, less brass but retaining the Vintage U-shaped neck. Modern samarium cobalt noiseless Tele pickups are fitted as standard on this and the Custom Deluxe, which has a bound body and Fender/Schaller Deluxe Staggered Cast/Sealed Tuning Machines.

Custom Shop

The Corona Custom Shop offer 'team-built' classics in limited runs alongside Masterbuilt one-offs in just about any colour or timber that takes your fancy. They also do a run of Nocasters and Esquires perfectly emulating what might have appeared in 1950–1, including the original eccentricities of EQ and pickup windings – irresistible!

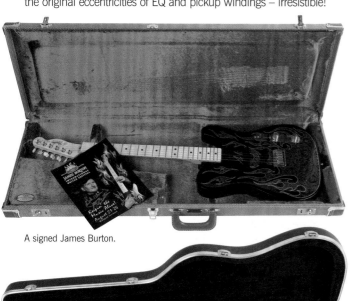

A signed James Burton.

A 'Partscaster'
(see Case studies).

Relics

These are new but 'worn-in' replicas of '50s and '60s classics. Also made by the Custom Shop, these guitars feature distressed ash and alder bodies, rusty straight-slot screws and faded pickups – all available on a bank loan rather than a second mortgage.

Closet Classics

Also distressed but not 'gigged', as if you had found the guitar in Grandpa's closet, like something he bought in the old days and forgot about – you wish!

N.O.S.

The original specification but newly built – hence 'New Old Stock' – the '50s or '60s Tele of your dreams *new*, just arrived in Bill and Ted's time machine from an era of innocence and chrome tail-finned Chevys.

'Road Worn'

The more affordable 'Relic', distressed on an assembly line to a tolerable amount of wear and tear. With some tasteful updates including 'Tex Mex' pickups and modern frets.

Signature series

These carry the signature of the classic Tele players, from James Burton to Merle Haggard and Jerry Donahue. They display that artist's favourite modifications and finish.

Tribute series

A Tribute series has kicked off with an exact replica of Andy Summers's heavily modified 'Custom' with a ferocious Humbucker and on-board preamp and extra knobs and toggle switches – *'Every Breath You Take I'll be watching you!'* Phone The Police if you break a tendon on those arpeggios.

Highway One and Vintage Hot Rods

Kinky variants with pickup and hardware options such as a 'grease bucket' tone circuit which rolls off the highs without adding bass and a Seymour Duncan humbucker pickup for that Albert Collins attack.

3 Second-hand Telecasters

It's very tempting to buy guitars online from a website, but I strongly suggest that buying a musical instrument may be a little too personal for this. No two guitars are exactly identical – wood varies and so do finish and set-up. To really know if a guitar is right for you, you should play it. If you are a beginner get a teacher to play it for you – he can advise on the pros and cons of an instrument appropriate for your stage of learning.

Also buy from someone who offers after-sales service – preferably a music shop, which will be able to help if two years down the line the guitar needs attention. Look for accreditation: is the shop affiliated to any of the retail trade associations, do they offer a guarantee?

Only buy privately if you really know guitars. The Tele is a classic and virtually every part you may need to replace is still currently available in at least a good replica form. The issues then become provenance and authenticity – is the guitar really what it seems? See 'Verifying authenticity' boxout on the facing page.

LEFT The Esquire of your dreams.

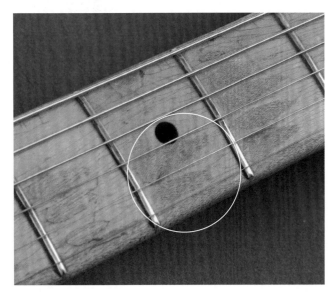

Some issues to address when buying second-hand

■ Corrosion of metal parts
Typical club playing conditions mean that electric guitars are exposed to a lot of condensation and sweat – parts will corrode and rust, but this need not be a serious problem given a little care and maintenance.

■ Fret wear
This can be a bit more of an issue, especially on a maple fingerboard, but is not insurmountable. Ask your dealer for a discount and perhaps an in-house or affiliated re-fret? Go for an authentic and appropriate fret type and gauge, especially on a vintage instrument. Failure to do so will result in a plummeting future valuation.

■ Fingerboard wear
A replacement fingerboard can be pricey and you will have to weigh up the value of the individual instrument plus the repair/replacement costs. Nothing is impossible, but some repairs are very labour intensive. Consult a luthier first before committing to a currently unplayable guitar.

■ Machine heads
These do fail but new ones are readily available. Look out for gaps in their compliance and over-stiff mechanisms.

■ Noisy pots and switches

This happens, especially on older guitars. The answer is cleaning or replacement – but keep the old pots for provenance.

■ Pickups

Are they working? Do they hum? Is the sound what you expect? Good replacements are readily available but a vintage guitar with modern pickups will lose some intrinsic collector value.

■ Missing parts

Loose attachments, such as the 'ashtray', often go astray from vintage guitars. Consider the replacement cost and factor in a discount.

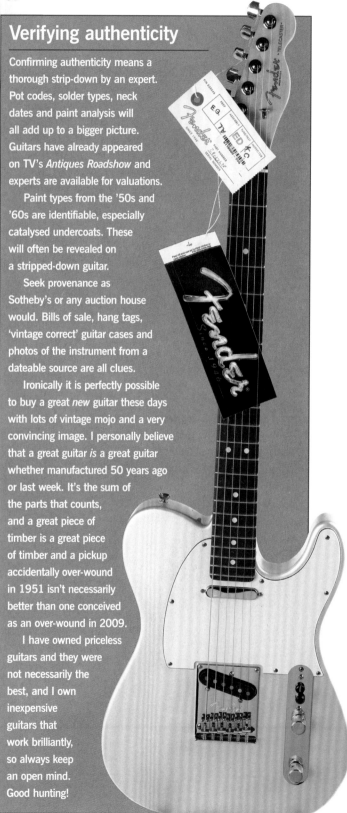

■ Authenticity

Buyer beware. As the vintage guitar market flourishes, unscrupulous individuals are stooping to all sorts of tricks to 'age' newer instruments – buying old pots with 1950s pot codes, buying cloth-covered wire or borrowing it from old radios, and so on. You may be asked for £24,000 for a '50s Tele, so the rogues have incentive!

An expert guitar tech will have seen a lot of guitars and will know the telltale signs of skulduggery, so consult one when buying a vintage guitar, just as you might consult an automobile association over a used car purchase.

Consider keeping an old guitar for special gigs and recordings and using a viable replica for rough stage handling. This is common practice amongst the rock and pop elite.

NB: *For valuable information on authenticating early Blackguard Teles 'The Blackguard' by Nacho Baños is invaluable.*

Verifying authenticity

Confirming authenticity means a thorough strip-down by an expert. Pot codes, solder types, neck dates and paint analysis will all add up to a bigger picture. Guitars have already appeared on TV's *Antiques Roadshow* and experts are available for valuations.

Paint types from the '50s and '60s are identifiable, especially catalysed undercoats. These will often be revealed on a stripped-down guitar.

Seek provenance as Sotheby's or any auction house would. Bills of sale, hang tags, 'vintage correct' guitar cases and photos of the instrument from a dateable source are all clues.

Ironically it is perfectly possible to buy a great *new* guitar these days with lots of vintage mojo and a very convincing image. I personally believe that a great guitar *is* a great guitar whether manufactured 50 years ago or last week. It's the sum of the parts that counts, and a great piece of timber is a great piece of timber and a pickup accidentally over-wound in 1951 isn't necessarily better than one conceived as an over-wound in 2009.

I have owned priceless guitars and they were not necessarily the best, and I own inexpensive guitars that work brilliantly, so always keep an open mind. Good hunting!

Know your Vintage Tele/Esquire

The guitar we now know as the classic early Telecaster actually evolved through two prototypes and four production models – a one-pickup Esquire, the two-pickup Broadcaster and 'Nocaster' and a few rare two-pickup Esquires. All these minor variants have a common genesis in Leo Fender's concept of an electro-Spanish guitar based on his successful Lap Steel Guitar. The features that evolved from the Lap Steel include through stringing, an integral bridge and pickup, Kluson tuners with a 'straight' string pull and a chrome 'ashtray' to hide the obvious mechanics of the bridge.

LEFT Typical 'Relic'.

RIGHT '51 Nocaster.

LEFT No dust on this fingerboard!

■ Slab construction

The simple Tele is, as its derogators say, 'a plank of wood' – usually ash – a practical rigid anchor for the strings with a nod towards conventional guitar shape. The 'plank' isn't always one piece and the ever practical Leo never insisted on this. Two pieces of wood can be more stable and have a lower fundamental frequency – an advantage.

■ Maple neck

The first Esquires had a one-piece maple neck/fingerboard with a radius of approximately 7.25in (184mm). The maple neck was clear, novel, exciting and radical, and when it wore out Leo could mail you a new one in a postal tube. This and every other part of the guitar is held together with regular straight-slot woodworker or machine screws.

■ Single radical cutaway

Though there had been many previous references to fingerboard access beyond the 12th fret, Leo, from his first prototype and clearly in response to players' ideas, gave good access to the 21st fret. This bold step gave players an unprecedented freedom and that higher octave soon became legitimate musical territory.

■ 21 accessible frets

Giving a top C# in the guitar's home key of E – this is enough for most mortals! You *can* have two octaves of frets, but you then lose the position of the neck pickup at the critical second octave harmonic. If you want high E on a Tele you just bend the string – which sounds more interesting.

■ Nut

There had never been such a narrow, skinny or low nut, and it made playing seem child's play.

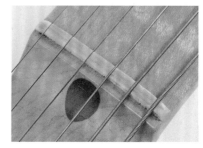

LEFT '51 Relic.

■ Adjustable truss rod

The first Esquires had no truss rod, but Leo's colleague Don Randall insisted on the installation of one, following the advice of Al Frost – the Gibson patent had just expired, and no gigging guitar should be without one. The original butt-end adjustment slot isn't very accessible.

■ Position markers

These were $\frac{1}{4}$in and black on most Maple necks and were much appreciated by players not yet familiar with this radical access to the previously dusty end of the fingerboard. The 12th fret spacing of the two dots changed in 1952 from $\frac{5}{8}$in to a slightly more aesthetically pleasing $\frac{3}{16}$in wider, thus lining up with the strings.

■ Saddles in detail

The 'vintage' saddle varies according to year. Early 1950 guitars have steel saddles, whereas the depicted '51 form is brass with no string slots. During the '50s other variants appeared with steel saddles and also threaded and individual string grooves. Some late '50s versions have notches just for the two E strings. The bridge is semi-adjustable with both intonation and height compromised by the 'two strings per saddle' sharing arrangement. Many players prefer this compromise, citing better downward pressure from two strings giving a sturdier fix and better tone.

■ Body mounted jack-socket

This seems logically placed but wasn't always a success – the original design is prone to dropping out at the wrong moment! However, slight modifications have ensured fewer disasters.

■ Integral bridge and pickup with through stringing

All borrowed from Leo's steel guitars and probably designed as much for ease of assembly as anything else. However, this close relationship establishes the Tele's classic sound with a strong affinity to its steel guitar roots. The three-saddle semi-adjustable brass bridge is important both for intonation and string radius and is found on most classic Teles. The first prototype had a slide-away metal bridge cover, so Leo was not unaware of a Spanish guitarist's need to achieve palm muting, or 'etouffe' as it was then called. The first Esquires and Teles had a removable 'ashtray'. This absorbs stray capacitance and subtly alters the guitar's sound.

■ Strap buttons

The Telecaster was born to western swing and sits nicely balanced on its often flimsy '50s guitar straps.

■ String guide

Leo Fender was soon alerted to the need for more downward pressure at the nut on the first and second strings and fixed it practically 'while you wait' with a screw and a handy ferrule. Later guitars have more sophisticated arrangements.

■ Two 'different' pickups

Leo was keen to have a two-pickup guitar as rivals appeared with two and three-pickup arrangements. However, he reasonably felt that these pickups should have markedly different tones. So although the two pickups are very similar in construction they have different coil wire gauges, a different number of windings and a consequent different 'Q' or audio frequency peak. Additionally the two pickups are handled differently at the resistive capacitor EQ stage (tone controls). As if this wasn't enough the chrome cover on the neck pickup isn't just cosmetic – it soaks up stray capacitance, diminishing some high frequencies. The neck pickup is positioned exactly at the point of the open string second octave harmonic, and the bridge pickup is angled to favour a little more of the bass frequencies. The early guitars have no pole-piece compensation – all the poles are the same height. This changed by 1955 as players noticed the different magnetic responses of different gauge strings and Leo accommodated the need for change.

■ Enclosed machine heads

These Kluson tuners had previously featured on Fender steel guitars and the first prototype Esquire has the conventional 'three each side of the headstock' arrangement. From the second prototype onwards the Tele has had this distinctive six-in-a-row 'straight pull' design. Leo says he borrowed the idea from Istrian folk guitars and he'd also certainly seen Paul Bigsby's Merle Travis prototype solid guitar, which employed the same idea.

■ Three-way pickup selector

Though now familiar and taken for granted, in 1950 its integration into an easy-assemble module was both novel and useful. Note that the early two-pickup Esquires, and Broadcasters and Nocasters, had a unique switching arrangement that was not at all what you might expect. The forward or neck position had an extra capacitor in circuit for bass guitar impressions (Leo thought guitarists might replace bass players, and he was right, but they would take up his precision bass in 1951 and not this rear pickup option). Middle switch position gave the neck pickup without the extra capacitance – a normal sound, though still mellow due to the chrome cover soaking up stray capacitance. The 'back' position, with the knurled blend knob flat out, gave the bridge pickup alone, and as it was turned anticlockwise the neck pickup was blended in for a mellower sound. Brilliant and very 21st century, but too far ahead of its time for '50s western swing.

■ Volume and 'blend' potentiometers

Extraordinary as it may now seem these early electric guitars had no tone control but instead had a volume and 'mix' control, as well as some novel resistive capacitor circuits. Guitarists found it all too complicated and the arrangement was altered in 1952, giving 'bass' guitar in the neck position, neck pickup with tone control in the middle position and bridge pickup with tone control in the back position. The conventional three-position switch arrangement didn't arrive on the Tele until 1967! In the meantime many working Teles were custom modified.

■ Four-bolt neck

A radical notion in 1950, in a world where guitars were hand-glued by luthiers, not parts-assembled as per Leo's 'model T Ford'.

■ Five-screw pickguard

Made of fibrous Bakelite these single ply boards are not yet an integral part of the electrics assembly – they are simple, cosmetic, practical and usually black, though there *are* a few early '50s Teles with white boards. White became the norm in 1954 and the triple-ply board arrived in 1959.

■ The logo

Shown here in its unofficial 'Nocaster' form, but also seen with Broadcaster, Telecaster and Esquire attributions.

Bakelite

'Bakelite' is the Union Carbide trademarked name for a phenolic 'resinoid varnish' impregnated paper fibre composite material, an early (and *cheap*...) form of plastic. It was commonly used in the past to make telephones, radio cases, bowling balls and many other consumer and industrial items – including guitar pickguards. The 1941 *Electrical Buyers Reference* explains that 'Laminated products are fabricated from superimposed layers of paper, canvas, cotton duck, or asbestos fabric impregnated with Bakelite resinoid varnishes and hardened by heat and pressure. Characterized by unusual strength, resiliency and toughness, Bakelite laminates possess high dielectric strength; are exceptionally resistant to heat, water, oil and most chemicals. Will not warp nor deteriorate with age. Extensively employed for radio and electrical insulation, instrument panels, etc.'

Know your American Standard

The American Standard has been in a state of evolution since its introduction in 1988. Intended to reflect the best of current standard American production, the guitar retains the essence of the original alongside all the accumulated wisdom of the almost 60 intervening years. The present guitar remains simple, effective and rugged – no frills, just built to boogie. Whether you think the current Standard is a *better* guitar or not is up to you *and you still have the choice*, with everything including a '51 spec still available. Extraordinary! Imagine the look you might get trying to buy a '51 spec car or washing machine?

LEFT The 'no ashtray' bridge.

RIGHT An American Standard.

■ Vintage '52 body shape
In the past the classic Tele shape had occasionally been distorted by misaligned jigs and cutters – the American Standard reverses the trend.

■ Solid slab construction
Currently made of alder and with a new thinner urethane finish. There *have* been contoured Teles, but that's gilding the lily.

■ 22 medium 'jumbo' frets
More substantial than the vintage wire, and with the extra semitone giving top 'D' the minor or flattened 7th in the home key of E.

■ Position markers on a rosewood fingerboard
The Standard is also available with a more traditional maple fingerboard but the simple dot markers remain. 'Clay' or Pearloid dots all do the same job. A bigger 9.5in (241mm) fingerboard radius accommodates modern playing styles without too much chocking on string bends. The Standard has sometimes had a 12in (305mm) radius. The tougher rosewood fingerboard first appeared in 1959. The neck itself has a modern 'C' shape.

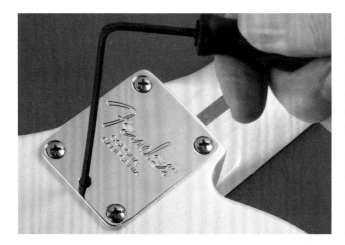

■ Integral bridge and pickup

This fundamental aspect of the Tele has been tinkered with on other models but the Standard returns to basics on a new bridge, with improved bent-steel saddles mounted to a stamped-brass bridge plate for increased resonance and sustain. Six saddles make for a Stratocaster-like appearance and many players like the improved flexibility of adjustment. However, traditionalists prefer the old three-saddle bridge (this being available on Vintage reissues and Relics). The 'ashtray' has been discarded and there is no lip to retain it (nobody smokes any more!). Though occasionally absent on some Teles, 'through stringing' is firmly applied on the American Standard.

■ Four-bolt neck with Micro-Tilt

In the bad old days a dodgy neck slot or consequent bad neck angle was solved with a primitive shim of wood. The Micro-Tilt arrangement provides precise adjustment.

■ Better truss rod access

Access at the nut is more convenient, with no need to part unbolt the neck.

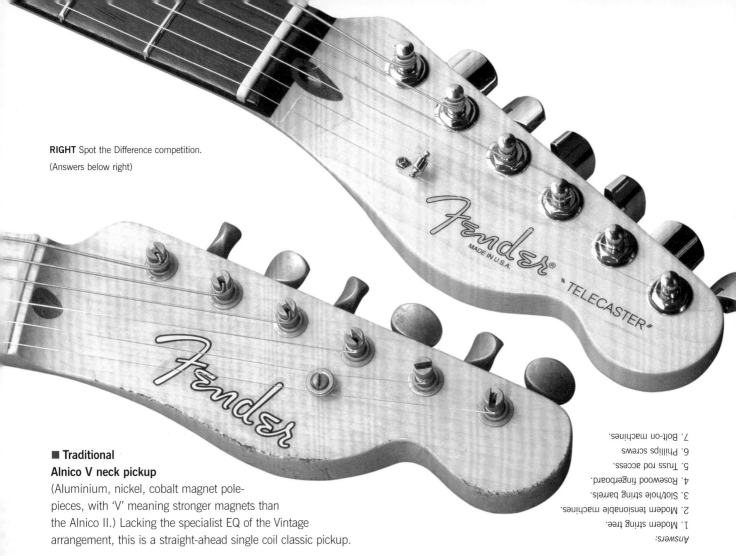

RIGHT Spot the Difference competition.
(Answers below right)

Answers:

1. Modern string tree.
2. Modern tensionable machines.
3. Slot/hole string barrels.
4. Rosewood fingerboard.
5. Truss rod access.
6. Phillips screws
7. Bolt-on machines.

■ Traditional
Alnico V neck pickup

(Aluminium, nickel, cobalt magnet pole-pieces, with 'V' meaning stronger magnets than the Alnico II.) Lacking the specialist EQ of the Vintage arrangement, this is a straight-ahead single coil classic pickup.

■ Modern machine heads

Staggered for a better string angle at the nut, bolted for stability, and with a better gearing ratio than the vintage Klusons.

■ Modern design string tree

The simple ferrule and screw of the Vintage model has now been superseded by an elegant polished designer 'tree'.

■ Phillips screws

Since 1952 most Teles have had assembly-line-friendly Phillips screws in all but the control knobs, which require an Allen key.

■ Simple electrics with 'Delta Tone'
Ironically the Tele electrics have gradually
become simpler and *more* minimal. The
complicated blend facility of the Vintage
guitar has been rationalised to one volume
one tone and a conventional three-position
switch. 'Delta Tone' provides an end détente
on the tone control that puts even that out
of circuit – for straight-ahead rocking.

■ Three-ply pickguard
The old single-ply boards tended to buckle
and crack, and the addition of extra layers
and three more screws makes for
a neater finish.

■ Jack socket
More secure than
the Vintage spec.

Setting up and tuning

Having played hundreds of guitars old and new, I firmly believe the set-up on a guitar is much more important than the vintage or the price tag. A well set-up budget Squier is a far more useful instrument than a poorly set-up '51 Nocaster. Most importantly, a poorly set-up guitar is impossible to get in tune.

LEFT Checking for neck relief.

RIGHT A '50s Vibe Squier

1 Bridge adjustment

Setting the string height

Three-saddle type
(Early Esquires, Broadcasters, Nocasters & Vintage reissues)
What we see in the classic Telecaster bridge is an early attempt at an engineering solution to the problems of 'electric Spanish' guitar intonation and compensation for a (then relatively novel) curved fingerboard radius.

One of the problems raised by the clarity of the Broadcaster sound – a real shock in 1950 – is that any intonation discrepancies stand out as never before. Leo tried to solve this with a 'two strings per saddle' approach to bridge intonation setting. Ironically this *does* have advantages over both a universal saddle and an 'individual saddle per string' approach. However, setting up these 'compromise' saddles does involve some extra thought.

Note too that there are many types of Vintage saddles – brass without any string grooves, brass and steel with grooves and steel with multiple grooves are the most common. Leo added the grooves because players complained that sometimes unfettered strings would catch on the height grub screws, producing an interesting sitar-like effect that was not ideal for western swing!

Innovation
Leo Fender wasn't alone in trying to improve electric guitar intonation and alignment. The Gretsch company would introduce *individual* string length adjustment in 1952 with the six-saddle Melita Synchro-sonic bridge designed by Sebastiano (Johnny) Melita, and Gibson introduced their 'Tunomatic' bridge circa 1953.

■ Action
Before making any adjustment, it is extremely important to note that a guitar's 'string action' is affected by a complex interplay of factors, *not* just the saddle height setting. Factors to consider are:

■ The nut height setting and individual nut grooves.
■ Neck relief – is the neck flat, convex or, ideally, slightly concave along its length?
■ Fret wear – are the frets correctly 'stoned' to shape or is wear causing them to become uneven?
■ The fingerboard radius – is this reflected in the individual bridge saddle alignment?
■ Does the neck/body angle – as determined by shims or by Micro-Tilt adjustment in later post-Vintage Teles – require attention?
■ String gauges – are these appropriate and matched as a set?

All these issues are addressed below.

■ So why might you want to adjust paired string heights?
The most likely reason is to correctly reflect the radius of the fingerboard, but it might simply be because you are curious. Leo would approve – he built his whole Fender guitar concept around satisfying individual players' requirements. This built-in versatility has resulted in one genius design being used happily by players as diverse as James Burton, Andy Summers and Jerry Donahue.

More likely you are trying to achieve a lower more playable action or are experimenting with string gauges. Following a change of gauges – particularly moving up to a heavier gauge – you may observe that the neck has become more concave along its length, or 'done a Robin Hood', as it is sometimes affectionately described. You may first need to adjust the truss rod to compensate for this. If you suspect this is the case

see page 81 for neck relief specifications and remedies. Having adjusted the truss rod it's likely you may also want to reset the string action for optimum playing comfort appropriate to your own style.

If you are playing bottleneck guitar you may need to set the strings quite high to avoid catching the frets with your slide. If you are playing slinky blues with a light picking style you may find a very 'low' action workable.

String height parameters eventually come down to personal taste and your individual sound. However, Leo did offer some recommendations for 'average' set-ups:

Neck radius	String height Bass side	String height Treble side
7.25in Vintage	$^5\!/_{64}$in/.0781in (2mm)	$^1\!/_{16}$in/.0625in (1.6mm)
9.5 to 12in	$^1\!/_{16}$in/.0625in (1.6mm)	$^1\!/_{16}$in/.0625in (1.6mm)
15 to 17in	$^1\!/_{16}$in/.0625in (1.6mm)	$^3\!/_{64}$in/.0469in (1.2mm)

For details of your specific Tele neck radius refer to the relevant case studies and/or the Fender website.

ABOVE Muddy Waters with his Mojo working.

■ The nut
Before adjusting the saddles it is also important to check the nut. A good guide for correct Tele nut-height for conventional playing (*ie* non-slide playing) is approximately .008–010in at the first fret. Check this by inserting a car feeler gauge (.010in) at the first fret. It should be a close fit but should not be lifting the string. If the nut is too high or too low, either generally or on one particular string, then refer to *'Adjusting the nut', page 82*.

■ You can adjust the sixth string bridge saddle to the Vintage ⁵⁄₆₄in height according to the Fender chart recommendations, then adjust the other bridge saddles to follow the neck radius as indicated by the appropriate proprietary under-string radius gauge.

1 Check the current action height at the 17th fret with the car feeler gauge. In practice this means combining several individual feeler gauges to make up ¹⁄₁₆in or the decimal equivalent value of .0625in. A Tele *will* work with a lower action than this but in certain playing styles it will be prone to a lot of fret buzz. Alternatively, using a 6in ruler (with ¹⁄₃₂ and ¹⁄₆₄in increments) measure the distance between the bottom of the strings and the top of the 17th fret.

2 Use the two pivot adjustment screws – requiring an Allen key on newer Teles or a 3mm straight-slot screwdriver on very early Vintage models – to achieve the desired overall string-height for the first and second strings at the 17th fret. Note that the Allen wrench size varies depending on the model. Modern reproductions use a 1.5mm. See the individual case studies for more on this.

■ **You will now need to retune the guitar**
Note that these recommended action settings and radius measurements are, of course, only a guide. You can obviously experiment with the individual saddle heights until *your* desired sound and feel is achieved.

Note that adjusting string *heights* affects the effective sounding *length* of the string and this naturally affects intonation, so you will now need to refer to *'Setting the working string lengths'* (opposite) to compensate for this.

It is also important to note that the magnetic field of the conventional Tele pickup can be strong enough to interfere with the strings' normal excursion and this can have further implications for accurate intonation. *See page 101 for more on this.*

Six-saddle type
(Most post-'70s Teles and American Standards)
All the set-up principles are naturally the same as the three-saddle, as outlined above – you just have more individual flexibility over string height and length.

1 Check the current string height as described above. Use the two pivot adjustment screws and an Allen key to achieve the desired overall string height for the first string at the 17th fret. Guide height is ¹⁄₁₆in on the modern radius. The Allen wrench size varies depending on the model – the American Standard uses a .050in. See the individual case studies for more on this.

■ You can adjust the sixth string bridge saddle to the ¹⁄₁₆in height according to the Fender chart recommendations, then adjust the other bridge saddles to follow the neck radius as indicated by the appropriate under-string radius gauge.

Setting the working string lengths

Three-saddle type
(Early Esquires, Broadcasters, Nocasters & Vintage reissues)
Leo Fender's original design incorporated the facility to adjust
paired string lengths.

■ **So why would you want to
do this?**

If the guitar has not been
maintained for some years or
if you have recently changed
your string gauges, you may
notice that as you ascend the
fingerboard in normal playing
the guitar does not sound
in tune. Adjusting the paired
saddle arrangement to correct this naturally involves
a compromise when contrasted with the individual saddles
of many modern guitars.

■ **A little background**
As you know, there are two basic ways of changing the pitch
of a vibrating guitar string – you can increase or decrease the
string tension by adjusting the machine heads, as in normal
tuning, or you can alter the string length by normal fretting on
the fingerboard.

The frets on the fingerboard are arranged in a mathematical
series of ascending decreasing intervals. The frets get closer
together as we ascend to what guitarist Martin Taylor refers to as
'the dusty end of the fingerboard'. We won't get bogged down in
the maths here.

The assumption of the correct function of the carefully
worked-out fret intervals is that the string itself has a defined
length. If all your guitar's strings were the same gauge or
thickness we could dispense with Leo's innovation and simply
have a straight line arrangement of the bridge saddles.

In the real world your first string could be .009 gauge and
your sixth string .042. The four other strings are usually gauged
somewhere between these two. Fretting a string changes its
tension slightly. A difference in string diameter affects the
amount of change in string tension as it is fretted. This means
that to sound 'in tune' the first string benefits from having a
shorter effective sounding length than the second string and so
on. Hence Leo's innovation.

Tools required

■ **Phillips-type screwdriver
size '0', '1' or 5mm
straight-slot for early
'50s models and Relics**
■ **Electronic tuner
(optional) and guitar lead**
■ **Duster**
■ **Masking tape**

1 If present the chrome bridge cover should be removed.
(Though the bridge cover is part of Leo Fender's original
concept it is rarely found on Teles in practical use, as it
prevents the use of right-hand damping or 'etouffe' effects. Guitarists
affectionately refer to these redundant parts as Fender 'ashtrays'.)

2 Before you begin, take care to protect the guitar paintwork
with a duster taped in place with a low adhesion masking
tape. Tune the open string to E concert. Check the harmonic
note at the 12th fret of the first string as compared to the same
fretted note. All the sounded notes should be precisely the same
pitch, though in different octaves. In practice a compromise will have
to be reached as it isn't possible to get both the first and second
strings 'scientifically' correct on a Vintage-type Tele, as they share a
saddle. Jerry Donahue has actually devised a cunning solution to
make this work in our favour, for which see the boxout on page 37.

When setting intonation a practised ear will detect any
discrepancy. An alternative solution is to use an extremely
accurate electronic tuner, which will visually display any
discrepancy in 'cents', either flat or sharp.

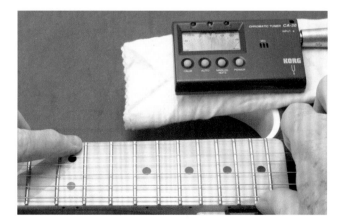

3 If the string sounds or indicates flat at the 12th fret when compared with the 12th harmonic, turn the longitudinal screw anticlockwise, thereby moving the saddle towards the neck. You will need a '1' point Phillips for most Teles and a 5mm straight-slot for a Broadcaster.

If the note at the 12th fret sounds sharp as compared to the harmonic then the string length is too short and the saddle should be adjusted clockwise.

Adjust until the harmonic, open string and 12th fret all indicate or sound at an appropriate compromise 'tempered' pitch. Repeat this procedure for all six strings.

NB: Since raising or lowering the string saddles as in *'Bridge adjustment part 1'* will effectively alter the string length these two operations essentially need to be considered together.

✎ Tech Tip

It's worth checking the intonation at the 19th fret of the first string (B natural) against the open B string. If the open B and E are in tune then the 19th fret and open B should not 'beat'. This applies equally to the 20th fret on the B string and the open G string. Similar checks should be tried on the 19th fret for all the other strings.

John Diggins – Luthier

Six-saddle type
(Most post-'70s Teles and American Standards)
Modern Teles have the facility to adjust *individual* string lengths.

1 Tune the open string to E concert. Check the harmonic note at the 12th fret of the first string as compared to the same fretted note. All the sounded notes should be precisely the same pitch, though in different octaves.

When setting intonation a practised ear will detect any discrepancy. An alternative solution is to use an extremely accurate electronic tuner, which will visually display any discrepancy in 'cents', either flat or sharp.

Take care to protect the guitar paintwork with a duster while you work.

2 If the string sounds or indicates flat at the 12th fret when compared with the 12th harmonic, turn the longitudinal screw anticlockwise, thereby moving the saddle towards the neck. You will need a '1' point Phillips for most Teles.

If the note at the 12th fret sounds sharp as compared to the harmonic then the string length is too short and the saddle should be adjusted clockwise.

Adjust until the harmonic, open string and 12th fret all indicate or sound at the same pitch. Repeat this procedure for all six strings.

Saddle up your Telecaster, by Jerry Donahue

We asked 'Bendmaster of the Telecaster' Jerry Donahue to share some of his secrets for setting up a Telecaster bridge and keeping it properly intonated (Jerry demonstrates this technique in his guitar clinics):

'Attention all current and would-be Tele slingers! You needn't resort to six individual bridge saddles to improve your intonation. The original Broadcaster design called for three brass saddles: and that's still the best design today. The larger saddles mean more mass, providing greater output, sustain and tone. Also, with two strings per saddle you have twice the string pressure against the body!

'Now, on to intonation. Until fairly recently, I felt that a guitar couldn't really play in tune unless each string's 12th fret harmonic and 12th fret note had the exact same reading on the electric tuner. And of course, they never do on a three-saddle bridge. I finally settled on a technique that not only deals with this problem but, to my delight, addresses other inherent problems also. Here it is: adjust the middle saddle's intonation screw so that the D string's 12th fret note reads slightly flat of the 12th fret harmonic on your tuner. Then, check out the G string's 12th fretted note. This note should be only *marginally* sharp of the harmonic. Are you with me? Now tune your guitar, with the open G string reading somewhere between A440 and A439 (so that the 12th *fretted* note is at A440). Tune the other strings as one would normally. Final adjustments can be made by ear when you compare first position E major and E minor chords. The E major's G# note (third string, first fret) should no longer seem sharp in the chord; and the open G string should still be perceptively in tune within the E minor chord.

'Here's another for instance: an A chord barred at the fifth fret sounds fine. But when the nearest E is played (fifth string, seventh fret; fourth string, sixth fret; third string, fourth fret;

second string, fifth fret), it typically sounds "off". The major third is the culprit (fourth string, sixth fret): it typically sounds sharp. But with my adjustment (the fourth string's 12th fretted note being slightly flat) that problem no longer exists. There is a small margin of error here, which actually works to the guitarist's advantage!

'*Occasionally*, depending on the gauge of your strings and the force of your picking hand, it might also serve you to marginally flatten the low E string. I do this as I use a 42 and like to hit it fairly hard sometimes. Trust your own ears, though, as each instrument tends to be different, too.

'A final qualification in adopting all the aforementioned technique: a piano tuner may use an electronic tuner as a point of reference. But if he tuned the entire keyboard to be "perfect", it would sound awful. The bottom keys actually must be tuned sharp and the high ones tuned flat. This is the only way the human brain will perceive the piano to be in tune. It's essentially the same concept I've applied here to the Telecaster. I really like this method. Once I adopted it, my Teles sounded noticeably more in tune than my Strats (across all of the chord shapes) ... so I've since made the same adjustments to the Strats!

'Remember, life is about compromise. Check it out!'

Jerry Donahue

Neck adjustment

Due to the 'handmade', pre-computer nature of early Tele manufacture there may often be a slight variance in neck pitch in relation to the body. This can have critical implications for perceived action, string height and the setting of the bridge saddles. Correcting this in practice means placing a wooden shim approximately .010in (0.25mm) thick in the neck pocket, underneath the butt of the neck.

Shimming the neck on a Vintage-type Tele
■ **Why would you want to do this?**
The need to adjust the pitch of the neck occurs in situations where the string height is high and the action adjustment is as low as the saddle adjustment will allow.

'Shimming' is the time-honoured procedure used to adjust the pitch of the Vintage Tele neck. But note that the pitch of the neck on your guitar should have been preset at the factory and in most cases will not need to be adjusted. However, old Fenders have often been repaired/adjusted and shims are often lost or removed accidentally.

1 Remove the strings. I suggest removing them one at a time – sixth, then first, then fifth and second. This spreads the tension loss evenly as opposed to removing all the strings at once, as a sudden change of tension can impose tremendous shock to the timber of the neck, with potential for distortion.

2 Unscrew the four neck screws using a '2' point Phillips screwdriver.

3 Remove the neck gently from its seating in the pocket of the body. Note carefully the position of any existing shims if present.

4 A new shim approximately ¼in (6.4mm) wide x 1¾in (44.5mm) long x .01in (0.25mm) thick will allow you to raise the action approximately ¹⁄₃₂in (0.8mm).

5 Ease the new shim into position and carefully maintain it in place whilst replacing the neck in its slot. Replace the neck fixing screws.

✎ Tech Tip

Shims can be made of card or bits of old-fashioned electrical insulating board, but I prefer thin wood veneers. This seems more organic – wood to wood contact.

John Diggins – Luthier

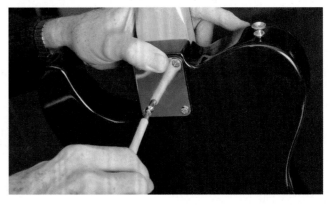

Replacing Kluson tuners

Early Teles are usually fitted with Kluson Deluxe semi-enclosed machine heads. These are often unbranded. They were the most easily available at the time of manufacture but are not perfect. They have a tendency to a 'dead spot' phenomenon where turning the tuner in opposite directions often has no effect on the string post and therefore the string tension. The dead spot is caused by poor manufacturing tolerances and the use of brass for the worm gear as opposed to steel.

Fortunately Spertzel and Gotoh now manufacture an exact lookalike with the advantage of a better gearing ratio (15:1 rather than the old 12:1) and the fact that they come with nylon washers to take up any slack on the worm gear. There may, however, be some slight difference in the size of the bushings on replacements. The solution is to file the serrated teeth on the new bushings rather than deface a vintage guitar.

1 Remove the strings. Always take the time to reduce the neck tension in a slow and methodical way to reduce the risk of upsetting the balance of the timber neck.

2 The very old Kluson fixing screws require a straight-slot 4mm screwdriver for removal, while most post-'52 guitars need a '1' point Phillips.

3 When positioning the new machine head remember to replace the metal ferrule.

Keep old parts

To preserve its looks and value, when replacing any parts on a vintage guitar always get the nearest you can to an identical replacement and store all the vintage parts safely. They will help provide 'provenance' for the instrument at any future sale.

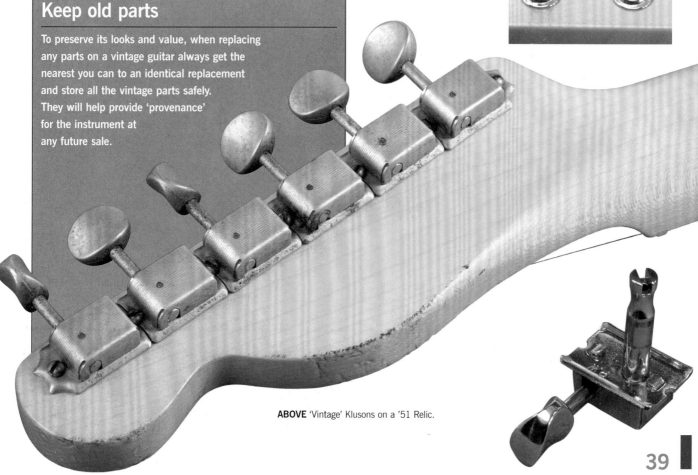

ABOVE 'Vintage' Klusons on a '51 Relic.

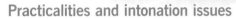

The Paul Bigsby vibrato

Designed by Paul Adelburt Bigsby (1899–1968), and currently made in Savannah, Georgia, USA (as well as being licensed for Far Eastern copies), the Bigsby guitar vibrato arm is probably the second most famous vibrato after Leo Fenders 'synchronised floating trem'.

The Telecaster is the classic 'hard tail' guitar, and in his further attempts to give the guitarist access to the pitch vibrato of the steel guitar Leo Fender would eventually develop the Stratocaster with its integral 'floating trem'. However, many Tele fans *have* craved a vibrato option and Telecasters from as early as 1953 can be found with prototype Bigsby units.

Bigsby came up with a specific Fender-branded unit in 1967. This is now known as the FB5. In truth the Bigsby arm is not as innovative as Leo's and is both very heavy and perhaps a little less responsive in operation. However, it does have its own distinctive character of vibrato, heard to great effect on the recordings of Duane Eddy, Chet Atkins and many rockabilly guitarists.

The Bigsby is most often associated with hollow-body Gretsch and Gibson models, *not* solid-body guitars.

Practicalities and intonation issues

Perhaps the first thing to consider with a Bigsby is weight! It may look great but it puts about a pound (0.45kg) onto the weight of your guitar.

Although the Bigsby is less subtle and responsive than Leo Fender's or any of the other 'synchronised' trems, there *are* plus factors to Paul Bigsby's design:

■ The extra weight behind the bridge does give more rigidity and 'tone' to the guitar's acoustic and amplified sound, perhaps lowering the guitar's principle resonant frequency – often a beneficial effect.

BELOW The 'Fender' Bigsby.

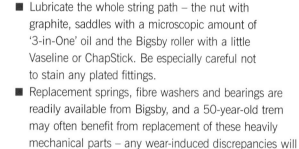

- Unlike a 'floating' trem, the single powerful 'motorcycle compression' spring of the Bigsby causes much less pitch discrepancy when physically bending strings, *ie* you can manually pitch bend strings one, two and three whilst sustaining a pedal bass note and the latter remains *relatively* stable. Try this on a floating Strat trem and you may unintentionally enter the world of bitonality!
- By the same token a broken string on a correctly set-up Bigsby will leave the rest of the guitar fairly in tune. On a floating trem you enter the world of atonality.

However, keeping a Bigsby working well and even replacing strings does set certain unique challenges.

The first thing to know is that there are at least 12 different variants of the Bigsby vibrato, some cosmetic but many critical to its effective use. If you have a Tele with a factory-fitted Bigsby it will be the correct type. However, retro-fitted Bigsbys need to be carefully selected and Bigsby currently offer aluminium and 'gold'-plated types specifically with the Tele in mind. These are the B5, FB5, B50 and B16, all offered in plain aluminium or 'gold' plated.

Maintenance

- If required, lubricate the spring extremely sparingly – over-lubrication may cause damage to the all-important 'cushion' washer.

- Lubricate the whole string path – the nut with graphite, saddles with a microscopic amount of '3-in-One' oil and the Bigsby roller with a little Vaseline or ChapStick. Be especially careful not to stain any plated fittings.
- Replacement springs, fibre washers and bearings are readily available from Bigsby, and a 50-year-old trem may often benefit from replacement of these heavily mechanical parts – any wear-induced discrepancies will naturally affect the precarious stability of the mechanism.

- For tuning stability it is essential to ensure that all the fitting screws are tight. This requires a '2' point Phillips.

- Sometimes the vibrato arm itself can become loose. This is held in place by a spring washer and nut arrangement which requires an 8mm socket for a little tightening – not too much, just enough to keep the arm in a convenient playing position.

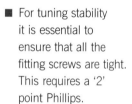

Stringing a Bigsby-fitted Telecaster

1 Crimp the new string into a curve at the ball end – an awkward job. Rounded jewellers' wire-working pliers are the ideal tool but ordinary long-nose pliers will do the job.

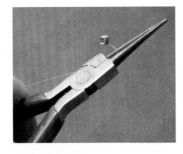

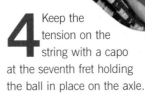

4 Keep the tension on the string with a capo at the seventh fret holding the ball in place on the axle.

2 Feed the string underneath, around and over the axle.

3 Place the ball end of the string onto the axle pin.

5 You could alternatively try pushing a wedge of bubble wrap into the space under the axle to keep the string in place on the pin during winding.

6 Wind the string onto the tuning machine, tune to pitch, remove the capo and/or bubble wrap.

✎ Tech Tip

Any factor that lowers a guitar's fundamental resonant frequency will help amplified 'tone'. The lower the fundamental frequency of the body and neck of the instrument, the less cancellation of relevant string frequencies at the pickup.

John Diggins – Luthier

Survival of the species

In 1965, Paul Bigsby was in poor health and wanted to sell his over-stretched company. He telephoned his old associate Ted McCarty, the ex-president of Gibson guitars. Ted purchased the Bigsby name and inventory in January 1966, and Paul passed away in 1968. On 10 May 1999 the Gretsch Guitar Company purchased Bigsby Accessories from Ted McCarty and the brand lives on.

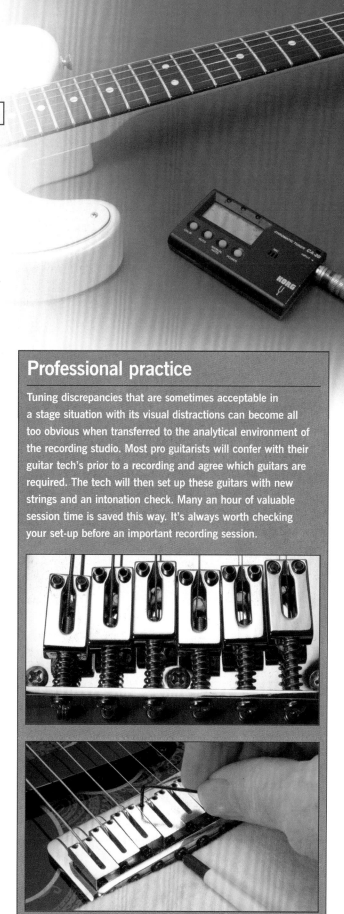

Tuning

A well set-up Tele will tune up and stay fairly in tune even in the most demanding stage situations.

When the Esquire first appeared the only reference options available for accurate tuning were tuning forks, as used by violinists and piano tuners, and 'pitch pipes', a device similar to a mouth-organ with six 'open string' reference pitches. Pianos when available were often pitched fractionally 'flat' due to neglect.

The introduction of electronic tuners since the early 1980s has offered guitarists an increasingly accurate reference tool. The key word here is 'reference'. The open strings of a guitar tuned to correspond with an accurate electronic tuner provide a great starting point for accurate tuning. However, it is essential to remember that the guitar, like the piano, is a 'tempered' instrument. Even the most accurately fretted and set up guitar is built on a tempered tuning system that compromises the science of pitch by considering 'enharmonic' notes such as C# and Db as the same note, which they are not!

■ Tempered tuning

If we all played fretless guitars this would not be an issue. However, there are very few fretless Teles and even less fretless guitarists.

■ Tempered tuning in practice

In the real world a tuning compromise has been reached, referred to as 'equal temperament', and most rock and pop musicians will happily accept the faint 'out of tuneness' associated with certain chords in certain keys and positions on the fingerboard.

In fact in single-string solo playing many players consciously or unconsciously 'temper' certain notes slightly sharp or flat by a combination of listening and microtonally 'bending' notes as they play. This technique, combined with pitch-dependent vibrato, is so indigenous to the guitar as to be second nature. This factor even contributes to the guitar's expressive 'human' quality – keyboards, for instance, can never really do this.

For accurate rhythm playing which naturally incorporates chords many guitarists will 'tune to key', using an electronic tuner for reference and then 'tempering' the relevant notes within the pivotal chords of a song to reach an acceptable compromise that 'sounds' musical.

■ The bottom line

Tune your guitar to EADGBE (or whatever exotic tuning you favour) using a tuner for reference, then 'temper' as required.

Professional practice

Tuning discrepancies that are sometimes acceptable in a stage situation with its visual distractions can become all too obvious when transferred to the analytical environment of the recording studio. Most pro guitarists will confer with their guitar tech's prior to a recording and agree which guitars are required. The tech will then set up these guitars with new strings and an intonation check. Many an hour of valuable session time is saved this way. It's always worth checking your set-up before an important recording session.

Repairs, maintenance and adjustments

This first production electric guitar is a rugged workhorse that has often survived 50-plus years of sex, drugs and airport security. However, a little maintenance and lubrication will ensure that the guitarist's focus can be on performance and remembering the lyrics, not a wonky string!

LEFT A custom tool for an awkward intonation adjustment.

RIGHT 1957 Esquire.

Safety first

Generally speaking a Vintage Telecaster electric guitar is no more dangerous to play or work on than its acoustic ancestor. However, there are some hazards of which you should be aware.

Electric shock

Sadly many guitar players have either been killed or badly burned through accidental exposure to mains current. Though the UK's adoption of 240V may seem to present a greater risk than the USA's 110V, it's actually the amps that are the killer not the volts! Amperes are the measure of current, and high currents are the ones to avoid.

Guitar amplifiers run happily on domestic supplies at relatively low current ratings, so the situation of one guitarist one amp is a pretty safe scenario, especially if we observe a few precautions:

■ Always ensure a good earth or ground connection. This allows a safe path to earth for any stray current, which always flows along the easiest path. The earth or ground wire offers a quicker route to earth than through you and therein lies its safety potential.
■ Never replace fuses with the wrong value, eg a 5-amp fuse in a 3-amp socket. Fuses are there to protect us and our equipment from power surges. A higher value means less protection. Never replace a fuse with a bodge such as silver foil or similar. This offers no protection at all.
■ Consider using an earth leakage trip or circuit-breaker in any situation where you have no control of the mains power.
■ Maintain your mains leads. Check them regularly for damage and strained wires. The earth wire must be in place.
■ Never operate an amplifier with the safety cover removed, especially valve amplifiers known for their HT circuits.
■ Never put drinks on or near amplifiers.
■ Never touch a stage lighting circuit or lamp. Apart from mains electricity issues they are often also dangerously hot. Leave stage lamps to qualified electricians.

Beware of
■ Multi amp/multi PA scenarios that aren't professionally administered. Professional PA and lighting supervisors are very safety-conscious and trained in health and safety to a legal minimum requirement. The danger comes with 'semi pro' and amateur rigs which are not closely scrutinised. If you're in any doubt don't plug in until you've talked to the on-site supervisor and feel you can trust his assurances.

■ Unknown stage situations, especially those which feature big lighting rigs. This is easily said but hard to adhere to. Even the most modest gigs nowadays have quite sophisticated lights and sound. The crucial issue is that all the audio equipment is connected to the same PHASE. Danger particularly arises when microphones are connected to one PHASE and guitars to another. A guitar/vocalist could find himself as the 'bridge' between 30 amps of current! If in any doubt be rude and ask.

Hearing damage

Leo Fender's first guitar amp, the K&F of 1945, knocked out a feverish 4W of audio. In fact they were so mild-mannered that some of them lacked so much as a volume control.

The first Fender Bassman amps boasted 26W and by 1964 The Beatles had the first 100W VOX amps, specifically made to cope with concerts in vast football stadiums and the noise of immense screaming crowds.

By 1970 100W was the norm for a guitar 'head' in a small club and the first 10,000W PA systems had rocked Woodstock.

Pete Townshend of The Who first complained of the hearing impairment tinnitus in the mid '70s and for many years refused to tour with a band as his hearing worsened.

The key to saving your hearing is 'dose' figures. Research has shown that you risk damage if exposed to sound 'dose' levels of 90dB or above for extended periods. Health and

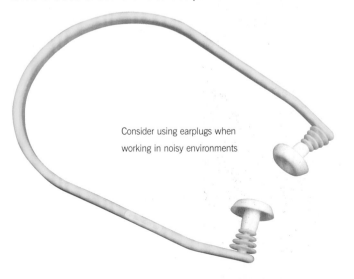

Consider using earplugs when working in noisy environments

Chemical Hazards

Paints and solvents

Traditionally the Telecaster is painted with nitrocellulose lacquer and this practice continues on many guitars, especially Vintage reissues. Nitrocellulose lacquers produce a very hard yet flexible, durable finish that can be polished to a high gloss. The drawbacks of these lacquers include the hazardous nature of the solvent, which is flammable, volatile and toxic. The dangers inherent in the inhalation of spray paints are serious enough to be covered by legal statutes in the USA, the UK, and Europe.

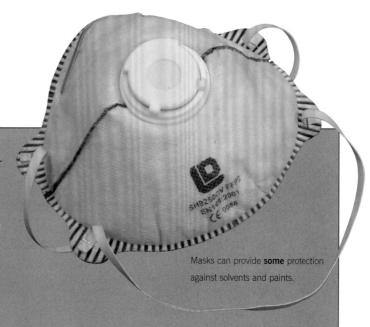

Masks can provide **some** protection against solvents and paints.

Symptoms

- **Acute and chronic ingestion:** Large doses may cause nausea, narcosis, weakness, drowsiness, and unconsciousness.
- **Inhalation:** Irritation to nose and throat. At high concentrations, same effects as ingestion.
- **Skin:** Cracking of skin, dermatitis, and secondary infections.
- **Eyes:** Irritation.
- **Symptoms of overexposure:** Repeated skin contact may cause dermatitis, while the skin defatting properties of this material may aggravate an existing dermatitis. (Source: Material Safety Data Sheet.)

Polyurethane

Vapours may accumulate in inadequately ventilated/confined areas. Vapours may form explosive mixtures with air. Vapours may travel long distances and flashback may occur. Closed containers may explode when exposed to extreme heat.

Symptoms

- **Ingestion:** May be similar to inhalation symptoms – drowsiness, dizziness, nausea, irritation of digestive tract, depression, aspiration hazard.

- **Inhalation:** Dizziness, drowsiness, fatigue, weakness, headache, unconsciousness.
- **Skin:** Drying, cracking, dermatitis.
- **Eyes:** Burning, tearing, reddening. Possible transient corneal injury or swelling of conjunctiva. (Source: Carbon Black Carcinogen by IARC, Symptoms of Overexposure.)

Recommended precautions

Always wear goggles/full face shield and other protective equipment. Avoid skin contact by wearing protective clothing. Take a shower and bathe your eyes after exposure. Wash contaminated clothing thoroughly before reusing it.

...So, with all this in mind, remember that the addresses of recommended guitar repair men and spray shops can be found in your local *Yellow Pages*.

If you really feel you want to customise your Telecaster body then you must take extreme precautions, particularly to avoid inhalation of the dangerous mist created by the spray process.

A passive mask available from DIY stores will only offer the most minimal protection. If in any doubt consult the paint manufacturer for detailed precautions specific to the paint type you've chosen.

---

safety limits for recording studios now recommend no more than 90dBA ('A' standing for average) per eight-hour day, these levels to be reduced dramatically if the period is longer or the dBA higher.

Transient peaks, as in those produced by a loud snare drum or hi-hat, can easily push levels beyond these figures. Be careful where you stand in relation to drums and amplifiers – a small movement can effect a dramatic change in transient

sound level. Don't be afraid to ask about peak and average levels. Your ears are your greatest asset as a musician, so don't be embarrassed into thinking you can't question sound levels.

Repetitive strain injury

Guitarists need to think about posture, warm-up routines and avoiding over-practising. RSI is not funny and affects millions of guitarists. Generate good habits early and stick to them.

Tools and working facilities

Many Tele adjustments can be done using regular domestic workshop tools. Leo Fender rightly felt that a good working instrument should be easy to maintain.

Necessary workshop tools

Many of the tools listed below can double up as your essential gig bag wrap, but as you don't have to carry all these tools around we can be less concerned about weight and portability. Consequently it's very convenient, for instance, to have separate screwdrivers rather than the interchangeable-bit variety. Heftier wire cutters also make string changing a little easier.

■ Set of Phillips-type screwdrivers sizes '0', '1' and '2' point
It may seem a small point but we recommend using the correct size and type of screwdriver. Many valuable Telecasters have survived 30 years on the road but often have a selection of odd screws and 'stripped' screw heads. These look unsightly, slow down maintenance and make the simplest job a chore. The correct 'point' size screwdriver will reduce screw stripping and is also less likely to skate across your prized paintwork.

BELOW The tools used in our case studies.

■ Use type '0' point for some Kluson machine heads.
■ Use type '1' point for pickguard, rear access covers, jack socket, some machine head screws and strap buttons.
■ Use type '2' point for neck bolts.

A screwdriver with interchangeable heads is an alternative option. However, you will often need several heads at the same time, which means a lot of changing around. This option is nevertheless useful on the road, when a compact toolkit is more practical.

Sometimes an electric screwdriver can take the strain out of repetitive tasks, but be sure to protect the guitar as the screwdriver 'torques out'. *Never* use one on plastic parts, as old plastics become brittle and easily crack under sudden pressure.

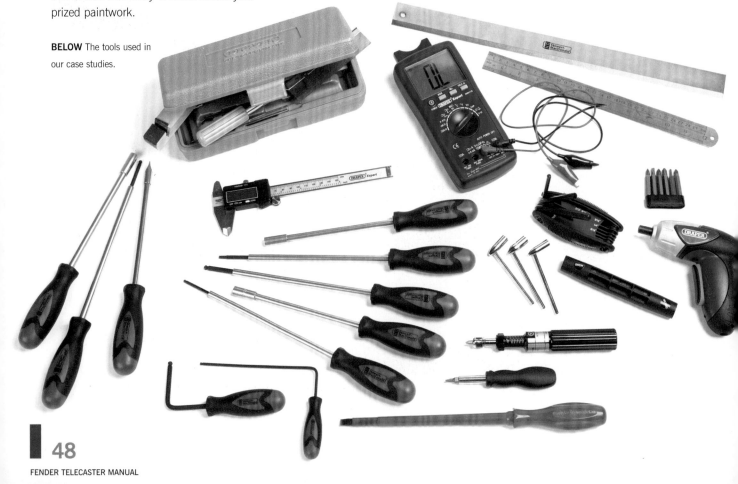

■ **Set of car feeler gauges
(.002–.025) (0.05–1mm)**
These are used for assessing
and setting the string action height.

■ **12in (150mm) ruler with ¹⁄₃₂in
and ¹⁄₆₄in increments (0.5mm increments)**
Also used for setting and assessing the string action.

■ **Light machine oil ('3-in-One' or equivalent)**
This can be used sparingly for lubricating the string path.

■ **4mm straight-slot screwdriver**
For early Esquires and Broadcasters.

ABOVE Useful tools for 'action setting'.

■ **Large straight-slot
screwdriver, 8–9mm**
For some truss rods.

■ **Portable suction fixing vice**
This ingenious device is
terrific if you have no suitable
permanent workbench. Ideal
for nut filing.

■ **Screw extractor HSS drills and tap wrenches**
For removing broken screws.

■ **Zap-It electric screwdriver attachment**
Makes light work of de-stringing guitars.

■ **Stewmac jack socket fixer**
Great for securing the traditional
Vintage Tele socket.

Tech Tip

When working
on vintage brittle
plastics consider
using a fixed-torque
screwdriver
– adjusted to avoid
the kind of damage
seen on the '57
Esquire. Once set
these screwdrivers
cannot over tighten.

Consider also having a set of bench draws and tidies
for all those often misplaced odds and sods that are
essential for guitar maintenance!

■ **Electronic tuner**
An accurate electronic tuner with a jack socket as
opposed to an internal microphone will make short work
of adjusting the intonation of individual string lengths. The
Peterson strobe-type is ideal.

■ **Wire cutters**
For cutting strings to length. Overlong strings at the
headstock are a safety hazard and tear up your gig bag.

■ **Peg winder**
Time saving, and avoids RSI when changing strings.
Fit one to your electric screwdriver.

Henry Phillips

Have you ever wondered why Leo Fender switched to Phillips-type screws?

In the 1950s many fledgling companies were taking lessons from the streamlined assembly process at Henry Ford's car lines in Detroit. For these, Henry Phillips (1890–1958) had developed the cross-head screw. In 1936 The American Screw Co persuaded General Motors to use the Phillips-head screw in manufacturing Cadillacs, and by 1940 virtually every American automaker had switched to Phillips screws.

This new screw worked well with ratchet and electric screwdrivers, had greater torque, was self-centring and didn't slip from the slot so easily, avoiding damage to the valuable paintjob. The speed with which Phillips screws can be used was crucial to the auto assembly line. In addition, Phillips screws are almost impossible to over-screw, which was very important.

However, cam-out or torque-out makes tightly-driven Phillips screws fiendishly hard to remove and often damages the screw, the driver, and anything else a suddenly loose driver happens to hit. And whereas a coin or a piece of scrap metal can often be used to loosen a slot screw, nothing takes the place of a Phillips screwdriver. A flat-bladed driver or even a wrong-size Phillips just makes cam-out worse.

AMERICAN **PHILIPS** SCREWS
with the patented *recessed head*

a source of Profit to Industry in
ASSEMBLY DOLLARS SAVED

HOURS SAVED

OPERATIONS SAVED

WORK SPOILAGE SAVED

SCREWS SAVED

ACCIDENTS PREVENTED

Beware: Phillips screwdrivers should not be used with Pozidrive screws (and vice versa). They are subtly different and when mixed they tend to ride out of the slot as well as rounding the corners of both the tool and the screw recess.

■ Soldering iron
This should be at least 25W with a penlight tip. An iron is essential when replacing worn-out volume pots and three-way switches etc. It's worth investing in a stand with a sponge cleaner attached (Draper components 23554 or similar). A crocodile clip multi-arm is also useful for holding small components in place.

■ A tube of solder
Multicore-type non-acid resin.

■ Tweezers
For rescuing dropped screws from awkward cavities and removing hot wires during soldering.

■ Crocodile clips
Can be used as isolating 'heat sinks' – but not too close to the joins, as they'll hamper the operation by drawing away too much heat.

■ Solder syringe
Makes light work of drawing old solder from previous electrical joints.

 **Tech Tip**

The worst-case scenario with soldering is melting the plastic on interior wires – so be quick! But also keep the components steady: a wire moved while solder is setting may cause a 'dry joint' and poor conductivity.

John Diggins – Luthier

■ **A small penlight torch**

Useful for closer examination of details. Useful any time but especially in a stageside emergency.

■ **Polish and cloth**

A soft duster for body and back of the neck, a lint free cotton hankie for strings and fingerboard. Proprietary guitar polishes differ from household furniture polishes, which often contain silicone. The wax used in guitar polish is emulsified to avoid any sticky residue, especially under the heat from stage lighting.

Some vintage guitars still retain cloth-wire insulation, which doesn't melt but may start to disintegrate – I don't think anybody expected electric guitars to last 50 years!

ABOVE The insulated handles on these tools are soft rubber – less likely to scratch the guitar.

Useful accessories

- Vaseline or ChapStick for lubrication.
- Silicone or graphite locksmiths' nut lubricant.
- Matchsticks or cocktail sticks for lubrication application and 'rawlplugging' loose screws.
- Pipe cleaners and cotton buds for cleaning awkward spots; an old electric toothbrush can also be useful.
- Radius gauges for setting the bridge saddles.
- An electronic multimeter for testing pickup circuits.
- A set of socket spanners are good for removing and tightening pot nuts, jack sockets and some modern machine heads.
- Mechanical and digital callipers, great for all sorts of detailed measurements.
- Loctite or similar multi-purpose superglue.
- Craft knife for nut work.
- Thread gauges, useful for checking for correct threads on replacement screws etc.
- Rubber hammer, safer in many situations on valuable instruments.
- Wire stripper.
- Lemon oil for rosewood fingerboards.
- Spare jack socket, 250K pot, knobs and pickup switch.
- Dental abrasives and/or abrasive cord for fine-tuning a nut slot.

Working environment

Many guitar repairs and much maintenance can be safely carried out with the guitar resting in its hard shell case on a normal kitchen table or on a Workmate-type DIY bench, suitably padded. The photographs in this book are 80 per cent of work done at home on a Draper Workmate. However, *see page 46* for precautions regarding the inhalation of cellulose etc.

Outside the guitar case environment, a small 1m square of carpet sample bluetacked to a workbench can avoid a lot of inadvertent damage to guitar paintwork.

All the guitar techs and luthiers consulted for this book seemed to have their own ingenious home-made tools for very specific jobs.

Essential gig bag accessories

Carrying a few spares can save you a long walk, but you have enough to carry to a gig without hauling your whole toolkit around. The mere essentials compactly rolled in a tool wrap will potentially save a lot of pre-gig hassle, and may fit in your gig bag or guitar case compartment.

Tech Tip

Beware of 'guitar multi-tools' – they look great in the shop, but are difficult to use without damage to the guitar.

Frank Marvel

We suggest...

A multipoint screwdriver with Phillips or cross-screw type '0', '1' and '2' point bits and small and medium point conventional straight heads. Early Teles sometimes utilise straight-slot screws as opposed to the Phillips variety found on the modern guitar. A conventional screwdriver is useful to have around anyway for dealing with broken mains plugs and blown fuses. Also:

- A small pair of wire snips for emergency string changes.
- Small 'emergency only' soldering iron and 6in of solder.
- Some 13-amp and 5-amp (UK) fuses as well as any specific to your area of touring (*ie* USA and European equivalents, etc).
- A PP3 battery (for FX).
- A penlight torch.
- Spare plectrums and/or finger picks.
- Allen or hex keys for truss rod, etc.
- A nail file.
- A Leatherman or similar multitool – useful for a sharp blade and decent pliers.

- Capo.
- Insulating tape.
- Feeler gauges.
- 6in rule.
- An electronic tuner.
- Spare strings.
- Plumbers' PTFE tape – useful for securing loose control knobs.

Unfortunately, by having these with you you'll acquire a reputation as Mr Ever Ready, and before long everybody in the band will come to depend on your tools!

It's worth doing a little maintenance

…Or getting an expert to do it for you. Leo's 'canoe paddle' is proving to be a classic survivor. Even the rigours of the world tour have been surmounted with the help of a good flight case and a little loving care. Clearly few of us would risk taking a '51 Nocaster on the road, but barring abuse and given a few careful tweaks it would undoubtedly acquit itself well. The '57 in our case studies is still being gigged.

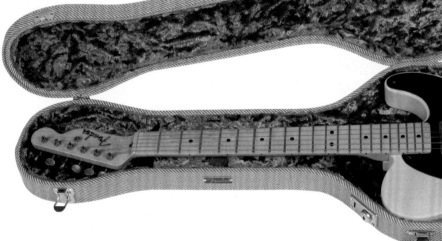

Vintage antiques

If you're lucky enough to own a vintage Esquire then what you have in your possession is not just a good instrument but a piece of popular music history. Given its rarity, you must regard the guitar as you would any other valuable 'antique'.

Whilst such guitars are considered a valuable investment, I personally share the view of many antique furniture collectors that design and function are part of the charm of such items and therefore they are best kept in use. I wonder about the 'investor' who thinks a guitar is best consigned to a bank vault. For me this is missing the point, like the owner who never actually drives his Ferrari. On visiting the world's museums I've observed that unplayed instruments simply wilt and die. So I recommend you enjoy your guitar whilst observing a few precautions:

BELOW Everything mechanical wears out.

- Never subject the guitar to any extremes of change in temperature and humidity. The chief victim here is the finish, which can crack or 'pave' as the underlying wood shrinks or expands. Vintage guitars are more prone to this as their paints and glazes are pervious – which may contribute to the character of their sound as the wood continues to 'breathe'.

- Give the guitar a good wipe down with a lint-free cloth after playing. This will reduce any damage to metal parts and finish caused by perspiration – the main cause of rust to the bridge and machine heads. This, of course, also preserves the strings, often doubling their useful life.

- Keep all the moving parts suitably lubricated.

- Use a good stable guitar stand. This sounds so obvious, but many once fabulous instruments turn up on the repair bench having been accidentally knocked off some precarious perch. John Diggins repairs one broken neck a month.

RIGHT Hangtags and inventory cards are useful sources of 'provenance'.

Authenticity

Many true 'relics' of the '50s have parts missing, particularly knobs and switches. It is perfectly natural to want to replace these. However, it is almost a custodial responsibility to replace them tastefully. These guitars will outlive us and carry on being worthwhile instruments for centuries. I predict the authentic 'early music' enthusiasts of 2050 will include people performing James Burton licks on authentic '50s Teles with 'tweed' Fender amps. So seek out the most authentic replacement parts possible. It's relatively easy to buy 'aged' plastic parts with a suitable patina that ooze an atmosphere of smoky bars and long years on the chitlin circuit (see *Useful contacts* appendix). Do, however, make a careful note of any changes, as this will save arguments over authenticity at a later date.

Authenticity remains an issue 'under the hood', and with an old instrument it is extremely prudent to conserve any original cloth-covered wiring and even use authentic '50s-type solders. This may sound over the top at present but the collectors and players of the next century will remember you warmly for taking that extra bit of trouble.

■ Keep the originals parts

Over the years I have personally accumulated a small collection of bits from previous guitars, including a couple of bridge parts from a '62 Fiesta Red Strat, my first proper guitar. Now in 1969 when I sold the guitar, these seemed to be scrap metal and it never occurred to me to pass them on. But if the guitar still exists, and it probably does (serial no 87827 – let me know if you have it!), these old parts are an important piece of what antiquarians call 'provenance'. A dealer may spot the 'new' saddle pieces I obtained with great difficulty in 1966, and wonder if the guitar really is a '62 Fiesta Red, but if the present owner had the old parts it completes a part of that story which supports the authenticity of the overall instrument. So put those old parts in a safe place and label them with any information you have.

ABOVE In search of that elusive fourth chord!

When not to respray

Never be tempted to respray a '50s, '60s or '70s Tele. However tatty it may have become it's worth more in its original state. Again it's like the 'bruises' on a piece of Chippendale furniture – they are a testimony to the artefact's history. The same, of course, applies to younger guitars, but somehow they don't resonate with quite the same history (yet!).

■ An exception

John Diggins, the brilliant guitar maker behind the basses of Mark King and the guitars of Tony Iommi, does marvellous 'patch blends' on old finishes. I now think this approach is a good working compromise for newer instruments. A few years ago I presented him with a sunburst Fender Precision bass that some punk had sanded down to the wood, but only on the front! I thought that only a complete respray would provide a pleasing finish but John immediately recommended a 'patch'. I was sceptical but on seeing the results I was stunned, the guitar looks wonderful and is still 50 per cent original finish; the odd 'ding' on the original finish gives the guitar a bit of history, but it no longer looks like an industrial accident, which it did before. As a mark of John's true craftsmanship you cannot see the joins. He fastidiously found accurate paints and carefully test-matched the colours, achieving a great result. But this is a drastic step and you wouldn't do it to Andy Summers's modified Custom – that would clearly be erasing history.

Do-it-yourself versus calling in an expert

We all have varying levels of competency in carpentry, electronics and painting. When I obtained my first electric guitar at the age of 15 it was a complete mess. The teacher I bought it from had bought it on a whim in 1962 at the height of The Shadows' popularity. He learned to play *Apache* then consigned the guitar to a damp attic. When he retrieved it in 1966, 50 per cent of the metal parts were rusted red to the point where none of the saddles would move and the Klusons had huge gaps in their compliance.

What I did next as an innocent 15-year-old is testament to enthusiasm over experience and serves as a good list of 'do nots':

■ I completely disassembled the guitar, paying no attention to what came from where. Take guitars apart carefully and note where everything comes from, especially the screws, which come in many different sizes.

■ I replaced all the rusty screws with the wrong type of replacements. Phillips-type screws were virtually unknown in mid-'60s Britain, but exact replacements are now easily available from many websites (see *Useful contacts* appendix).

■ I over-oiled the rusty Klusons, thinking they would repair themselves – they didn't, and what's more the excess oil found its way into the neck grain! Again, Kluson replicas are now easily obtained.

■ I replaced the bridge with proper American replacements. These cost a fortune and took six months to arrive from California by ship! Now a websearch would replace them in 48 hours.

■ I rewired the electronics to obtain my favourite pickup combinations. Not fatal, but I failed to protect the pickups and capacitors with a heat sink and could have done a lot of damage.

■ I cleaned the volume and tone knobs so well I bleached off the numbers. I replaced a missing knob with a white and gold one – all that Frank Hessy's in Liverpool could offer.

Despite all this the guitar sounded great! I have it on record. However, it was never in tune. The combination of lost neck shims, a poor understanding of the saddle arrangement, rusty Klusons and a poorly set-up tremolo/vibrato meant it drove me nuts – so much so that I sold it for £90 (a fortune in 1969

and a 50 per cent profit on the £60 I paid
for it). I don't want to know its present
value, thank you very much.

This book is driven by the desire to help
others avoid my youthful errors.

So bottom line, if you are good with tools
and prepared to be diligent and extremely
careful, you can probably do most of what
this manual expounds and either maintain
a lovely instrument in peak performance or
radically improve a budget Squier.

However, if you have any doubt at
all about your abilities call an expert. In
1965 there were no guitar techs (not even
for Eric Clapton), only luthiers, who all
regarded my guitar as a bit of a joke. Today
there are at least half a dozen skilled techs in every major city
in the world and they all have a sneaking regard for the old
warhorses that keep bouncing back.

Never

- Practise refretting on a
  vintage instrument. Buy
  a budget Squier and
  learn the craft first.

- Attempt a respray
  unless you have all
  the required tools and
  skills and a dust-free
  environment. Always
  wear protective mask
  and clothing.

- Force the wrong size
  screw in a body or
  component. Consider
  using fixed-torque
  screwdrivers on
  vintage instruments.

- Always protect the
  guitar surfaces during
  any maintenance
  or lubrication.

But whatever else you do, enjoy that special piece of
popular music history by playing it every day and trying
very hard to wear it out!

I have seen and played a lot of guitars in the last 40
years and I have this thought to pass on:

A well set-up budget Vibe '50s Tele is a better working
instrument than a poorly set-up Custom Shop Relic. In crude
terms, a good working guitar is about 70 per cent set-up
and 20 per cent the synergy of the parts – all pieces of wood
are different and even machined metal parts vary in their
composition and microscopic detail. The last 10 per cent is
alchemy. A good guitar is a good guitar whether old or new.
As my great teacher Brendan John McCormack often said,
'It's just a plank of wood – you have to make the music.'

Does a guitar respond to being played well? Does the
prevalent temperature and humidity affect a guitar's sound?
Great guitars still have a certain mystery about them – long
may it remain.

Tech Tip

There is no such thing as one perfect set-up –
what's right for Mark Knopfler is not right for
Eric Clapton – so seek your own ideal set-up.

Glenn Saggers – Mark Knopfler's guitar tech

Stageside repairs

Given that the electric guitar always requires the rigging of some additional equipment, it's worth arriving at a gig at least one hour before showtime. This also allows for sound-checks and time for the things that inevitably go wrong to be put right. Sound-checks also give the PA man a chance to serve your needs better – to understand the likely combinations of instruments and any instrument changes during your set. Sound-checks are also great for fault-finding, and time to find solutions.

No sound from your guitar?

Step 1

- Work systematically through the cable chain starting at the guitar, as this is very unlikely to have failed completely.

- Try changing the pickup selector to another pickup. Is the volume control turned up?

- Still no sound? Try replacing the cable between the guitar and the amplifier with a new cable (one you are sure is working – for instance, the one the bass player is successfully using).

- The above step should bypass & eliminate any effects chain.

- If you then have sound, try reinserting the effects chain. (Still no sound? Go to Step 2.)

- If you have sound then you merely had a faulty cable, the most common cause of onstage sound failure.

- If the sound fails again then it would seem that some component of the effects chain is faulty – work through the chain removing one cable at a time to isolate the fault.

- If cable replacement doesn't solve the problem try systematically removing one effect at a time from the chain.

- If you find a 'dead' component of the chain try replacing the associated battery or power supply.

Step 2

- Still no sound, even though you're now plugged directly into the amplifier with a 'new' cable?

- The likely scenario is a 'failed' amplifier. Try checking the obvious causes such as:

  - Has the volume been inadvertently turned down to zero?
  - Check the master volume and channel gain.
  - Is the standby switch in the ON position?
  - Does the mains light (if fitted) show 'ON'?
  - Is the amplifier plugged into the mains? Is the mains switched on? Does the stage have a separate fuse?
  - Are other amplifiers on the same circuit working?

- If yours is the only failed amp look to the fuses. There are likely to be fuses on the amplifier (usually a screw-type fuse cartridge near the mains switch). There may also be fuses in the mains plug. Try a replacement.

- If all of this fails then you must assume the amplifier has a major fault and try a 'work around' – eg sharing an amplifier with the other musicians etc. A band should carry at least one spare amp.

- The crucial thing here is to be systematic – work through the chain logically, eliminating elements of the chain until the fault is isolated.

The guitar won't stay in tune?

Strings!

The most likely cause of tuning difficulties on an otherwise well-maintained guitar is poor or worn strings. The bad news is that changing strings one hour before a gig is also a formula for disaster, as the strings really need time to settle. In an emergency try replacing any individual strings that seem particularly troublesome – rusty first, second and third strings will inevitably cause severe tuning problems.

NB: A machine head that is securely fitted but turns without altering pitch needs replacement. In practice this is unlikely to happen suddenly and should be picked up during routine maintenance.

■ If the guitar has a Bigsby fitted is it poorly set up? This is unlikely to respond to a quick fix. *See 'The Paul Bigsby vibrato' maintenance, page 40.*

Loose components?

■ Have the neck securing screws worked loose? A quarter-turn can improve the neck stability, but don't go mad – beware of cracking the surrounding lacquer by overtightening.

■ Are the machine heads loose?

In practice any loose component in the string path will cause instability and hence tuning problems – examine the guitar for loose screws and lost or corroded securing springs. If the strings are OK and there are no obvious loose components then perhaps you have changed string gauges without realigning the guitar?

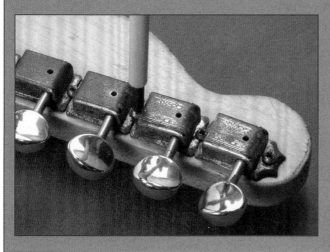

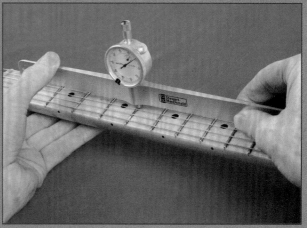

Three-monthly checks

The Telecaster is a rugged workhorse, a low-maintenance classic that Leo Fender and his team designed for simple and easy upkeep. A few simple checks will keep your Tele at peak performance for the next 50 years.

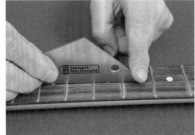

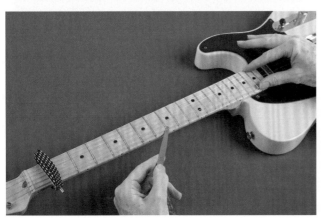

Strings

Change these according to use, perhaps weekly if you're a gigging professional and at least every three months for students. Use the same brand consistently and use the same gauge and metal type, as this will save time-consuming adjustments to the action and intonation. Different strings have different tensions, and gauges can vary from heavy to extra light. Cheap strings are always a false economy – they are inconsistent and wear out quicker. I personally find D'Addario's consistent and good value.

A good 'benchmark' in stringing a Tele is .009–.042 – light gauge strings for flexibility and ease of string bending. Experiment around this area for your own sound. Some Tele players prefer medium to heavy gauge, but these are usually players who are using the Tele as a good solid rhythm guitar.

Experiment with gauges, but refer to *'Setting up and tuning', page 30*, to ensure your guitar is adjusted to cope.

New strings are consistent in their profile and hence more 'harmonically correct' along their length – this makes them easier to tune. Old strings are worn by fret contact, are inconsistent and above all sound dull.

Keep new strings sounding good longer by wiping them after every use with a lint-free cloth. This removes corrosive perspiration and prevents premature rusting.

Early Fenders came fitted with burnished strings and some players even fitted flat-wound strings of a type more usually associated with mainstream jazz styles. Today's fashionable guitar sounds tend to be bright and crisp and this is best achieved with conventional roundwound strings, usually made of nickel wound on steel. Stainless steel is another long-lasting option, though

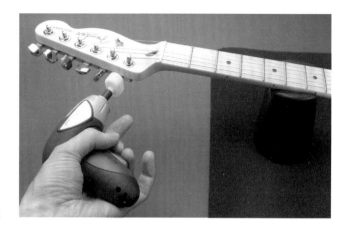

beware of using strings that are made of a material harder than your frets, as inevitably this will result in quicker fret wear.

'Coated strings' are more resistant to corrosion though initially more expensive.

Always use electric guitar strings. This sounds obvious but acoustic guitar strings are not designed for magnetic pickups and are therefore not always magnetically consistent – electric strings are! Stick to one brand as these will be balanced across the gauges both physically and magnetically. If you want to hear the results of acoustic strings on an electric guitar listen to the 1946 Django Reinhardt sessions – even Django struggled to get a consistent response.

To reduce string breakage, lightly lubricate any metal string/saddle contact point. Do this every time you change your strings. The lubricant acts as an insulator against moisture, and reduces friction and metal fatigue. '3-in-One' oil should be applied very, very sparingly to a metal saddle and graphite to a plastic or bone saddle.

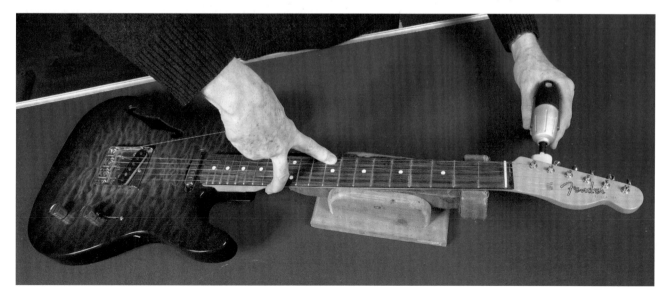

2 Pull the sixth string to the 4th key (make sure you're pulling the string taut). Bend and crimp the string to a 90° angle and cut to length.

Stringing a Vintage-type Telecaster

- When possible always change one string at a time to avoid drastic changes in tension on the slim maple neck. This is especially true if you have a very early Esquire with no truss rod!

- Cutting the curled ends off old strings makes for easier passage through the body ferrules.

3 Insert into the centre hole in the tuning key, then wind neatly in a downward pattern, carefully preventing overlapping.

1 Thread the new strings through the rear ferrules. Due to the unique 'slot and hole' Vintage design you will need to pre-cut the strings to achieve a working length and a workable amount of peg winds.

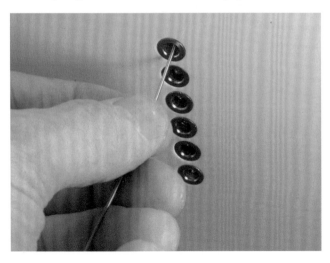

4 Pull the fifth string to the 3rd key. Crimp and cut it. Repeat the procedure as above. Pull the fourth string between the 2nd and 1st keys. Crimp and cut it. Pull the third string just about to the top of the headstock. Crimp and cut it. Pull the second string about ½in (13mm) past the headstock. Crimp and cut it. Finally pull the first string 1½in (38mm) past the top of the headstock. Crimp and cut it. Thread and wind each string as above.

Stringing a modern-type Telecaster

■ Many modern Teles have a conventional hole in the barrel of the machine head.

■ As a rule you should change strings one at a time to maintain an even tension on the neck and thus avoid any movement in the neck angle.

■ When removing old strings, cutting off the curly ends will assist their passage through the body.

NB: If your tuning keys have a screw on the end of the button, as with most Standards, check the tightness of the screw as this affects the tension of the gears inside the tuning keys. You should slacken this tension for ease of restringing. Unusually the Standard requires a 4mm straight-slot screwdriver – many Teles use a '1' point Phillips.

1 Thread the string through the rear ferrules and insert it into the centre hole in the tuning key.

2 In order to reduce string slippage at the tuning key, I recommend that you use a tie technique. This is accomplished by pulling the string through the keyhole, then pulling the string clockwise underneath itself and bringing it back over the top of itself, creating a knot.

Do this under tension and leave just enough string to achieve a few turnings on the machine head barrel. Wind neatly in a downward pattern – carefully, so as to prevent overlapping the windings. Keep the string under tension with your fingers.

3 Repeat the procedure as above for all strings. Crimp any excess string with wire cutters.

Obviously Bigsby and non-through strung Teles require different approaches. These are covered in the relevant case studies on *pages 102 onwards*.

Bridge and saddle corrosion

The saddle components on all Teles are prone to corrosion due to perspiration and condensation. This is easily prevented by a light application of '3-in-One' oil or lighter fluid.

Too late for this Relic! – so always dry off your guitar after a sweaty gig. It's the first thing a pro guitar tech does after a guitar is retrieved from the stage.

✎ Tech Tip

After stringing it is very important not to over-tighten the machine head locking screws. They should be tightened only to 'finger-tight'.

Frank Marvel

Repairing or replacing a jack socket

Loose retaining nut?

A common problem is a loose jack socket retaining nut. This needs attention, as if the jack socket revolves the internal wires often break, causing a disastrous mid-gig loss of output! Normally you will need to remove the socket to tighten the external nut.

An alternative solution is to use a special tool called 'Jack The Gripper', which enables you to tighten the securing nut without having to remove the jack socket – particularly useful in a last-minute stageside repair. The tool fits in the socket, and with a turn its eccentric cam locks to the socket barrel. You can then tighten the external nut without the barrel turning! A special lever fits over a ⅜in socket and allows 'Jack The Gripper' to access the jack socket.

Loose retaining spring?

Heavy use may result in the jack socket spring retainer becoming loose. This can often be easily solved.

1 Most Telecasters have a fairly rudimentary jack socket retainer which is removed by brute force (and sometimes removes itself mid-gig). If it's a tight fit you can ease it out with a little leverage from a jack in the socket and a push from inside the control cavity. Alternatively you can use a reversed Tele jack installation tool (*see page 65*).

2 Once removed a gentle squeeze of the 'earth' springed connector may suffice to give a little more tension to the socket.

■ If the jack still seems a little loose then it's worth replacing this *and* the retainer with a high-quality guitar-type socket – one that's designed to take heavier use. It's worth paying a little extra for a quality component which won't let you down in a pressured stage environment. The jack socket retainer itself can be usefully replaced by an Electro-socket, which is screw-fastened.

The socket on this '50s Vibe guitar is retained by a rudimentary 'claw'.

3 Remove the old socket first by loosening the retaining nut with a 0.5in socket spanner.

4 There should be no need to label the two wires – just remember the single core is 'hot' or 'tip' and the screened/braided wire the earth or return, and then carefully unsolder.

■ Some replacement jack sockets *may* have a longer 'earth prong'. If so a little wood may need to be removed from inside the body socket – a small wood rasp should do this with little trouble.

5 Solder the new socket in place, retaining the correct polarity as per your labelling. **NB:** *Use .32 60/40 resin core electrical solder and a small iron rated at 25W and above.*

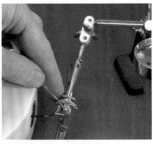

Note the mechanical third hand – indispensible!

6 Position the new Electro-socket, taking care not to twist the wires as you reinsert the socket. Pilot the screw holes with a bradawl. Secure the Electro-socket with its two Phillips screws.

7 Position the nut and bolt the new jack in place. **NB:** *You may not need the retaining nut, as the Electro-socket casing is already threaded.*

■ **Three-monthly checks**

Vintage cool

If you wish to preserve the integrity of an 'original' socket on a vintage guitar, stewmac.com supply a brilliant little gizmo for revitalising the grip of an old retainer clip. This is the 'Tele Jack Installation Tool', which expands the clip so that its corners bite into the walls of the jack cavity.

Stewmac Tele jack installation tool.

1 Disassemble the tool. Place a pre-bent retainer clip over the bolt with its wings pointing out of the guitar socket – the retainer clip slots into the special nut. Screw the lower part of the tool on to the bolt, just enough to retain the 'retainer' but not flatten it!

2 Insert it into the guitar and tighten with the supplied 8mm Allen wrench. Keep the bolt from revolving using a suitable 22mm or adjustable spanner. Note the low adhesion masking tape on the guitar body.

3 When the retainer feels secure remove the bolt by unscrewing the Allen wrench, thus freeing the tool from the cavity.

NB: *If the hole containing the jack cup has been badly damaged by the old retaining clip, you can rebuild the wall of the hole with a mixture of Araldite 2-pack resin and sawdust. Dried out this works like a new wood surface and the replacement clip bites.*

Note that the same tool can also be used *in reverse*. Used this way it collapses an old retainer clip, making it easy to remove. (Detailed instructions come with the tool.)

Frets

Have a look at your frets, particularly in the playing positions you use the most. Slight wear may not pose a problem but severe wear with 'grooving' will affect intonation and perhaps create some 'fret buzz'. See overleaf for a simple fret polish and *page 74* for more drastic measures.

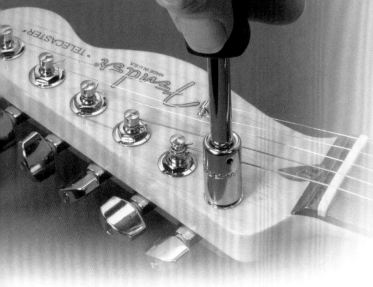

For details of your specific Tele neck radius refer to the case studies section of this book. If the action is too high or too low, *see 'Setting up and tuning', page 30*.

Volume and tone controls

Check these for electrical crackles and 'dead spots'. If these problems are present then the pots may respond to a treatment with switch cleaner. *See 'Volume and tone controls', page 90*.

Loose strap retainers

A simple problem that can cause havoc if the guitar is eventually dropped! If the retaining screw remains loose when fully tightened a cocktail stick or split matchstick will work effectively as a rawlplug.

Machine heads

Newer Teles may have Schaller or Gotoh machines which are secured by a locking nut on the face of the headstock. These work loose, causing intonation problems, so a periodic tighten is in order.

Check for loose machine head retaining screws and tighten if necessary. This usually requires a '1' point Phillips.

Also check for any 'dead' spots in the compliance – *ie* you turn the peg but no pitch change occurs. These will need replacement.

Vintage Teles have Kluson-type machines and many later guitars have Kluson lookalikes – these are generally interchangeable, though be aware that the later machines have different gearing ratios and this can be disconcerting if the types are mixed on the same instrument. *See 'Replacing Kluson tuners', page 39*.

Tremolo/Vibrato

If fitted, the tremolo/vibrato unit should be silent in operation, with no 'spring pings'. For adjustment and lubrication, *see 'The Paul Bigsby vibrato' maintenance, page 40*.

Fingerboard wear

Check for fingerboard wear. Superficial wear is not in itself a problem, but the appearance of dips or grooves in the wood is more worrying – this requires professional attention.

Action

Check the action height with the car feeler gauge (.002–.025), applying Fender recommended specifications:

Pingy strings?

Check for a pinging noise whilst tuning each individual string. This is often caused by the string sticking in the nut grooves at the top of the neck. A light lubrication of graphite dust or silicone projected into the grooves will usually solve this annoying problem and even help tuning stability. A cocktail stick can be used both to mix a little Vaseline and locksmiths' graphite and apply it to the nut grooves.

Less serious cases often respond to a simple run with a pencil lead or a polish with Mitchell's gauged abrasive cord.

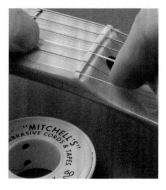

Neck radius	String height Bass side	String height Treble side
7.25in Vintage	⁵⁄₆₄in/.0781in (2mm)	¹⁄₁₆in/.0625in (1.6mm)
9.5 to 12in	¹⁄₁₆in/.0625in (1.6mm)	¹⁄₁₆in/.0625in (1.6mm)
15 to 17in	¹⁄₁₆in/.0625in (1.6mm)	³⁄₆₄in/.0469in (1.2mm)

A fret polish

Budget Teles sometimes arrive with rather unfinished frets. They are workable but feel a little rough, especially when 'bending' strings. The solution is a little simple polishing.

1 After removing the strings mask the fretboard with some low adhesion masking tape (this is less likely to leave a sticky deposit).

2 Wearing protective gloves and eye protection, carefully dress the frets with some 000 grade wire wool. Beware of overdoing this, as you can change the shape of the frets and cause much worse problems. Remove the masking tape.

3 A light finishing polish with a lambswool buffer is good for a maple fingerboard, while the finish on a rosewood fingerboard will respond to a light application of a little lemon oil. This will also help remove any adhesive deposit left by the tape.

String breakage

The foremost contributor to this is moisture collection at the point of contact on the bridge saddle. This can be attributed to the moisture and acidity that transfers from your hands or can be a direct effect of humidity in the air.

■ Metal conflict

Metal-to-metal friction and fatigue is a scientific fact that affects any mechanical device employing a combination of metal materials.

Different metal components, in contact over a period of time,

An alternative approach

D'Addario, the renowned stringmakers, have recently come up with an alternative solution which saves a little time. They offer a simple card fingerboard mask which literally masks the fingerboard whilst you polish the frets with their supplied light abrasive paper.

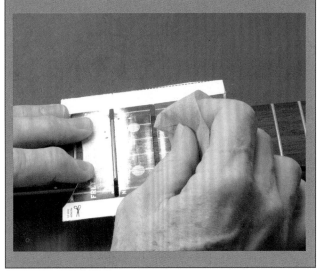

react to each other and break down the integrity of, for instance, guitar strings. A stronger metal will always attack a softer metal (this is why a stainless-steel string may wear a groove into a metal saddle). Finally, you will also find that different string brands will break at different points of tension, due to the metal make-up and string manufacturing techniques.

One of the ways to reduce string breakage is to lubricate the string/saddle contact point with a light machine oil ('3-in-One' oil, which also contains anti-rust and anti-corrosive properties, is ideal). The oil acts not only as an insulator against moisture, but also reduces friction and metal fatigue. This lubrication needs to be done sparingly. Use a matchstick or 'Q'-tip end to transfer a minimum of oil to each bridge saddle.

For the string tree or ferrule a small amount of Vaseline or ChapStick applied with a cocktail stick does the trick.

Earthing and RF induction issues

The electric guitar can be prone to a lot of 'Rattle and Hum'.

However, there are steps that can be taken to improve matters.

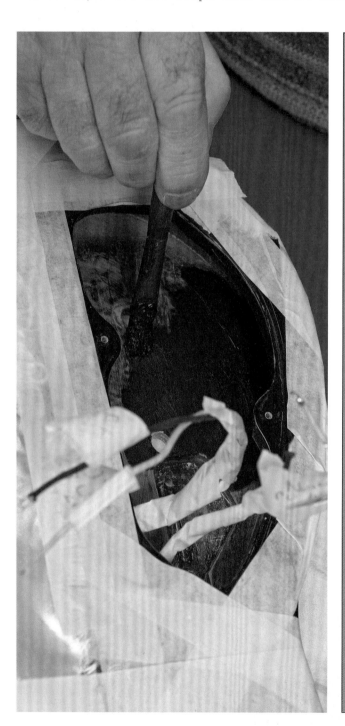

The historical perspective

In the 1950s western swing guitarists were playing bars, lounges and small dancehalls. Early rock'n'roll players such as Paul Burlison were playing in small clubs with no PA system and no stage lighting. In these conditions an unscreened and electrically 'unbalanced' single coil pickup was no real problem. If the player heard a little hum from his amp he could just shift around a little until his pickup was 'off axis' to the hum-generating radio frequencies emanating from his valve amp's huge transformers.

By 1957 this situation was changing, as artists like the Johnny Burnette Trio might play some theatres and even some television shows. The lighting dimmers in such situations often induced a lot of hum into audio circuits, and not just at the low 50–60Hz frequencies that were easily 'lost in the mix'. Soon the audience were hearing nasty 'spikes' in the vocal frequencies where our ears are most sensitive.

The early PA pioneers like Leo Fender were drawn towards 'balanced' line audio circuits with their 'hum bucking' properties, but guitarists were left with a growing noise problem.

Today popular music of all kinds has gravitated to stadiums and auditoria bristling with hundreds of computer-programmed lighting dimmers, electric server-driven lighting changes, smoke machines, radio microphones, intercoms and millions of watts of amplification putting every tiny buzz and hum under a microscope.

Humbucking guitar pickups are a part solution but they do sound different. Many guitarists prefer the classic character of electrically 'unbalanced' single coil pickups as found on most Teles. In search of a solution, some makers started looking at better electrical 'screening'.

The screening concept is to build a metallic 'shield' around sensitive 'unbalanced' guitar circuits and connect that screen to an earth potential. The screen effectively intercepts any interference – noise – and drains it away to earth before it can affect the signal passing along the guitar circuits.

Supplementary screening

One part solution to induced hum suggested by guitar craftsman John Diggins is a screening paint, applied in the pickup cavities. John specifically recommends carbon graphite paint but also advises that it won't *completely* solve the problem in today's increasingly electronically 'busy' world.

SAFETY FIRST: Always use a vapour barrier facemask/respirator and eye protection when applying specialist paints. Shown on a 'thinline', but effective on *any* Tele.

1 Remove the guitar strings and carefully remove the covers from all the cavities you intend to screen. Keep all the screws together in a series of pots and trays – it's worth labelling these NOW, as putting the wrong screws back in the wrong holes will inevitably cause problems.

2 Carefully unsolder the connections and *label* the cables. Consider drawing a diagram of 'what goes where'. I made a loom of the remaining wiring with some low adhesion masking tape – this prevents paint adhering to the wiring and causing confusion later.

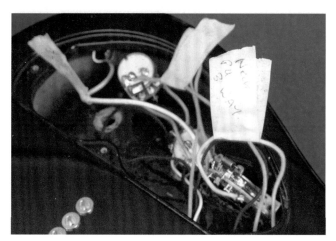
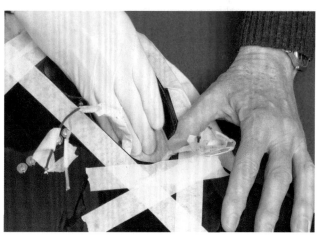

3 I also masked the edges of the cavity and then prepared the surfaces for painting, removing any grease or rough edges that might hamper paint adhesion. It's worth masking the other side of the control cavities too, to prevent paint spilling out onto the front of the guitar.

6 Carefully reassemble the pots and wiring, checking for all points of contact with the new screened surface. All pickups and potentiometers (volume/tone) and switches must be clear of contact with the new surface *unless* they are to be 'grounded'. When soldering, a dab of 'tinner cleaner' RS561 533 will improve the conductivity of the solder iron heat and aid a quicker, more effective solder joint.

4 Apply the first coat of paint and allow to dry (John uses Carbon Graphite paint). Sometimes a second coat helps electrical conductivity, but in this case testing with a multimeter set to 'beep' indicated that all was good with one coat. To check, place your multimeter prongs at several spaced points on the finish and see what continuity you've achieved. Add a second coat when and where necessary.

WARNING: This paint will be a very effective conductor, so be careful to only apply it where a route to earth or ground is desirable. A bit of paint in the wrong place, which on reassembly touches a 'hot' wire, can of course short circuit the guitar.

Guitar leads as aerials

As well as noise induced into the pickups, guitarists have increasingly long guitar leads to contend with. A long length of 'unbalanced' guitar lead can act as a giant aerial, picking up all sorts of electrical noise and radio frequencies (RF), all of which will be amplified just as effectively as any audio signal running down the line. We have all been to a gig where you suddenly hear taxi radios and ambulance messages blaring through the PA. This is usually the result of RF picked up by unbalanced guitar pickups or leads. Better screening can sometimes help.

Mains hum

In order to reduce mains hum 50–60Hz from induction, it's very important to route *all* your audio cables (guitar FX and microphones) physically away from the mains cables from your gear, as well as elements such as power amplifiers and external power supplies (wall warts). A good rule of thumb is, when an audio cable *has* to cross the path of a mains cable, make sure it crosses at a right angle – this minimises the induction of this type of hum.

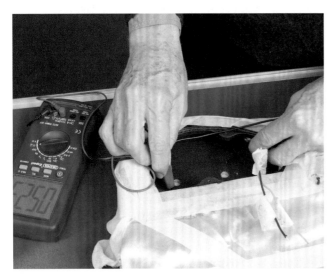

5 If necessary solder a wire from your new screen to the earth side of your jack socket. The need for this will depend on the extent of your painting and whether or not the paint is going to contact an existing earth point on reassembly.

Earth loops

An even more common source of hum is the infamous earth loop, also known as a 'ground loop'. These are often difficult to track down and isolate. However, once you've applied most of the common-sense measures to reduce hum, any hum remaining will usually be attributable to a ground loop. It is possible to completely eliminate earth loops if you take the necessary steps, but it involves a systematic process of eliminating problems one component at a time.

■ So what is an earth loop?

Earth loops occur because most modern equipment is fitted with three-pin mains plugs. The third pin on the plug connects the chassis of your gear to AC earth, which ensures that your body cannot become the earth path for AC current. All well and good.

However, when two pieces of equipment both have three-pin plugs and are connected together with cable, the shielding on the cable is also responsible for 'grounding', and an earth loop is possible.

What we now have are two paths to earth (one, through its own AC cable; the other through the audio cable connected to the other unit, and consequently through *that* unit's AC cable). Thus a loop of current is formed that can act like an aerial, perfect for inducing hum. You can even pick up radio interference this way as you have effectively created a 'tuned circuit'. If you were doing this on purpose you would call it a radio, but Marconi beat you to it!

■ Troubleshooting

Most earth loop problems can be solved by plugging all of your stage gear into a single earthed AC outlet. However, it's easily possible to overload the AC outlet, so make sure the AC source is rated to handle all the gear you have plugged into it. A guitar amp itself and a couple of FX will certainly be less than the UK-standard 13 amps, but beware of plugging the whole band into one socket! And remember that different countries have different standards or ratings for AC outlets. It's in the interests of your safety to know these.

The only way of being sure you have a potential earth loop problem is to listen carefully for a slightly edgy hum as you're assembling, wiring and cabling your system. Have your gear powered and monitor for hum after each audio connection. This way you can quickly determine and isolate the source of the problem.

Once you identify the unit that is causing the hum then you have to find a 'work around'. This may mean a compromise on the number and position of the units in your audio chain.

It's worth physically moving the unit that seems to be causing the problem and trying again. Sometimes the close proximity of items such as mains transformers can be aggravating the induction problem. You can eliminate battery-operated gear or gear with two-prong adapters, as they cannot contribute to earth loop problems.

■ Earth lift

Some people solve earth loop problems by using a 'lifting' device (three-prong to two-prong adapter) on one of the units, thus breaking the earth route and severing the loop.

However, NB: This is a *very* dangerous option that should not be used. You are negating the safety factor that the AC earth wire provides. If you choose to use three- to two-prong AC adapters, electrocution may result.

■ Isolating transformers

The best (but more expensive) way to fix a persistent earth loop problem is through the use of a transformer. The job of the transformer is to ensure there is no electrical contact between two pieces of equipment, except for the audio signal. Transformers have no earth connection between the input and output connections, thus effectively breaking an earth loop.

When buying transformers for earth loop problems, it's important to realise that the cheaper variety may colour the sound a little due to frequency response irregularities. Buy the best you can afford – it's worth it.

Intermittents

In my experience these are the worst sort of interference as you're never sure if they've been 'cured'.

If you hear a buzz that only appears for a short time and at a constant level, you may have a pulse in your mains lines, which can be caused by the switching action of fluorescent lighting, dimmer switches, window air conditioners, or a refrigerator turning on and off. Again it's a matter of working through the possibilities in a systematic way.

If you must share an AC circuit with any of these elements, and if it's a long-term gig, somebody needs to install a proprietary noise-suppressed AC distribution panel, which will give you a clean power supply for your stage.

String guide variants

From its inception the Fender guitar was different. Virtually every other guitar ever made up until 1950 had a headstock that angled back away from the nut. This convention ensured a good downward pressure on the nut, which both keeps the strings in place and ensures a good tone.

But Leo's approach was different. His 'working man's' guitar would be lean, mean and efficient. Curiously his innovation also saves wood, which is good for productivity and also the environment. Having saved some wood and created a distinctive and very different headstock (based, he says, on some Croatian guitars he had seen*). Leo was left with a problem, which he pragmatically solved for the Esquire in 1950 by introducing a round string guide to pull the first and second strings in towards the neck.

This round string guide is still found on some very early Teles but is more often replaced by a custom-made 'string tree' which does the same job.

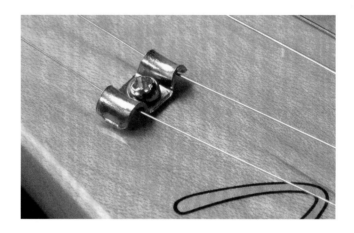

■ The slightest touch of lubrication (using ChapStick or Vaseline) applied under the tree will avoid any 'sticking' causing intonation problems. This particularly applies when heavy use is made of any vibrato/tremolo arm or onstage retuning. Note that the newer 'classic ferrule' type has a grooved rear which needs careful realigning after lubrication.

*The Croatian guitars still used in Istria have this distinctive Stauffer type of headstock, but I'm not sure of how Stauffer links with Istria, though I suspect the link is Istria's cultural connection with Venice.

■ The adoption by many guitarists of a plain unwound third string may have been the prompt for Fender to adopt a second string tree in the early '70s. This covers the third and fourth strings and is aesthetically a neater solution than a single or triple 'tree'.

American Standard onwards

A third option found on the American Standard Teles features a neat combination of a low friction 'roller' type string tree for the first and second strings combined with staggered lower string posts for the top four strings. This is an effective solution to the 'nut tension' issue.

Some 'specials' such as the Clarence White and James Burton have a deeper angle at the headstock, which also aids nut tension.

The latest Teles have staggered tuner pegs to assist with correct nut angle issues – so the evolution continues.

Very occasionally string trees may have been positioned incorrectly at the factory. This means that the desirable 'straight pull' which Leo intended is distorted. Remedying this without leaving unsightly holes in the headstock is a job for a well-equipped and skilled luthier.

✎ Tech Tip

The extra string tree helps when an inexperienced player replacing his strings doesn't allow enough windings on the string post, leaving a fairly gentle slope up to the nut – the string spacer provides the necessary pressure at the nut.

Andy Gibson of London's Tin Pan Alley

A little fretwork

Our Partscaster featured as a case study on page 154 is not unusual in being poorly set up as well as having a slightly unfinished feel to the frets and fingerboard. This is luthier John Diggins's solution:

1 John and the author checking the removed neck for excessive relief using an accurate straight edge held up to the light.

2 A quarter-turn with a '2' point Phillips screwdriver corrects the concave tendency in this Vintage-type neck.

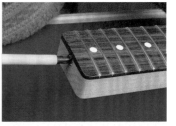

Tech Tip

Fret work isn't for the keen amateur, especially not on a vintage guitar. Practice the art on a cheap Squier first.

Frank Marvel

Fret wear is causing a little 'buzz'

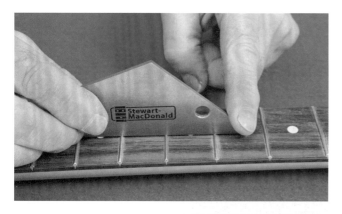

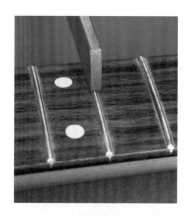

5 The 'flattened' frets are now restored to the correct contour with a large Stewmac fret file (John prefers to use the large file for both Gibson and Fender-type frets and then customise the fret contour by hand).

3 A 'fret rocker' reveals any proud frets. A diamond dressing stone is used to take the top off the proud frets.

6 The frets are then polished, initially with 400 free-cut paper and a soft-backed sanding block then a 1200 grit wet-and-dry.

4 Some protrusion of the fret edges due to wood shrinkage is also dressed.

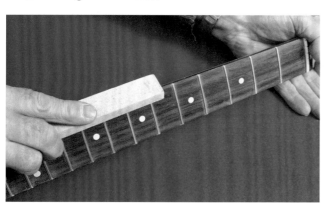

7 A final polish with a buffing wheel is ideal but a similar finish can be had with a D'Addario polishing paper and their small fret polishing template.

B-Bender maintenance

There are two main types of B-Bender for the Telecaster. These offer pedal steel-like effects at the tug of a guitar strap. They need occasional TLC.

Fender Parsons/White B-Bender

Lubrication
■ Apply a drop of lightweight oil on the B string bridge, where the string contacts the saddle. This is the only recommended regular maintenance for the B-Bender.

Tuning
■ First, tune all of the strings including the B string to pitch, using the regular tuning machines on the headstock of the guitar.

■ The B-Bender is actuated by pushing down on the neck of the guitar. The 7mm straight-slot screw located on the top bout of the guitar adjusts the raised pitch of the note on the B string.

■ Turn the screw clockwise to sharpen the pitch of the actuated note and anticlockwise to flatten the pitch of the affected note.

Strings
■ Gene Parsons recommends a B string gauge of .013 to achieve the best tone and performance.

Spring tension
■ Fender do not recommend DIY adjustment of the spring tension on the Fender B-Bender.

Fender Parsons/Green B-Bender

The technical information below addresses particular issues relating to the Parsons/Green version of the B-Bender, which is significantly different to the Custom Shop Parsons/White model. It is given here by kind permission of the co-inventor Gene Parsons.

The Fender B-Bender was designed by Gene Parsons and Meridian Green. When properly set up it will provide smooth, silent, trouble-free operation for many years.

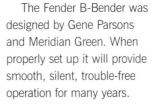

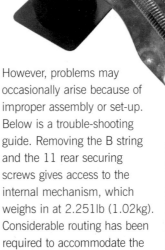

However, problems may occasionally arise because of improper assembly or set-up. Below is a trouble-shooting guide. Removing the B string and the 11 rear securing screws gives access to the internal mechanism, which weighs in at 2.251lb (1.02kg). Considerable routing has been required to accommodate the substantial engineering.

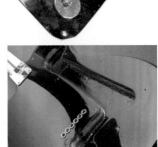

■ Problem A

Squeaking sound when the Bender is actuated

Possible cause 1: If, having oiled the bridge saddle, a squeaking sound persists, or if several B strings have broken, the bridge saddle may need to be filed and smoothed where the B string contacts, or in rare cases replaced. Some Fender American Standard bridge saddles are made of powdered metal and are crystalline in structure. A coining process carried out during their manufacture is intended to harden and smooth the surface of the saddles where the strings contact them. However, in a few of the early runs this coining process was not perfected and the smooth surface would wear away quickly, exposing the string to the abrasive and crystalline metal underneath. More recent bridges have solved this problem.

Possible cause 2: The return spring may be rubbing on the side of the connecting rod clevis.
Remedy: Bend the end loop of the return spring where it attaches to the clevis pin so that the spring is not in contact with the side of the clevis body.

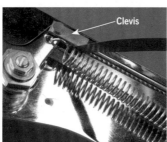

Return spring and clevis showing a .0015in feeler gauge in this gap.

Possible cause 3: The felt pad under the connecting rod is either loose, in the wrong position or missing.
Remedy: Secure the pad with glue and/or replace it.

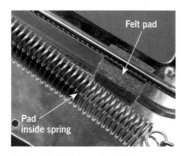

Felt pads in their correct positions.

Possible cause 4: In rare instances the strap lever may be loose, causing it to rub on the surface of the back cover plate.
Remedy: Tighten the screw that fastens the strap lever spindle on to the back cover plate. Make sure that all other components are securely fastened and working absolutely freely.

■ Problem B

Clicking sound when the Bender is released

(*ie* when the strap lever is allowed to return to home position)

Possible cause 1: Components are loose where they're fastened to the back cover plate.
Remedy: Tighten the fastening screws.

Possible cause 2: The connecting rod is coming in contact with the tower.

If this is the problem it will be easy to identify even before the unit is removed from the guitar, because the B string hole in the string pulling pendulum (visible through the slot in the back

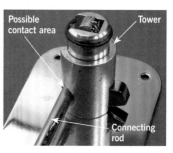

Tower and connecting rod.

cover plate (see photo below) will be positioned too far back in the slot to allow the insertion of a new B string without moving the strap lever. If the lever has to be pulled in order to insert a new B string this is a sure sign that the unit was improperly set up and needs to be adjusted. This problem with improper initial set-up is almost always accompanied by a resounding 'click' when the StringBender is released and allowed to return to home position.

Remedy: Shorten the length of the connecting rod by removing the screws that secure the tower and rotating the tower and connecting rod as a unit, so that the rod threads further into the clevis. One or two clockwise turns should do the trick.

Reattach the tower to the back cover plate and check to make sure that the connecting rod isn't touching it when the StringBender is in the 'home' position. The unit should function silently and smoothly now when pressure on the strap lever is released and the mechanism returns to its 'home' position.

Pendulum, exterior view, correctly and incorrectly adjusted.

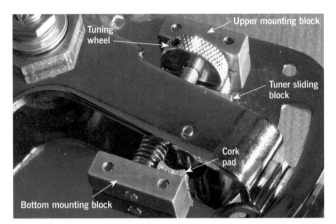

Tuning mechanism, interior bottom view.

Possible cause 3: The cork pad is missing from the bottom tuning mechanism mounting block.
Remedy: Replace the cork pad.

Possible cause 4: The strap lever stop is loose.
Remedy: Tighten the screw that secures the strap lever stop.

Possible cause 5: the tuning mechanism is loose.
Remedy: Tighten the screws securing the mechanism (see photo below). The Allen key required is a 1.4mm and the screws are '1' point Phillips.

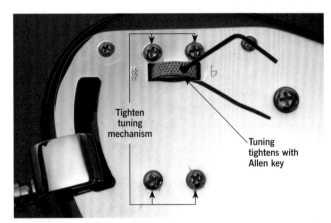

Tuning mechanism, exterior view.

■ Problem C
Clicking sound at end of stroke when Bender is actuated

Possible cause 1: Components are loose where they're fastened to the back cover plate.
Remedy: Tighten the fastening screws.

Possible cause 2: The cork pad is missing on the tuning mechanism sliding block.
Remedy: Replace the cork pad.

Tuning mechanism, interior top view.

Possible cause 3: The strap lever stop is loose.
Remedy: Tighten the screw that secures the strap lever stop.

Possible cause 4: The tuning mechanism is loose.
Remedy: Tighten the screws securing the mechanism.

■ Problem D
Loose tuning mechanism sliding block

Possible cause: There are rare instances when even though the tuning mechanism is securely tightened by its attaching screws the sliding block has too much clearance between its underside and the back cover plate. If this is the case it will tend to flop around during the function of the StringBender and will produce noise.
Remedy: Insert a small piece of rubber or cork between one corner of the sliding block and the back cover plate. Another more permanent solution is to disassemble the tuning mechanism and carefully sand, mill or file some material from the bottom of the mounting blocks until the excess clearance between the sliding block and the back cover plate is eliminated. Be careful, though – don't take off too much!

■ Problem E
The StringBender can't be tuned

Possible cause: The tuner wheel is loose on its shaft.
Remedy: Using the proper size Allen hex wrench, tighten the set screw in the tuner wheel.

■ Problem F
The B string returns sharp when StringBender is used

Possible cause 1: The B string is binding in the B bridge saddle groove.
Remedy: Lubricate the bridge saddle where the B string rides over it. Alternatively the bridge saddle may need to be carefully filed and smoothed where the string contacts it or in rare cases may need to be replaced.

Possible cause 2: The B string is binding in the nut.
Remedy: Re-file the B string groove in the nut so that the string rides freely. Alternatively lubricate the nut with graphite or another suitable lubricant (Gene likes to use oil).

Possible cause 3: Tuning problems can result if any of the components aren't working absolutely freely without binding, or if any component mounting screws have become loosened, or if there is some foreign object or objects inside the guitar.
Remedy: See solutions outlined above.

■ Problem G
Spring sound (boing!) when Bender is actuated

Possible cause: The felt pad is missing from inside the return spring.
Remedy: Replace the felt pad.

■ Problem H
StringBender won't return all the way to home position

or the player finds that it's being actuated unintentionally

Possible cause: Not enough return spring tension.
Remedy: Increase return spring tension by cutting off a loop or loops from the end of the spring where it attaches to the return spring anchor. Simply cut off one loop at a time and bend down the next loop in line so that the return spring can again be attached to the anchor. Reattach the return spring, reinstall the unit and check the return action. If enough tension isn't achieved with one loop removed, then a second, third or more loops may need to be removed until the right action is achieved.

If after removing up to six loops the tension is still insufficient, a new return spring may be necessary. Some of the first Fenders fitted with Parsons/Green B-Benders were somewhat heavy and were more often troubled with inadequate return spring tension.

Some players like more return tension than others. Gene's personal preference is just enough tension for the unit to completely return from any position (even when the strap lever is just slightly pulled up), but no more tension than is necessary. Too much tension will make the Parsons/Green B-Bender difficult to use, particularly when playing up the neck where there's less leverage available.

■ Problem I
String breakage 1½in from the string ball

Possible cause: The string pulling pendulum is manufactured with a 'vee' slot milled into the back of its top which is intended to centre the B string so that it rides over the rounded crown of the pendulum rather than on the edge of the slot. However, on some pendulums the slot is milled too deep, with a sharp edge at its top. The B string must then make a sharp bend over this edge as it changes its vertical direction from inside the pendulum and rides over the crown on its way towards the bridge saddle. If the string is riding on the crown of the pendulum it is unlikely to break – but if it is riding on the sharp edge of the 'vee' slot it is quite likely to break.

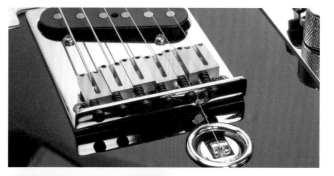

The string rides over the 'vee' slot.

Remedy: Using a small jewellers' file or Dremel, carefully round off the area at the top or point of the 'vee' so that the B string has a smooth, rounded crown to ride over rather than a sharp edge.

Alternatively shorten the connecting rod by threading it further into the clevis (refer to the remedy for Problem B, possible cause 2). This changes the position of the pendulum, rocking it back slightly, which will cause the string to ride more as it should, over the rounded crown rather than over the sharp slot edge.

Another solution is to insert ³⁄₁₆in (inner diameter) spacer washers between the base of the tower and the backplate. By doing this the string pulling pendulum and tower are made to protrude a little higher through the ferrule ring on the face of the guitar body, thus causing the B string to ride more on the rounded crown of the pendulum.

See www.stringbender.com for more information

Vintage truss rod adjustment

N.B. *See the relevant Case studies for the adjustment of headstock truss rods.*

Some very early Fenders had no truss rod at all but Leo soon realised the benefit of being able to correct any concave tendencies resulting from a maple neck succumbing to the stress of six metal strings. The Vintage Tele truss rod adjusts at the heel of the neck, which is difficult to access.

Vintage Telecasters, Broadcasters and Esquires

1 Check your tuning (which should be at standard A440 pitch or your preferred and consistent 'custom pitch'). Next you need to check the neck for relief – is it straight, or bowed either convex or concave? Install a capo at the first fret, depress the sixth string at the last fret.

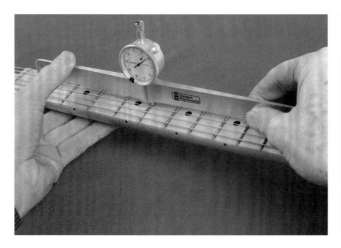

CLOCKWISE

ANTICLOCKWISE

2 With a feeler gauge, check the gap between the bottom of the string and the top of the eighth fret. See the specification chart below for the correct gap. This will vary depending on the radius of your particular neck type. An alternative approach used by luthiers is to use a proprietary relief gauge. If the neck is too concave (indicated by too big a gap measured with the feeler or relief gauge) then you may consider adjusting the truss rod.

DO NOT adjust the truss rod on a rare and precious guitar if you feel unqualified. Talk instead to an experienced guitar tech via your local music shop.

3 Slacken the strings. Then, using a '2' point Phillips screwdriver carefully unscrew the four neck bolts approximately $\frac{1}{8}$in at the top and $\frac{1}{2}$in at the back – this should be enough to tilt the neck back for access to the truss rod screw.

Access to the truss rod on Vintage and Reissue '50s and '60s Teles varies as some have a small cut-out indentation in the pickguard to enable easier access. Generally the earliest guitars and their reissues do not have this. With these guitars you may have to unscrew the neck bolts slightly more to access the truss rod and avoid risking damage to the pickguard. **NB:** Be very careful to note the position of any neck shims (small slivers of wood or card in the neck pocket) if present, as they must remain in the same position when the neck is reseated.

4 Adjust the truss rod screw a quarter-turn clockwise. **NB:** Although this is really a job for a straight-slot 8mm or $\frac{11}{32}$in screwdriver, with the difficult access involved a '2' point Phillips often works well and risks less damage to the plastic pickguard. If you have a Stewmac truss rod driver that's obviously perfect. Note in the picture that the chrome/gold pickup cover is protected by a little low adhesion masking tape.

5 Alternatively, if the neck is too convex (strings are too close to the fingerboard), turn the truss rod nut a quarter-turn anticlockwise to allow the string tension to pull more relief into the neck. **NB:** For obvious reasons the Vintage truss rod was originally conceived to adjust situations with too much relief – it is much more likely to be successful in this application.

6 Checking that any shims are correctly reseated, replace the neck and re-tension the strings to correct pitch. Recheck the relief gap with the feeler gauge and readjust as needed. **NB:** In either case, if you meet excessive resistance when adjusting the truss rod, or your instrument needs constant adjustment, or adjusting the truss rod has no effect on the neck, seek advice from a guitar tech via your local musical instrument shop.

Fender recommended neck relief

Neck radius	Relief
7.25in	.012in (0.3mm)
9.5in to 12in	.010in (0.25mm)
15in to 17in	.008in (0.2mm)

NB: You may need to reset the individual string height following truss rod adjustment – *see page 32.*

81

Nut adjustment and repair

A well set-up nut made of a suitable material can radically transform a guitar's performance. They're traditionally made of bone, but budget guitars often arrive with a cheap plastic substitute. Though I recommend sticking to bone on a vintage guitar for aesthetic reasons, one viable alternative worth considering is the graphite and Teflon impregnated composite, which offers the potential of a non-stick nut, further aiding tuning stability.

A word of warning

The nut is one of the most difficult and skilled adjustments/ replacements for an amateur. Correct nut shaping – which is essential to ensure stable tuning, good tone and correct string spacing – is not a job to be taken lightly. Even if you're buying a pre-formed Tele nut you'll need specialist tools to make minor adjustments. If you're at all unsure of your skills or tooling then I recommend you take your guitar to a qualified guitar tech or Luthier.

■ So why would you want to do this adjustment?
Wear in the nut slots, perhaps caused by the sawing action of extensive Bigsby use or just tuning and wear and tear, can make the action at the nut/first fret too low, resulting in buzzing and snagging.

Another reason is to replace a cheap plastic nut with a substitute which has better acoustic properties and is self-lubricating.

Replacing the nut

Tools required

- Small rubber hammer
- Feeler gauges
- Specialist precision nut-shaping files in the correct gauges for your strings
- Smooth-ended pliers
- Specialist nut seating file
- A sharp craft knife

- A sharp chisel, custom width slightly less than ⅛in
- X-Acto or equivalent razor saws

If you're not a skilled luthier I recommend protecting the fingerboard and headstock with layers of masking tape.

1 Remove the strings. It is important to reduce the shock to the neck by removing first and sixth, second and fifth, etc, in alternate pairs. Check for any overlapping polyurethane or lacquer around the old nut – if this is present then carefully score around the edges with a sharp craft knife. This avoids a messy extraction spoiling the finish on the neck. On our case study the nut was clear of any overlap.

2 Remove the old nut. Often you can tap the nut gently using a small hammer and it eventually becomes loose enough to be removed as one piece – however, this particular piece of plastic was brittle and eventually had to be removed with some hefty pliers.

■ Assuming you were happy with your original string spacing the old nut should be retained intact, as it provides a perfect template for the new string spacing.

3 If necessary clean the nut slot of any surplus adhesive, lacquer, etc. A narrow and sharp file can be used as an effective tool on both the end of the fingerboard and the bottom of the nut slot. A file slightly narrower than ⅛in is required. Also check the fingerboard radius – the new nut will need to mirror this top and bottom.

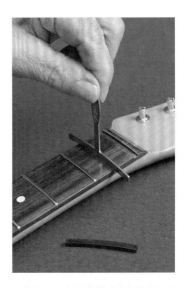

4 The nut we're using here is an oversize blank which has the correct radius but needs to be marked and cut to the correct width.

5 Placing the old and new nuts in parallel in a vice enables guide slots to be copied and cut accurately with an X-Acto saw. Pay particular attention to the spacing of the sixth and first strings from the outside edge. Having strings too close to the edge will make finger vibrato difficult.

6 The string slots can now be roughed in with the correct gauge nut slotting files – in this case .009–.042 (though John Diggins gives the strings a fraction more room than their actual width). Specialist precision nut files (see *Useful contacts* appendix) will allow smoothing of the nut slot bottom without damaging the sides of the slot. These files have smooth edges and a round bottom and are available in the precise size for your chosen string gauges. In practice a luthier would use a slightly smaller file than the requisite slot and use a rolling technique on the forward motion to widen the slot with more control and less chance of the file snagging.

File at a back angle, to shape the floor (or bottom) of the slot correctly. This enables the string to slide through freely. If the slot isn't correctly shaped it will prevent smooth tuning and will hamper the instrument's ability to return to tune, particularly after using a Bigsby vibrato.

The back angle of the slot will give good contact for the string, important for tone, whilst a first contact point at the front (fret end) of the nut will ensure correct intonation.

Ideally the bottom of the nut slot should be rounded as per the relevant string radius. Mitchells gauged abrasive cord is perfect for this.

7 Glue the new nut in place with a *small* amount of Loctite – you may need to remove it in the future!

8 With the nut in place you can fine-tune the depth of the nut slots with the X-Acto saw and nut files.

Feeler gauges

Feeler gauges usually come in sets with a number of blades. The thickness of each blade is marked in thousandths of an inch and hundredths of a millimetre. A marking of 0.040 indicates the feeler is 40 thousandths of an inch thick. It may also indicate a measurement of 1.02mm. A feeler marked 0.005 indicates the thickness is 5 thousandths of an inch. It may also indicate 0.12mm.

In practice most skilled luthiers do this work by 'eye' and 'feel'. The correct thickness of feeler gauge placed in front of the nut can, however, serve as a barrier against over-filing.

■ If you have access to a specialist nut slotting gauge this can be used to accurately measure the nut height of the individual strings and calculate the exact depth of each slot.

This works by 'zeroing' the gauge on the top of the unfretted string and then depressing the string to indicate an accurate measure of the unfretted height of the string, at that fret, in thousandths

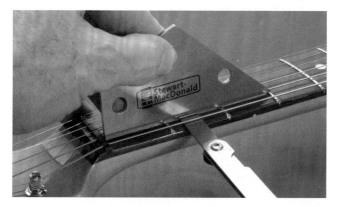

Emergency measures

An alternative to a complete nut replacement, and useful in an emergency – especially if only one or two nut slots are too deep – is to recycle some material from the top of the nut (assuming excess is available) and use this as infilling material.

To do this, tape both sides of the nut with masking tape then take a coarse file and file the top of the nut approximately half the depth you expect to raise the slots. Catch the loose filings on a piece of paper.

Fill the offending slots with the loose filings. Then carefully soak the filings with thin superglue. Press the solution into place with a toothpick.

When dry, refile the slots, referring to the methods described above. As before, the slots should be made so the string sits in about half to three-quarters of their diameter, though the guitar will cope quite well with deeper nut slots, especially if you're a 'heavy picker'. Slots should taper downwards on the tuner side, and again the strings' first point of contact must be at the fret side of the nut.

✎ Tech Tip

Graphite dust used for lock lubrication makes a good nut lubricant but it does tend to go everywhere when applied using the blower provided. Mixing a little graphite with some Vaseline petroleum jelly makes a useful and controllable lubricant paste. Apply it very sparingly.

John Diggins – Luthier

of an inch. Otherwise you could use some feeler gauges to calculate the height of the first fret. The correct depth for the string slots is slightly more than the fret height, which can be calculated using a feeler gauge and a straight edge.

■ If for some reason you don't have the old nut then a specialist tool, a 'compensated nut spacing template', is the easiest way to get even spacing between the outsides of adjoining strings – a more important factor than equal spacing at their centres. Use this or the old nut to determine the position of the remaining string slots.

■ Surprising as it might seem, expert luthiers often determine the individual string spacing by eye. Though this sounds a little unscientific, the precise calculations in thousandths of an inch are made very complex by the fact that each string is a different gauge. (This is were the 'compensated nut spacing template' makes a useful reference.) You can adopt this pro method to a degree by positioning the strings in very shallow 'pilot' slots and then making any minor adjustments by eye before completing your actual filing of the final slots.

■ When a string binds in the nut slot, it makes a pinging sound as it breaks free of the slot. This ping is often attributed to the tremolo/vibrato, as it's the use of this device that triggers the release of the snagging. However, it's most often the nut that is the real problem.

■ Any nut will eventually need lubricating with graphite (*see page 66*).

Pickup replacement

Arguably the most distinctive aspect of the Tele's sound originates from its single coil pickups, particularly the bridge pickup which is integrated into the bridge.

Superficially all single coil pickups may look the same, but a closer look reveals many subtle and some not so subtle variations.

As the case studies in this book reveal, pickup outputs can vary, and different types of coil windings, wire thicknesses etc all have a significant effect on the crucial sound.

Many budget Teles – particularly the Chinese made-Squier 'Affinitys' – have cost-efficient but (some would suggest) 'sound compromised' pickup arrangements. For instance, there have been some Tele pickups without the metal plate on the base, with a resulting change of tone. For more on this see Appendix 2, Bridge pickup base plate functions.

The most common 'improvement' to a basic Tele is a pickup replacement. There are many replacement pickup options, but as we are dealing with a 'classic' Tele I will

detail a very popular change which entails fitting Seymour Duncan 'Five-Two' pickups to a retro-style Squier.

These unique pickups have Alnico V magnets for the three 'low' strings and Alnico II magnets on the treble strings – correcting the tendency towards slightly muddy bass and over-bright treble that some players perceive on classic Teles. (The II and V refer to the strength of the pickup magnets, II being weaker than V.)

1 Remove the strings. As usual, this should be done one string at a time and working in from the sixth and first to fifth and second etc, to save undue shock and strain on the neck. An electric string winder saves a lot of finger effort. Once the strings are all free of the machine heads, removing the 'curly ends' with a good set of wire cutters makes extraction through the bridge assembly a lot easier.

2 It's worth making a note of the existing pickup heights as a guide, especially if you are broadly happy with your guitar's performance and intonation (yes, due to magnetic interference pickup height can interfere with intonation!). A recycled business card makes an ideal memo card.

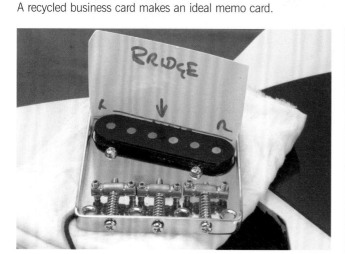

3 Unscrew the scratchplate with a '1' or '2' point Phillips screwdriver and store the screws safely in some sort of container.

■ Some modern Teles feature an extra fret, which means that care must be taken manoeuvring the scratchplate from under the lip that extends the fingerboard an extra ¼in or so to accommodate this additional fret.

4 Remove the control plate using a '1' or '2' point Phillips screwdriver, depending on the model (or a straight-slot on very old Teles and Broadcasters).

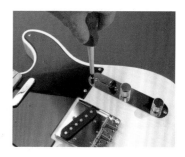

5 Make a careful note of where your original pickup wires are connected – label the connections or make your own sketch of what goes where.

■ Seymour Duncan supply a clear diagram with the 'Five-Two', indicating the correct wiring arrangement assuming that you have a standard three-way Fender switch installed. But since you may *not* have this switch it's doubly important that you draw yourself a diagram.

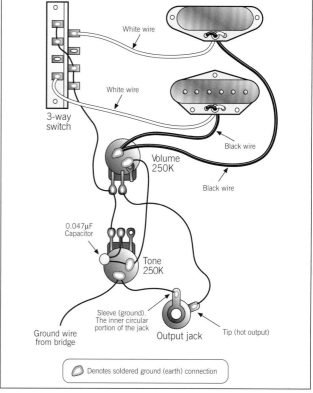

6 Unsolder the pickup selector and pot connections. For this you'll need a 25W soldering iron, an iron stand, and a wet sponge for removing redundant solder from the iron. When removing the wires from the back of the control pots and pickup selector be as quick as possible, to avoid any heat damage to the components.

8 Remove the four bridge plate screws with a '1' point (or sometimes a '2') Phillips screwdriver.

7 Unscrew the neck pickup, held in by two '1' point Phillips woodscrews.

9 With a '1' point Phillips screwdriver, carefully remove the old pickups. (Unsolder them if not already done.)

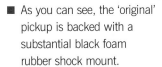

- As you can see, the 'original' pickup is backed with a substantial black foam rubber shock mount.

- This will have to be carefully removed and adhered to the 'Five-Two'. Fortunately this proves no problem and the new pickup sits quite happily on the original foam. Take care, however, when locating the woodscrews in the fibre mounting as this could easily be damaged. I prelocated the screws in the fibre and used the 'original' screws, as these were slightly longer than the Seymour Duncan ones.

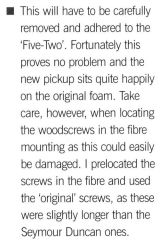

- Thread the new output wires through the small hole into the control cavity and replace the pickguard.

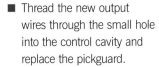

- Note that the original equipment has metal springs to facilitate adjustment of the pickup heights, whereas Seymour provides more traditional soft latex washers for this role. John Diggins tells me this is probably because the latex affords better acoustic damping than springs. The snag, however, is that they naturally perish over time. I will assume you *are* going to use the supplied authentic latex option.

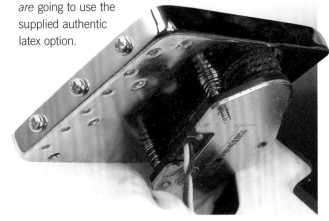

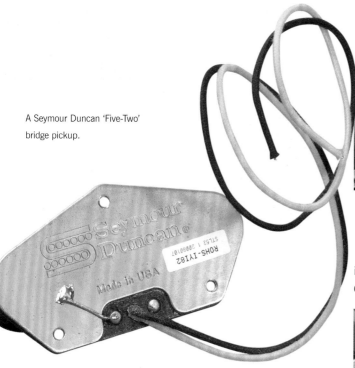

A Seymour Duncan 'Five-Two' bridge pickup.

11 Tin the new wires with a little solder for quicker and more effective joints.

12 Solder the new connections as per your drawing or the Seymour Duncan plan. The finished solder joint should be bright and shiny, indicating a good conducting medium – a 'dry' joint will be dull, indicating a potential problem. Reassemble.

10 Thread the new pickup wire through to the control cavity and carefully install the 'Five-Two' pickups using the latex washers. **NB:** It's often easier to 'screw' the washers on first and then fit the pickup.

- Note the use of the template for initial height setting. Be sure the ground wire protruding from the guitar body is going to make contact with the bridge plate.

- Also note the new pickups have authentic old-fashioned but wonderfully useful 'waxed' wire. An advantage of the old-fashioned stuff is that you can push the insulation back to expose the conductor for easy soldering.

- It's *very* important to use the minimum of solder, especially with frail economy-type switches, as stray solder can easily flow to the casing, causing a short to earth/ground and consequent loss of output.

In conclusion

The 'Five-Twos' do what they say on the tin – they provide a smoother, more even response across the strings and are less microphonic than the originals.

A word of caution, however, based on my long observation of 'guitar sound'. I think that perhaps the reason we like the characteristic sound of a Tele, a Strat, a Les Paul, a Gretsch, a Goldtop or a Rickenbacker is defined precisely by their quirks and character. Many 'Boutique' guitars are fabulous but can have less character – technically perfect is not the same thing as 'interesting'. Should we perhaps hesitate before we smooth out the wrinkles that give a face character?

Volume and tone controls

Testing, cleaning and/or replacement
of standard 250K pots

■ Why would you want to do this?
The Tele's volume and tone controls are
carbon-based potentiometers, an invention
of the late 19th and early 20th centuries.
They are crude and mechanical but they do
the job. They do, however, generate 'dirt'
by the nature of the mechanical friction of
metal on carbon. This loose carbon inside
the pot impedes the electrical contact and
often causes it to be intermittent and prone
to audible crackling. Corrosion of the metal
parts adds 'snap' to the 'crackle'. For our
purposes we shall concentrate on the volume
pot, as due to their more frequent use these
are the ones most likely to fail.

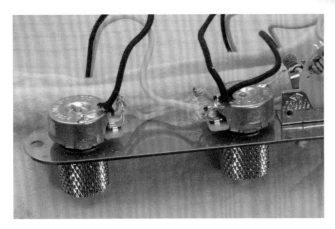

■ A little background
Leo Fender left school in 1928, the year the first viable
thermionic valves became commercially available. He was
already an enthusiastic radio ham and was soon in business
building and renting PA systems for local fairs. His formal start
in business came in 1938, with Fender's Radio Service. He
literally knocked on doors in the neighbourhood of his shop at
the corner of Spadra and Santa Fe Boulevard, Fullerton, and
offered to repair broken radios.

The simple tone and volume controls found in 1930s radios
– the 'resistive capacitor' circuits – are the basis for those still
found in most Fender guitars.

■ Understanding the
resistive capacitor circuit
If you alter the resistance
of a circuit (in this case by
turning your guitar's tone
control) and that circuit also
has a capacitor in circuit,
which it does, the frequency
response of that circuit will
alter – we perceive this as a
change in tone.

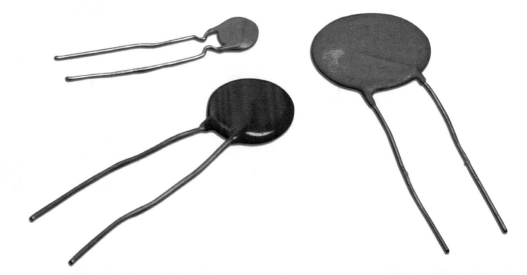

Testing a pot to see if it is still functioning

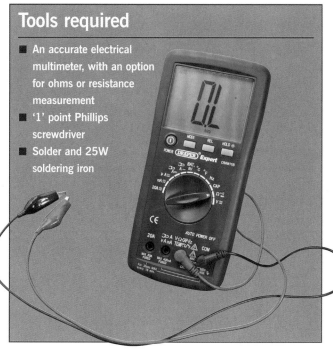

3 Set the multimeter to 'ohms' measurement in the R x 10K range. Zero the meter. Bring the multimeter probes into contact with the two outer connection prongs. A vintage Fender volume or tone control should present a reading of 250K, give or take 20 per cent. A figure higher than this suggests the pot should be replaced. **NB:** It's worth checking that the guitar has the correct pots fitted, as with an old guitar they may have been changed at some point. Sometimes the resistance value is marked on the pot casing.

■ Some later Teles can have higher pot values, so it's important to check Fender's website for the appropriate values for your specific model.

4 If the pot is giving the correct resistance value you can also test the smooth working of the carbon track.

■ Apply one of the multimeter probes to one of the pot's outer prongs and the other to the middle prong. Use crocodile clips to hold the probes in position. The resistance value indicated on the multimeter should smoothly alter as you rotate the pot control. If the needle shows an intermittent response the pot may need cleaning.

1 Remove the strings from the guitar and access the electrics by carefully removing the control panel with a '1' point Phillips screwdriver (or for this Relic a 4mm straight-slot). Keep the screws together in a small container (a pickup box is perfect).

2 Isolate the pot by first labelling then unsoldering the internal wiring. If you're slow with your soldering iron then use a pair of crocodile clips or something similar as effective 'heat sinks' to draw heat away from other damageable components. John Diggins actually uses a set of surgical forceps that not only draw away heat, but have enough mass to hold things in position if required.

5 Repeat the process, this time testing the other outer prong in relation to the middle prong.

Cleaning

Sometimes a well-used pot can be restored to useful service by simple cleaning/lubrication. However, the replacement pots are so cheap and readily available nowadays it's worth considering replacement. Also, 'switch cleaner' works well on switches but less well on carbon pots.

1 Using an appropriate screwdriver, unscrew the control panel and keep the screws together in a small container.

2 Beware of the metal parts of the electrical assembly scratching the guitar finish – you may want to mask the finish with a lightly taped duster. The control panel will not remove completely, as the wiring is soldered to the output jack. However, you should have enough slack to access the pots.

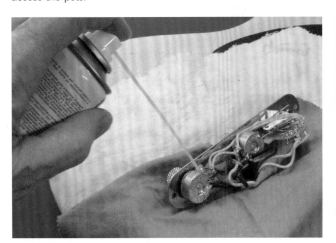

3 Using the supplied hose, squirt WD40 into the pot through the opening on the side of the case. If the pot is sealed, try cleaning via the microscopic gap around the shaft. You should try if possible to flush out any dirt. Also turn the pot shaft to allow the fluid to reach all of the contact points. Avoid getting WD40 on the guitar surface, and wear safety glasses to protect your eyes. Carefully replace the control assembly, and test the cleaned pot.

Noise problems or 'dead spots'

Everything mechanical eventually wears out, so consider a replacement pot. It makes a huge amount of sense to replace with an exact Fender specification pot, readily available via the Internet (see *Useful contacts appendix*). The type 250k pots are available slightly cheaper from radio supply shops, but all pots are not created equal and you may find slight variances in shaft sizes etc which can cause problems.

Replacing a volume or tone control

NB: This will involve electrical soldering, so protect your eyes with safety glasses and cover any guitar parts that may be spattered by stray solder.

1 Remove the domed knob from the offending control. These are attached with various grub screw types, 2.5mm straight-slots on the Vintage and American Standard, or are even just a push-fit on recent Squier guitars.

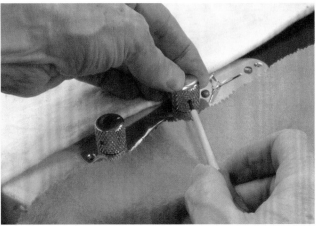

2 Using an appropriate screwdriver, unscrew the control panel and keep the screws together in a small container.

3 Beware of the metal parts of the electrical assembly scratching the guitar finish – you may want to mask the finish with a lightly taped duster or masking tape. The control panel will not remove completely, as the pickup wiring is soldered to the output jack. It is often worth separating the control assembly by unsoldering the output jack at the pickup end.

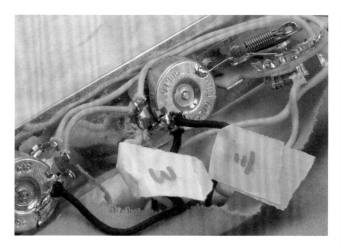

4 Label the cables connected to the old pot with some cloth-backed tape ('cloth-backed' is easy to write on, though a sticky label wrapped back on itself works just as well), assign each cable a number, and draw yourself a little sketch of what goes where. Some older cables are not colour coded and there are alternative wiring options, so taking this approach restores your wiring intact and gets you back to the sound you've come to expect.

5 Carefully unsolder the old pot with the lowest rating soldering iron you have – 15W may work but a higher rated iron used quickly will be fine.

6 Use a socket-type spanner – the size will vary from model to model but 0.5in is common (*see Case studies on pages 62 onwards*) – to unbolt the nut securing the pot to the control panel. (A socket-type spanner/wrench is less likely to mark the chrome than a conventional spanner.)

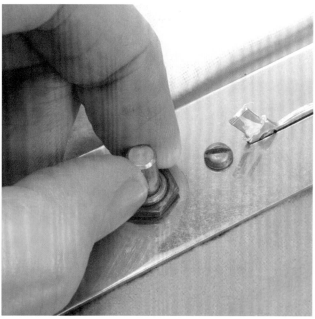

7 Place the new pot in position, retaining the old orientation (refer to your diagram), and fix with the new retaining nut.

8 Tin the new connecting tags for the replacement pot and solder them in place as per your labelling. A lollipop stick makes an effective steadying aid and also doesn't waste any heat. It's important not to move the joint whilst the solder is still molten. Reassemble as before.

Pickup selection options and rewiring

As we've seen earlier Leo Fender had very individual ideas about the three-way switch and was really an advocate of the idea that 'one pickup at a time is quite enough'. In fact some early Esquires are reported by *Gruhn's Guide to Vintage Guitars* as having only a two-way switch! However, things have moved on, and Leo himself would surely be surprised and delighted at the variety of switching arrangements available on the current batch of Telecasters.

Straightforward upgrade

We will install a robust Schaller T Model obtained from
www.stewmac.com.

1 Remove the control
plate using a '1'
point Phillips. Draw
a sketch of the current
wiring as a reference and
label the wires if you're
in any doubt about what
goes where.

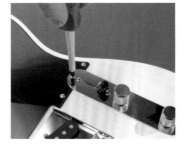

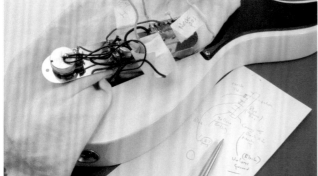

2 Unsolder the
existing switch.
Remove the switch
using a '2' point Phillips.

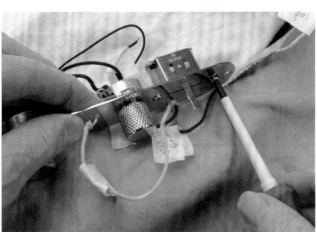

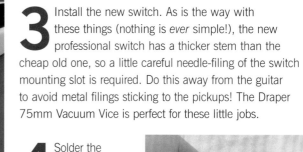

3 Install the new switch. As is the way with
these things (nothing is *ever* simple!), the new
professional switch has a thicker stem than the
cheap old one, so a little careful needle-filing of the switch
mounting slot is required. Do this away from the guitar
to avoid metal filings sticking to the pickups! The Draper
75mm Vacuum Vice is perfect for these little jobs.

4 Solder the
connections
as per your
drawing or the
manufacturer's
diagram (or a bit of
both). Pre-tinning
the connections
with a little solder
makes things simpler.
Reassemble the control
panel and install.

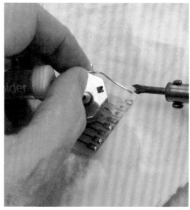

Humbucker options

The installation of a humbucker pickup on the Tele is a
common 'Hot Rod', pioneered by Albert Collins and exploited
by many others, including Keith Richards and Andy Summers.
I confess I used to share Roy Buchanan's view that this was
'like painting a moustache on the Mona Lisa', but having
enjoyed the versatility of Fender's recently reissued Deluxe
(*see page 158*) I'm a willing convert.

NB: I would never suggest doing this work on a real Vintage
Tele when a Vibe '50s Squier guitar is easily and economically
available. Like many modern Teles, the Squier guitar is already
pre-routed for this popular modification.

Routing for a humbucker

If you wish to rout an older guitar for a humbucker you'll need a guide template to avoid any unnecessary wood removal or damage to the guitar finish – you could make one from some scrap Perspex or buy one inexpensively from www.stewmac.com. Always use appropriate eye protection when using power tools.

John Diggins has made his own humbucker template and this can be safely used with a regular domestic router – the template is attached to the guitar with double-sided tape to prevent any movement.

The finished rout is the right size and depth for most humbuckers.

You may want to consider painting the interior of the new rout with some screening paint and connecting the new surface to earth/ground.

Option 1

How about we install a four-wire humbucker that has split coils and thus offers us the option to retain the classic single-coil sound of the Tele as well as a humbucker sound at the flick of a push-pull pot? The 'Stag Mag' Seymour Duncan pickup offers *true* single-coil sound as well as the option of a warm-neck humbucker.

1 The first challenge is the Bakelite pickguard that's so much a part of the classic Tele. If you have a vintage one of these set it aside and install a replacement, custom-cut for the much larger humbucker mounting. Ours came from WD Music Products.

2 Install the pickup to the guard. In this case the mounting holes were too small and needed careful enlarging with a round needle file.

3 Thread the height adjustment springs onto the pickup bolts and set the pickup at an approximate height.

4 De-string the guitar and undo the old guard and control plate. Draw a sketch of the current wiring as a reference and label the wires if you're in any doubt about what goes where. De-solder from the three-way switch and remove the single-coil pickup using a '1' point Phillips.

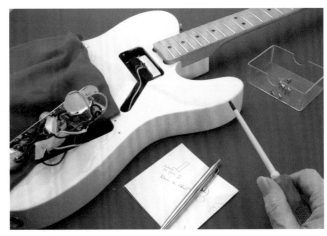

5 In this example installation of the new guard and pickup is a great success apart from the pickup mounting bolts, which are about 3mm too long for the depth of the pre-routed humbucker cavity. So a little hacksawing is required! Naturally this means taking the bolts off the pickup to avoid stray metal filings sticking to it. Be careful to cut the screws so as not to damage the end of the thread – you may need to gently file any sharp ends to provide a 'lead in' on the thread.

6 The height-setting springs are also often too long and reducing them to about 20mm will make this fiddly job that much easier. A bit of low adhesion masking tape protects that delicate Bakelite finish. Thread the new wires from the humbucker.

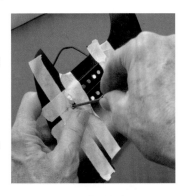

7 For a straightforward Seymour Duncan series humbucker arrangement, the ends of both coils (red and white in this instance) are joined. The black goes to the three-way switch pin one (live) and the green (start of coil one) and the ground wires go to ground (earth) on the back of the volume pot. However, these wiring colours vary from brand to brand so follow the diagram supplied with *your* pickup. Pre-tinning the wires aids quick soldering.

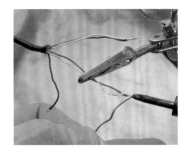

8 A little insulation tape prevents the bare ground wire from shorting.

9 Reassemble. A small misalignment of the new pickguard with the old one is compensated for by plugging the old holes with a cocktail stick and resiting some of the new screws.

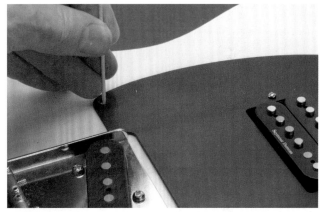

10 The new pickup balances well with the Tele and doesn't look to me as out of place as a chrome 'canned' humbucker. The sound is Fender in character but with more middle and low frequencies – I'll find a use for it. I like the authentic Bakelite scratchplate which now replaces the thicker original.

Bakelite pickguards

Early '50s Teles are prized for their frail Bakelite guards. Replacements are available:

'Our Bakelite is the real thing, 4X black paper phenolic sheeting that is .062in thick. It has a slightly grained appearance on the surface, and if you look carefully at the edges of any of the routs, you should see kind of a coarse edging. This material is also much stiffer than vinyl if you flex it.'

WD Music Products, UK

Option 2

How about we also install a split-coil facility, giving us ready access to a Strat-like single coil at the neck (without any more pickup installation)? This is achieved by tapping into the Seymour Duncan series humbucker wiring and shorting one of the coils to earth. Most modern replacement humbuckers are available in four-wire versions with this modification in mind.

The 'shorting' can be achieved in several ways but I personally favour the 'push-pull pot'. This avoids changing the outward appearance of a classic guitar. The push-pull pot functions exactly like its 'static' alternative except that it also contains a versatile double-pole double-throw switch activated by a pull on the shaft.

The only snag is the $1\frac{1}{8}$in depth required in the control cavity, and some careful routing may be required on some Teles. Please don't do this on a classic '50s guitar!

1 Remove the control plate and make a careful note of the current wiring to the existing volume pot. Label the wires if you have any doubts. De solder the original connections.

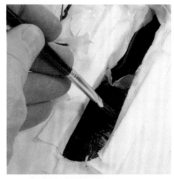

3 I then had to resort to a hand router and some fine chiselling to remove the excess pine, which was tougher than expected. If you have any doubts about your woodworking prowess now is the time to consult a skilled luthier!

4 The black screening paint will need touching up on the bare timber to ensure earth continuity. Physically install the new pot.

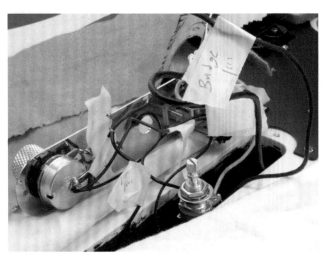

2 This reveals a snag – the control cavity isn't deep enough to accommodate the push-pull's extra depth! This means careful extraction of the problem timber and resiting of the earth connection for the cavity screening paint. Having carefully masked the guitar with low adhesion masking tape, a small X-Acto saw is used to define the enlarged cavity.

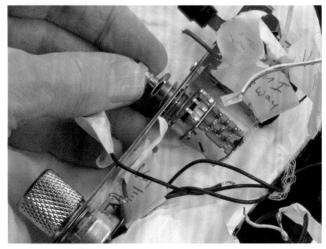

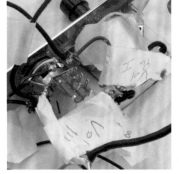

5 Solder the push-pull pot as a direct replacement for the volume or tone control.

6 Solder the red and white (coil ends) wires to the switch poles as shown in the figure below (these wire colours will vary according to manufacturer, so take note of your supplier's code) and make a jumper connection to ground or earth (the back of the pot will do fine). I used the tone control ground, as the back of the volume was getting a little crowded!

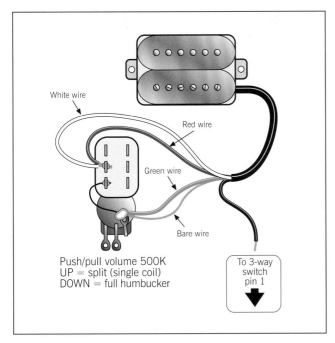

White wire

Red wire

Green wire

Bare wire

Push/pull volume 500K
UP = split (single coil)
DOWN = full humbucker

To 3-way switch pin 1

7 Reassemble. The guitar works fine, and despite all that surgery was still in tune! The neck single-coil option sounds brilliant – just like a Tele with a bit of Strat 'neck pickup' thrown in – and the double-coil humbucker option adds that bit of warmth when needed.

Option 3

Andy Summers of Police favours a 'one pickup out of phase with the other' capability on his Tele. This can be achieved by using a second push-pull pot.

1 Remove the control plate and make a careful note of the existing tone control wiring.

2 De-solder and remove the old pot. This particular pot required an 11mm socket, but this will vary depending on country of origin. Carefully de-solder the existing capacitor for reuse.

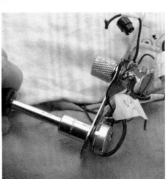

3 I suggest you do most of the push-pull switch and capacitor wiring on the new pot *before* installation. Note the 'loop wires' on the switch and the extra earth wire to the switch casing (see the figure below) – I initially forget this one and the pickup naturally ceased to work! (Thanks, JD, for putting me straight! Note also that this is my 'guitar player' soldering, not John's luthier standard!)

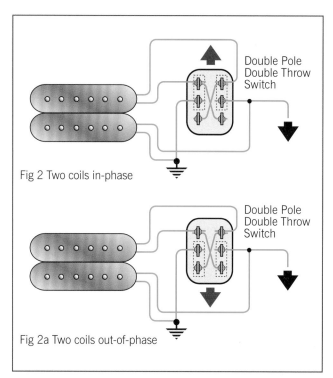

Fig 2 Two coils in-phase

Double Pole Double Throw Switch

Fig 2a Two coils out-of-phase

Double Pole Double Throw Switch

4 Fit the replacement push-pull pot and wire the tone control wires using the original wiring configuration as per your drawing. Note, however, that the live and earth wires from the bridge pickup now have to be routed to this new switch *before* the three-way selector.

5 The control cavity is now very crowded and I had to solder the switch output wires in situ then turn and fix the pot before attaching all the case-mounted earth/ground wires.

6 If you're using a Seymour Duncan pickup at the bridge as in our example you'll need to do one more thing. The SD pickups often have an extra jumper wire to ground the base plate. You'll need to cut this for phase reversal or the phase reverse switch will simply short the output to ground! Start by removing the bridge using a '2' point Phillips. The de-tensioned strings are here safely cushioned in a bubble-wrap bag.

7 Then snip the earth/ground jumper wire. You must now provide a ground from anywhere on the pickup base plate to the ground/earth of the output jack.

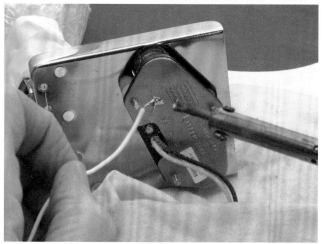

8 You may also need to provide a ground for the bridge now, though this is already in place on many Teles – as is the case here. This is simply a wire jammed behind the bridge that's connected to the earth side of the output jack.

■ This completes a versatile switching arrangement which enables the bridge pickup to be heard in *and* out of phase with either the humbucker or single-coil version of the neck pickup. If desired you could also rewire for optional series/parallel switching of the humbucker as detailed in Seymour Duncan's supplied diagrams. This may involve S1 'hidden switches' or mini toggle switches.

Personally I would consider keeping a stage guitar relatively simple, as time spent on switching is time away from the real business of communicating with your audience – so find a happy medium that works for you.

Studio and teaching guitars can be more complicated, as you may have a little more time to seek the ideal sound for specific overdubs and demonstrations.

Pickup height settings

It is reasonable to assume that having your pickups set high and thereby closer to the strings will produce more output from your Tele and possibly more 'tone'. However, be aware that the magnetic field from a pickup is strong enough to interfere with the natural excursion of the strings, which can result in very odd harmonic effects. Most notably the sixth string sounded at the 12th fret can produce odd 'beats' and very uneven intonation.

Fender have strict recommendations:

1 Depress all of the strings at the last fret. Using a 6in (150mm) ruler, measure the distance from the bottom of the first and sixth strings to the top of the pole-piece (top of the pickup on a conventional neck pickup). As a rule of thumb, the distance should be greatest at the sixth string for the neck pickup position, and closest at the first string for the bridge pickup position.

Follow the measurement guidelines from the Fender chart below as a starting point. The distance will vary according to the amount of magnetic pull of your specific pickup.

In the last analysis you'll have to decide for yourself on the most effective compromise between output and magnetic interference.

	Bass side	Treble side
Texas Specials	$\frac{1}{8}$in (3.6mm)	$\frac{3}{32}$in (2.4mm)
Vintage style	$\frac{3}{32}$in (2.4mm)	$\frac{5}{64}$in (2.0mm)
Noiseless Series	$\frac{1}{8}$in (3.6mm)	$\frac{3}{32}$in (2.4mm)
Standard Single-Coil	$\frac{5}{64}$in (2.0mm)	$\frac{1}{16}$in (1.6mm)
Humbuckers	$\frac{1}{16}$in (1.6mm)	$\frac{1}{16}$in (1.6mm)
Lace Sensors	As close as possible	

2 Neck pickup. Remove the pickguard using a '1' or '2' point Phillips depending on the model (straight-slots on some pre-'52 guitars). Then, using a '1' point Phillips screwdriver and an accurate metal ruler, adjust the height to the recommended starting point.

NB: Beware that when lowering the bridge pickup extensively the pickup screws sometimes becomes disengaged from their sockets. This procedure isn't recommended just before a gig, as relocating the screw usually means removing the bridge and strings!

Specific case studies

For approaching 60 years the Telecaster has changed very little. The iconic guitars of the early '50s are still the benchmark and are constantly emulated. There *have* been various attempts to improve the Tele, but these tend to merely 'gild the lily'. What makes the Tele such an icon is its simplicity. This chapter provides enough detail for the routine maintenance and appraisal of some common variants.

LEFT A 'broadcast' of Teles.

RIGHT James Burton signature model.

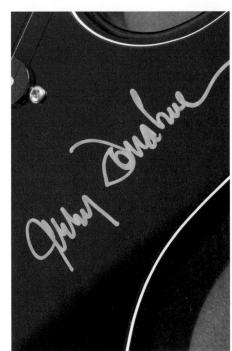

Case study variants

Fender currently offer everything from pre-aged replicas of the first Telecasters and Esquires to 'super Teles' with humbuckers and elaborate binding. The Fender USA flagship guitar is accompanied by licensed lookalikes originating in China, Indonesia, Japan and Mexico.

The guitars usefully fall into distinct groupings:

■ **Late prototypes and early production, 1949–51**
The Broadcaster, Telecaster and its companion Esquires, exhibiting the fine-tuning and hand-finish that defined a classic.

■ **The classic 'working man's guitar', 1951–present**
The 'canoe paddle' whose sound can complement every genre of popular music.

■ **'Super Teles'**
Thinline, humbucker, Bigsby and B-Bender fitted elaborations that take the guitar one step beyond.

Custom Shop reissues
Fender offer the guitar in every imaginable 'dressing', from Relic clones to 'Nashville Roses' and 'Rodeo Sweethearts'.

Relics, Vintage old stock, 'Road Worn' and Closet Classics
Distressed, as new, delivered by time machine or stored under the bed for 58 years – take your choice!

Artist series
Endorsees' guitars from James Burton to Jerry Donahue and Avril Lavigne, alongside a tribute guitar for Muddy Waters.

Budget Squiers
The classic Tele and most variants are available as budget guitars carrying the 'Squier' marque. The Vibe '50s model makes a brilliant starting point for an 'upgrade guitar'.

■ All these variants are to some extent covered here and the core elements of your guitar should be reflected in the following case studies, at least in principle.

USA-made Esquire '57–'59

Serial No. 22359

Assembled beside the railway tracks at the original Santa Fe Ave, Fullerton, California workshop in the late '50s, with Leo Fender on site, this guitar is typical of many '50s Fenders in that the parts and serial number imply different – and in this case earlier – dates: '57–'58 for the serial number stamping, '57 for the manufacture of the pots, '58 for the bridge saddles and March '59 as a neck date. All very plausible, given the nature of Leo's exponentially expanding workshop!

The single pickup guitar epitomises everything that Leo's original concept ever promised, but without the luxury that came with the hastily added second pickup. As it happens many guitarists largely ignore the neck pickup on their Tele – the sound they crave is locked in the bridge-encased single coil chime. This guitar could, in fact, have had two pickups had it been built in 1950, but from 1951 onwards the two-pickup guitar became the Broadcaster, Nocaster or Telecaster and the Esquire name was retained to denote the one-pickup version of the same body shape. There are a few very early two-pickup Esquires still extant.

Condition on arrival

This much-played guitar is still gigging after 50 years and once belonged to Bernie Marsden of Whitesnake. The present owner Richard (Paddy) Patrick, tone hound and Northamptonshire guitar legend, found Leo's original pickup unworkable at modern high volumes and has retro-fitted a Seymour Duncan Vintage-spec pickup (he has the original in a safe place!). He prefers a high action and heavy strings, so the guitar has a lot of neck relief, .022 at the ninth fret sixth string and .018 at the first. The strings are usually a set of custom-picked Ernie Ball .011, .014, .018, .030, .042, .052.

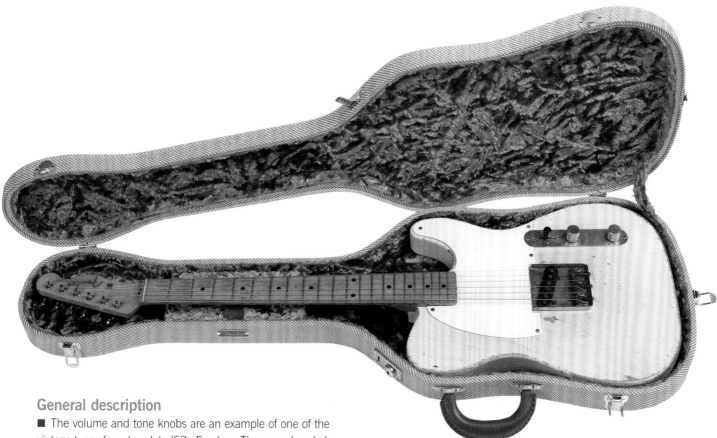

General description

■ The volume and tone knobs are an example of one of the vintage types found on late '50s Fenders. These are knurled and have a flat top without a dome. This, the truss rod, pickup height and the saddle screws are the components that Leo had not yet managed to convert to employing modern Phillips assembly-line-friendly screws.

■ The current pickup on this guitar is a Seymour Duncan 'identikit' replacement complete with the post-'52 staggered pole-pieces designed to give a more balanced output from all six strings.

■ The patented three-way switch has a distinctive early '50s black rounded 'top hat' knob made by Harry Davies Mfg Co of Chicago. The three positions are forward or neck position with an extra capacitor in circuit for bass guitar impressions, middle for the bridge pickup with tone control available, and back for straight-ahead 'no electronics in circuit' set the controls to 'sting' mode.

■ Interestingly the first one-pickup Esquires were supplied *without* a three-way switch. But Leo was clearly seeking something that would eventually emerge in 1951 as 'a bass for guitarists' – the first Tele-like Precision bass. He was also aware of the prevalent bass-heavy 'jazz' electric guitar sound of the time and didn't want to lose a customer.

■ The bridge, with its 'two strings per saddle' adjustable for height and length and its integral relationship with the pickup, is an important part of this guitar's sound, and many distinguished players prefer this arrangement to a more modern 'one string per saddle' set-up.

■ This specific instrument has steel saddles threaded for string positioning, an innovation of mid-1958.

■ Originally all '50s and many '60s Esquires had a chrome 'ashtray' cover over the bridge. This made good cosmetic and even electrical screening sense, but prevents the player from palm muting and 'playing on the bridge', both of which techniques are key to the classic Tele sound. Consequently most 'ashtrays' are 'missing in action'.

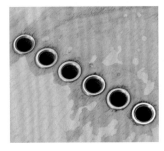

■ The 'through-body' stringing is an important part of the Fender guitar sound.

■ The battle-scarred ash body is a relatively heavy 7.75lb and approximately 1¾in thick at the edge.

■ The neck is a soft version of the '50s 'V' profile with a fairly constant depth of approximately 2.2cm, slightly thicker at the headstock and heel. The back of the neck has a distinct well-played-in appeal. The neck date is March '59. Note also the considerable rust on the truss rod slot. *See Appendix 8 for more specific information on neck profiles.*

■ The truss rod is accessed at the neck butt. Any adjustment requires a straight slot ⁵⁄₁₆in screwdriver. The 'Righty Tighty, Lefty Loosy' principle applies, particularly on an old and rusty rod – go left a bit first to check for freedom of movement! The channel Leo provided means the truss rod can be adjusted 'on guitar'.

■ The nut is a piece of yellowing shrunken bone which needs a little adjustment. The strings are, however, moving freely in the slots – bone has the advantage of being self lubricating.

■ The machine heads are probably '60s vintage-type replacement Klusons that exhibit the inevitable rust that follows heavy gigging in sweaty clubs and bars. The '62–'66 dating is attributed to the parallel arrangement of the words 'Kluson' and 'Deluxe' on the backplates. These machines still function quite well. Note that none of the Klusons actually fit properly – these are one of the few parts Leo could neither make himself nor get Kluson to redesign for his 'inline' concept. Early Fenders have crudely adapted Klusons originally conceived for conventional three-a-side arrays.

■ The headstock has the distinctive early '50s shape with the developing Fender logo and plain 'ESQUIRE' script. The logo is positioned correctly for a late '50s Fender, the introduction of an improvised string tree from serial number 0013 onwards causing a little reframing of the headstock layout. This improved 'gull wing' stringtree is itself a little loose and eccentric.

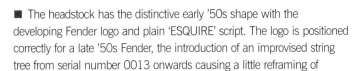

■ The plain unbound fingerboard is of maple and the radius is a traditional 7¼in, which is not currently mirrored at the bridge. The fingerboard is one-piece maple with considerable wear at the edges and lots of playing grooves in the bare wood. The frets are a slim 2mm gauge.

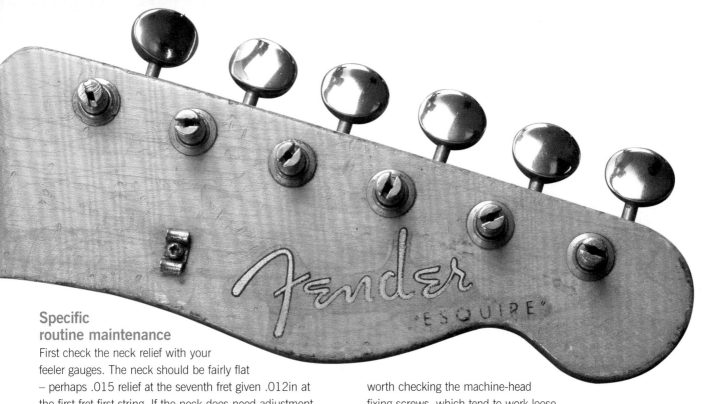

Specific
routine maintenance

First check the neck relief with your
feeler gauges. The neck should be fairly flat
– perhaps .015 relief at the seventh fret given .012in at
the first fret first string. If the neck does need adjustment,
the Esquire requires a straight-slot screwdriver. In this case
the owner likes his action set high.

worth checking the machine-head
fixing screws, which tend to work loose.
This requires a '1' point Phillips. Do not over-tighten them
– just enough to stop the machine head moving in normal use.

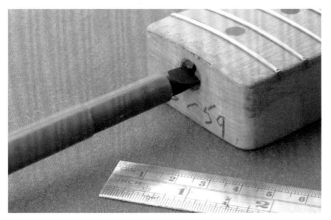

Follow the Vintage Telecaster set-up guide (*page 32*)
for any bridge height and intonation adjustments (you will
need a 2.5mm jewellers' straight-slot screwdriver for the
height adjustment). When adjusting the length of the string
travel for intonation the spring may not always actually
move the saddle – it will be inhibited by string pressure
– so remember to reset the saddle with a screwdriver as a
lever; it may not move otherwise. The string length adjustment
requires a '1' point Phillips. A little pre-lubrication with WD40
may be necessary on a rusted vintage guitar. Take care to
protect the body lacquer from any oil by using some low
adhesion masking tape.

The strings on this guitar are Vintage Reissue .011–.052,
heavier than would have been usual in 1957 but consistent
with the owner's requirements. When changing strings, it's

Whilst you have the tools out it's worth tightening the
infamous output jack retainer. This early design also tends
to work loose, causing crackles and intermittent output.
Tightening entails removing the chromed jack socket fitment
and getting a grip on the jack socket itself as you tighten the
exterior nut with a ½in socket spanner. In this particular case
the chromed fitment was
actually very secure and a
quick tighten of the ½in nut
was all that was required.
The screws and nuts used
on these vintage guitars
have often suffered a lot
of abuse over 50 years,
so tread lightly!

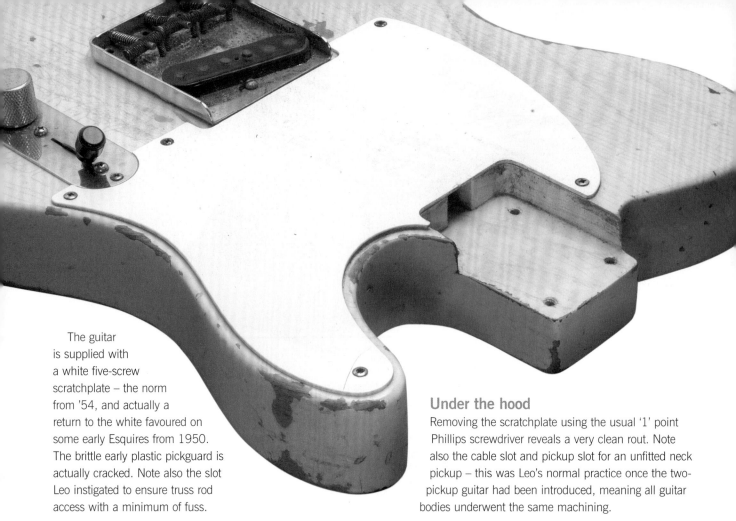

The guitar is supplied with a white five-screw scratchplate – the norm from '54, and actually a return to the white favoured on some early Esquires from 1950. The brittle early plastic pickguard is actually cracked. Note also the slot Leo instigated to ensure truss rod access with a minimum of fuss.

Under the hood

Removing the scratchplate using the usual '1' point Phillips screwdriver reveals a very clean rout. Note also the cable slot and pickup slot for an unfitted neck pickup – this was Leo's normal practice once the two-pickup guitar had been introduced, meaning all guitar bodies underwent the same machining.

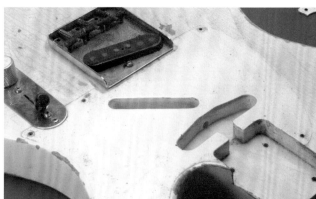

The strap 'buttons' are worth checking for secure fitting. If a '1' point Phillips screwdriver can't secure the screw then consider an improvised rawlplug made from a spent matchstick and a little superglue.

The frets are considerably worn and a good re-fret and fingerboard repair is imminent. If frets ever need a polish then a simple cardboard template and some light abrasive such as 'Planet Waves' fret polishing paper will do the trick.

The neck bolts often require a little tightening with a '2' point Phillips.

During these inspections an aerosol lid can make a useful 'screw keep', avoiding accidental losses.

■ The wiring is vintage wireless with two small 250K pots, two .47mF capacitors and a 3.3K resistor routed to a three-way switch.

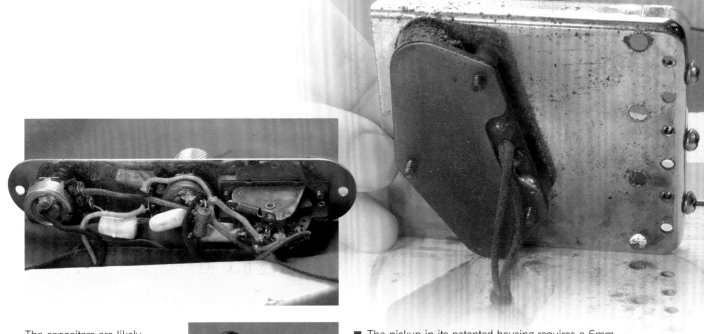

The capacitors are likely to be replacements, as the guitar was originally supplied with .05mFs. All the wiring is cloth-covered befitting the vintage. The pot codes indicate dates of late February '57 and are manufactured by one of Fender's regular suppliers, Stackpole.

■ The pickup in its patented housing requires a 6mm straight-blade screwdriver for adjusting its height in relation to the strings. Typically this has a three-point adjustment.

■ Removing the neck bolts reveals the original colour and a lot of screw rust, particularly around the heel bolt. Note that one of the neck bolts has sheared slightly – probably not a big problem, but if this happens ensure that the sheared bolt goes back in the matching cavity. Note the cavity into the neck pocket *(see page 110)*.

■ If loose, the volume and tone pots require a 3.5mm flat-head screwdriver to safely remove the grub-screwed knob and then a 0.5in socket spanner for removal or adjustment of the pot itself.

■ The three-way switch needs a '1' point Phillips for tightening and replacement.

Signed off

This guitar does require a little setting up. The saddles could be usefully adjusted to mirror the fingerboard radius, which would aid playability and intonation. But these are largely 'customer taste' issues wisely left to the owner's guitar tech. This is a classic, and when wound up delivers something very distinctive.

USA-made Custom Shop '51 Nocaster Relic

Completed in August 2007 at the Fender Custom Shop, this guitar features many of the key characteristics of three Fender guitars of the important early period 1950–51. Whilst no Fender guitar of this period was ever officially designated a 'Nocaster', several hundred guitars were manufactured during the period of transition from the copyright-infringing Broadcaster to the twin-pickup Telecaster and single-pickup Esquire marques.

These undesignated guitars simply had 'Fender' on their headstock transfers, the Broadcaster assignment having been hastily snipped off to avoid an expensive lawsuit with the Fred Gretsch company who, it transpired, made 'Broadkaster' drum kits.

Our specific guitar is designated a 'Relic' and as such has been skilfully aged to represent the wear and tear of 50-plus years on the road. It's interesting to put the Relic alongside the '57–'59 Esquire that has actually survived a similar lifespan. On the whole the patterns of wear are similar, but the Relic has had perhaps an easier life! There is more rust on the '57 Esquire and a lot more fret wear.

Condition on arrival

The 'ageing' work on this guitar is very consistent, with dings in all the expected places. Naturally the steel parts of the bridge have rusted but the brass parts remain relatively unscathed. The top bout elbow wear is perhaps a little unconvincing, as the bare wood is 'new' bare, not dirtied with a true patina of rock'n'roll excess (yet!). The frets are perfect as per a recent re-fret, and sensibly the fingerboard 'wear' does not include damage to the actual wood. Similarly, the machine heads look old but work fine.

General description
■ All the screws are rusty flatheads – Leo had yet to discover the virtues of automobile production line Phillips-type machine assembly.

■ The volume and tone knobs are an example of one of the vintage types found on '50s Fenders. These are knurled and have a flattish top with a slight dome. Period correct.

■ The patented three-way switch has the early '50s distinctive black rounded 'top hat' knob, a copy of the Harry Davies type seen in our Esquire case study. The three positions are forward or neck position with an extra capacitor in circuit for bass guitar impressions, middle for the neck pickup *without* the extra capacitance – a normal sound, though still mellow due to the chrome cover intentionally soaking up stray capacitance – and back, which when the knurled 'blend' knob is flat out gives the bridge pickup alone and as it is turned anticlockwise mixes in the neck pickup for a mellower sound.

■ The bridge pickup is an early '50s type wound 9,200 turns with finer 43 gauge wire and sounds extremely hot. Note the as yet un-staggered pre-'52 pole-pieces designed to replicate that eccentric unbalanced output from the six strings that Leo was still discovering had differing magnetic responses.

■ The neck pickup has 8,000 turns of 43GA wire and has six separate poles beneath the stray-capacitance absorbing chrome cover.

■ The bridge, with its 'two strings per saddle' adjustable for height and length and its integral relationship with the pickup, is an important part of this guitar's sound and many players prefer this arrangement to a more modern 'one string per saddle' set-up.

■ This specific instrument has brass saddles which, 'period correct', are not slotted for the strings.

■ Originally all '50s and many '60s Teles had a chrome 'ashtray' cover over the bridge. This made good cosmetic and even electrical screening sense, but prevents the player from palm muting and 'playing on the bridge', both of which techniques are key to the classic Tele sound. Consequently most 'ashtrays' are 'missing in action'.

■ The 'through-body' stringing is an important part of the early Fender guitar sound. Note the period correct slightly eccentric ferrule spacing – Leo and partners did this job by hand.

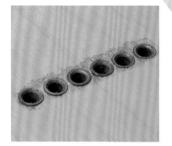

■ The lightly battle-scarred ash body of the guitar is light, for a two-pickup guitar, at 7.25lb and is approximately 1¾in thick at the edge – a 'handmade' shade thinner than our case study Esquire. Note the very thin Honey Blonde, nitrocellulose lacquer finish, designed to show off the ash.

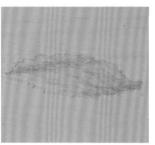

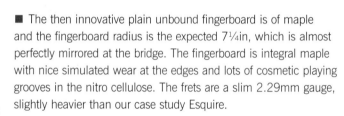

■ The then innovative plain unbound fingerboard is of maple and the fingerboard radius is the expected 7¼in, which is almost perfectly mirrored at the bridge. The fingerboard is integral maple with nice simulated wear at the edges and lots of cosmetic playing grooves in the nitro cellulose. The frets are a slim 2.29mm gauge, slightly heavier than our case study Esquire.

■ The truss rod is accessed at the neck butt. Any adjustment requires a straight-slot ⁵⁄₁₆in screwdriver. The 'Righty Tighty, Lefty Loosy' principle applies – go left a bit first to check for freedom of movement! The access channel Leo provided means the truss rod can be adjusted 'on guitar', but this is much easier with the neck off the guitar.

■ The nut is a nicely hand carved piece of yellowing shrunken bone which is perfectly cut and slotted – the strings move freely without that 'trapped' sound of a badly cut nut. Bone has the advantage of being self lubricating.

■ The neck is of a clubby early '50s profile with a fairly constant maximum depth of approximately ⅞in – huge by 21st-century standards, but it feels great and probably contributes to lowering the guitar's fundamental frequency, which is good for tone. The back of the neck has a satin finish with some cosmetic wear. The neck date is July 2007. The truss rod assembly is sensibly left rust free. *See Appendix 8 for more specific information on neck profiles.*

114

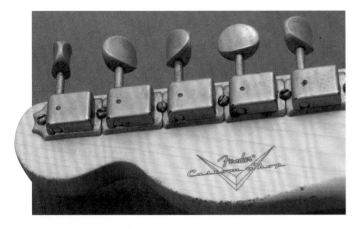

■ The machine heads are accurate reproductions of the second Chicago-made Kluson type that Fender employed from mid-1951 and correctly have no attribution. They're heavily oxidised and feel gritty but work fine, and the tuning is very stable.

■ The headstock has the distinctive early '50s shape with the developing Fender logo, correctly positioned for an early '50s model. The string tree is an improvised ferrule made from a nut and some washers – a very Leo Fender engineering solution.

The single improvised string tree had been absent from 1950 guitars and remained a practical solution as Leo realised guitars normally have a headstock tilt giving the necessary down tension on the nut. Note the artificially induced oxidisation.

Specific routine maintenance

First check the neck relief with your feeler gauges. The neck should be fairly flat – perhaps .015 relief at the seventh fret given .012in at the first fret first string. If the neck does need adjustment, the Nocaster requires a straight-slot 8mm screwdriver.

Follow the Vintage Telecaster set-up guide (*see page 32*) for any bridge height and intonation adjustments (you'll need a 3mm straight-slot screwdriver for the height adjustment). When adjusting the length of the string travel for intonation the spring may not always actually move the saddle – it will be inhibited by string pressure – so remember to reset the saddle with a screwdriver as a lever; it may not move otherwise. The string length adjustment requires a 5mm straight-slot screwdriver. A little pre-lubrication with WD40 may be necessary on a pre-rusted Relic guitar. Take care to protect the body lacquer from any oil by using some low adhesion masking tape. Note the brass saddles have no string slots on this 'early' guitar. I love this Meccano come Radioshack prototype feel!

The 'top hat' knob is inclined to fall off, but using a little PTFE tape to thicken the thin post will prevent a common loss.

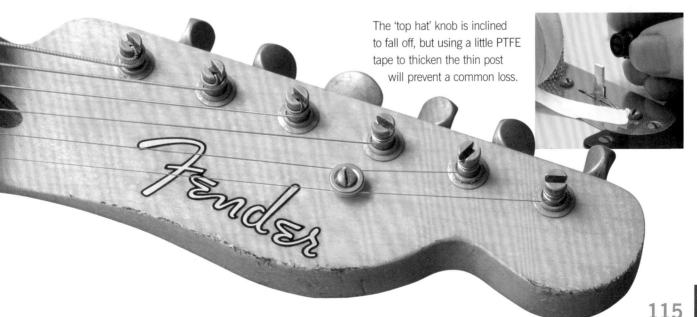

The strings on this guitar are lighter than any strings commercially available in 1951 at .009–.044. These are, however, consistent with Nashville stringing, *ie* employing a banjo string for a first and using the normal guitar first as a second and so on – a '50s solution to a craving for pliable guitar strings before the invention of light gauge Fender 'Rock'n'Roll'.

When changing strings, it's worth checking the machine-head fixing screws, which tend to work loose. This requires a 4mm straight-slot screwdriver. Do not over-tighten them – just enough to stop the machine head moving in normal use.

Whilst you have the tools out it's worth tightening the infamous output jack retainer. This early countersunk design also tends to work loose, causing crackles and intermittent output. Tightening entails removing the chromed jack socket fitment and getting a grip on the jack socket itself as you tighten the exterior nut with a ½in socket spanner. In this particular case the chromed milled fitting is actually very secure and a quick tighten of the ½in nut was all that was required – otherwise leave well alone, and if it ain't broke don't fix it! Note the induced rust.

Under the hood

Removing the scratchplate using a 5mm straight-slot screwdriver reveals a very clean rout. Note also the cable slot and pickup slot. The guitar is clearly stamped 'RELIC'. A nice touch of authenticity on the back of the scratchplate is the paint ring seen on the original Bakelite guards.

During these inspections an Asian food or canapés tray can make a useful 'screw and tool keep', avoiding accidental losses.

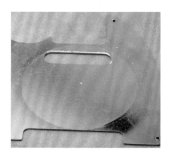

The guitar is supplied with a black single-ply five-screw scratchplate, with a typical wear pattern. Removing the plate reveals the slot Leo instigated to ensure truss rod access with a minimum of fuss.

The strap 'buttons' are worth checking for secure fitting. If a 5mm straight-slot can't secure the screw then consider an improvised rawlplug made from a spent matchstick and a little superglue.

The frets are beautifully finished. If they ever need a polish then a simple cardboard template and some light abrasive such as 'Planet Waves' fret polishing paper will do the trick.

The neck bolts often require a little tightening with a straight-slot 8mm screwdriver.

■ The truss rod adjustment is a single straight-slot 8mm type. Safe access to this is best achieved with the strings and front pickup removed.

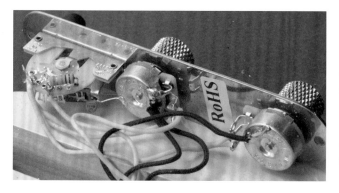

■ The wiring is the vintage arrangement but with modern components – two small 250K pots, one .05mF capacitor and a 15Kohm resistor wired to the three-way switch. All the wiring is cloth-covered befitting the guitar's 'vintage'.

■ Revealed by removing the backplate 6mm screws, the pickup is classic early Tele type, with wax string protecting the fine over-wound coil.

■ The neck pickup is a sophisticated six-pole device with some height adjustment aided by two small machine springs.

■ If loose, the volume and tone pots require a 2.5mm flat-head screwdriver to safely remove the grub-screwed knob and then a 0.5in socket spanner for removal or adjustment of the pot itself. I like the way Fender have installed '50s brass cored pots.

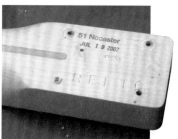

■ Removing the neck bolts with an 8mm straight-slot screwdriver reveals a neck date of 19 July 2007 and another two reminders of the Relic status of this guitar. The neck is a brilliant snug fit with no need of shims to achieve a good angle.

■ The three-way switch needs a 6mm straight-slot driver for tightening and replacement of its brass bolts.

■ The pickup in its patented housing requires a 6mm straight-blade screwdriver for adjusting its height in relation to the strings. Typically this has a three-point adjustment.

■ For the best tone and intonation be sure the bridge plate is well secured.

Signed off

This guitar is brilliantly set up and is the best 'vintage Tele' I've ever played. The back pickup has a real snarl and gave my amp a bit of a shock! Leo Fender would have loved this guitar – but then he would probably have set about 'improving' it. He'd start by correcting the eccentricity of the un-staggered pole-pieces – the plain third string sticks out from the crowd, but somehow that's part of the charm.

This is a classic and when wound up delivers something completely distinctive. A real fun guitar – I wish I could afford it!

Chinese-made '50s Vibe Squier

Completed in 2007, this guitar features many of the key characteristics of the original Fender design of circa 1952 at a very affordable price. The pine body is a reversion to Leo's early prototypes.

Serial No.
CGSO80400833

General description

■ All the screws on this guitar are the modern Phillips type employed by Leo Fender from 1952–53 as he realised the virtues of automobile assembly line practice.

■ The volume and tone knobs are similar to the vintage types found on '50s Fenders. These are knurled but have a flat top.

■ The three-way switch has the early '50s distinctive black rounded 'top hat' knob, a copy of the Harry Davies type seen on our Esquire. The three positions are a modern forward or neck position, middle for both pickups, and back for the bridge pickup alone. The tone and volume pots remain in circuit in all positions.

Condition on arrival

This new guitar arrives in a no frills cardboard box with no accessories or case. It needs a set-up, as budget guitars inevitably do. Disappointingly the guitar has a slight acid burn on the chrome control plate. However, this is easily remedied these days as Fender-type parts are readily available for all the classic models. Peter Cook's immediately supplied a replacement.

■ The custom Alnico III bridge pickup has the un-staggered pre-'52 pole-pieces designed to replicate that eccentric unbalanced output from the six strings.

■ The traditional look Alnico I neck pickup has six separate poles beneath the stray-capacitance absorbing chrome cover.

■ The bridge, with its 'two strings per saddle' adjustable for height and length and its integral relationship with the pickup, is an important part of this guitar's sound, and many distinguished players including Jerry Donahue prefer this arrangement to a more modern 'one string per saddle' set-up.

■ This specific instrument has brass saddles, and in a nice compromise of the authentic design it comes *with* the six slots you need!

■ Originally all '50s and many '60s Teles had a chrome 'ashtray' cover over the bridge. This made good cosmetic and even electrical screening sense, but prevents the player from palm muting and 'playing on the bridge', both of which techniques are key to the classic Tele sound. Consequently most 'ashtrays' are 'missing in action'. This guitar is supplied sans 'ashtray', but they are readily available for an authentic sound and look. George Harrison, Jimmy Bryant and Albert Collins are among the players who retained the 'ashtray' intact.

■ The 'through-body' stringing is an important part of the early Fender guitar sound. Note the ferrules are flush as on the Nocaster, not proud as on the American Standard.

■ The pine body is fairly light for a two-pickup guitar at 7½lb and is approximately 1¾in thick at the edge. The guitar has a very thin white finish, designed to show off the grain.

■ The neck profile is a slim modern 'C' shape, with a fairly constant maximum depth of approximately ¾in. The back of the neck and the integral fingerboard have a gloss polyurethane finish. *See Appendix 8 for more specific information on neck profiles.*

■ The once innovative plain unbound fingerboard is of maple and the fingerboard radius is a modern 9½in, which is perfectly

mirrored at the bridge. The frets are a medium 2.8mm gauge, heavier than our original '50s case study Esquire.

■ The truss rod is accessed practically in the 'modern' style at the headstock. Any adjustment requires a 5mm Allen or hex wrench. The 'Righty Tighty, Lefty Loosy' principle applies – go left a bit first to check for freedom of movement!

■ The nut is a piece of synthetic bone which is poorly cut. The strings are too high generally, but particularly on the treble side.

■ The machine heads are reproductions of the Kluson type that Fender employed from mid-1951 and have no attribution.

■ The headstock echoes the distinctive early '50s shape and carries the Fender Squier logo. The double logo takes up a lot of space and consequently the '50s-type string tree is moved back much further than is ideal. The tree echoes the original improvised ferrule made from a nut and some washers – a very Leo Fender engineering solution.

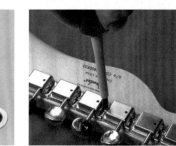

119

Specific routine maintenance

First check the neck relief with your feeler gauges. The neck should be fairly flat – perhaps .015 relief at the seventh fret given .012in at the first fret first string. If the neck does need adjustment, the guitar requires a 5mm Allen or hex in the 'modern' headstock access hole.

Follow the Vintage Telecaster set-up guide (*page 32*) for any bridge height and intonation adjustments (you will need a 1.5mm Allen or hex for the height adjustment). When adjusting the length of the string travel for intonation the spring may not always actually move the saddle – it will be inhibited by string pressure – so remember to reset the saddle with a screwdriver as a lever; it may not move otherwise. The string length adjustment requires a '2' point Phillips.

The 'top hat' knob is inclined to fall off, but using a little PTFE tape to thicken the thin post will prevent a common loss.

At .009–.044 the strings on this guitar are lighter than any commercially available in 1952. These are, however, consistent with Nashville stringing, *ie* employing a banjo string for a first and using the normal guitar first as a second and so on – a '50s solution to a craving for pliable guitar strings before the invention of light gauge Fender 'Rock'n'Roll'. James Burton first used this solution on his Tele in '58 on Ricky Nelson's *Believe What You Say*.

When changing strings, it's worth checking the machine-head fixing screws, which tend to work loose. This requires a '1' point Phillips screwdriver. Do not over-tighten them – just enough to stop the machine head moving in normal use.

Whilst you have the tools out it's worth tightening the infamous output jack retainer. This early countersunk design tends to work loose, causing crackles and intermittent output. Tightening entails removing the chromed jack socket fitment and getting a grip on the jack socket itself as you tighten the exterior nut with a ½in socket spanner. In this particular case the chromed milled fitment was actually very secure and a quick tighten of the 12mm nut was all that was required.

The strap 'buttons' are worth checking for secure fitting. If a '1' point Phillips screwdriver can't secure the screw then consider an improvised rawlplug made from a spent matchstick and a little superglue.

The frets are fairly unfinished. A polish with a simple cardboard template and some light abrasive such as 'Planet Waves' fret polishing paper will make for smoother string bends. Wire wool will also do the job, but take care to protect your hands and eyes. The neck bolts sometimes require a little tightening with a '2' point Phillips screwdriver.

Under the hood

Removing the traditional (but nicely bevelled!) five-screw scratchplate using a '1' point Phillips screwdriver reveals a clean rout which is humbucker-ready should you wish to go the Albert Collins/Keith Richards route. Note also the minimal screening on the back of the scratchplate.

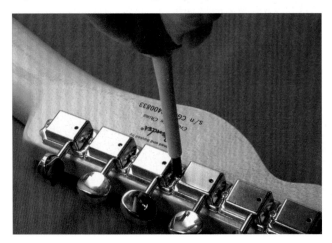

During these inspections an 'Asian food' or canapés tray can make a useful 'screw and tool keep', avoiding accidental losses.

■ The wiring is a simple vintage arrangement but with modern 'economy' components – two small 250K pots and one .05mF capacitor wired to the three-way switch. All the wiring is modern plastic-covered.

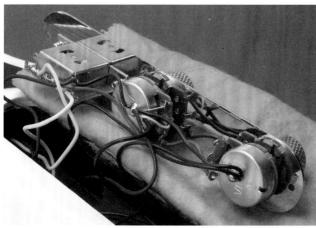

■ For the best tone and intonation be sure the bridge plate is well secured using a '2' point Phillips.

■ Removing the backplate with a '2' point Phillips reveals the pickup, which has the appearance of a classic early Tele with wax string protecting the fine over-wound coil. The pickup is designated TCA2B (Fender)-BK.

■ When removing a pickup a simple 'pencil line on a business card' template takes the guesswork out of getting the original height on replacement. This neck pickup is also a sophisticated six-pole device with some height adjustment aided by an integral pad of soft foam rubber. Note the odd routing of the neck pocket.

■ If loose, the volume and tone knobs are a simple push-fit. An 11mm socket spanner is required for removal or adjustment of the pot itself.

■ The three-way switch needs a '2' point Phillips driver for tightening and replacement of its steel bolts.

■ The bridge pickup in its patented housing requires a '1' point Phillips screwdriver for adjusting its height in relation to the strings. Typically this has a three-point adjustment.

■ The neck pickup is designated TCA2N (Fender)-NK and sits on an unusual ½in thick black foam rubber pad. It has six separate pole-pieces.

Signed off

This guitar has lots of potential. With a little nut work some fret levelling and perhaps some classic American pickups I'm sure it will make a useful professional guitar – which at the price is amazing. The sounds from the supplied pickups are all useful if a little microphonic, which adds some character. However, for serious stage use it's probably worth fitting some more expensive pickups.

USA-made American Standard, 2008 version

Made in Corona, California, this current updated version of the American Standard epitomises everything that the original design ever promised but with some later refinements that slightly update Leo's concept.

General description

■ The volume and tone knobs are modern 'flat-top' knurled cylinders and the three-way switch has a round head similar to the first '50s type. The three positions are forward or neck pickup alone, middle for both pickups and back position for bridge pickup alone. This is the modern arrangement and differs greatly from Leo Fender's original idea – see the Nocaster case study for more on this. The volume control works in all positions and the tone control is of Fender's 'Delta Tone' type. This has an end détente which enables the player to click the resistive capacitor tone controls 'out of circuit' for more direct punch from the bridge pickup.

■ The high-output type bridge pickup is still integral to the bridge itself – a vital part of the distinctive Telecaster sound. The pickup features vintage-style un-staggered pole-pieces, which also contribute to the classic sound.

Condition on arrival

This new guitar arrived factory fresh but in need of a basic set-up. It comes together with a robust ABS version of the Fender oblong case.

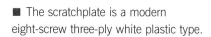

■ The scratchplate is a modern eight-screw three-ply white plastic type.

■ The guitar is ¾lb heavier than our Nocaster at 8lb, mostly due to more substantial hardware and a rosewood fingerboard, though the timber itself can vary in weight.

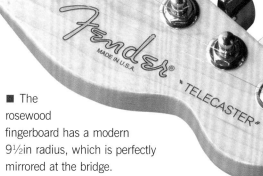

■ The bridge consists of six pressed steel saddles of a type usually associated with vintage Stratocasters, giving full individual adjustment of each string for intonation and height. The through-body stringing has been altered slightly to line up with this new arrangement. NB: Traditionally the strings come through the body at the *back* of the bridge plate. The strings anchor on a redesigned chromed brass bridge plate and substantial protruding rear ferrules which should make for ease of string changing.

■ The alder body is approximately 1¾in thick at the slightly more rounded edges. This minor variance from the classic 'slab' accentuates the flat edge required for the traditional-type recessed jack socket. The body is also available in a more traditional ash.

■ The satin finish neck has a slim oval profile with a fairly constant depth of approximately ¾in. The neck is one-piece maple with a walnut skunk stripe. The edges are rolled for a played-in feel. *See Appendix 8 for more specific information on neck profiles.*

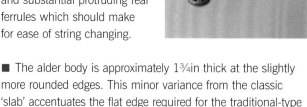

■ The neck joint features a new version of the '70s Micro-Tilt, but utilising the four traditional bolts *not* the much maligned CBS three-bolt system. This enables any necessary adjustment of neck pitch without resort to fiddly wood shims (3.2mm Hex wrench).

■ The rosewood fingerboard has a modern 9½in radius, which is perfectly mirrored at the bridge.

■ The truss rod is now accessed at the headstock. The rod requires a 3.2mm ⅛in Allen or hex key for any adjustment. The 'Righty Tighty, Lefty Loosy' principle applies – go left a bit first to check for freedom of movement! The photo shows a pro Allen/hex wrench which gives a bit more control and more torque. The frets are a substantial 2.65mm.

■ The nut is a nice piece of synthetic bone, which needs a little adjustment (it's just a little too high). This is expected on a new guitar. The idea is you set it to your preferred height – taking a nut *up* is harder than filing it down, and height raising shims can affect the tone.

■ The machine heads are modern Fender Deluxe cast/sealed types with tension adjust and have staggered pillars for better string-break angle at the nut.

■ The headstock is a version of the distinctive Telecaster shape, a little more substantial than the '50s original, with a modern single low friction string tree.

enough to stop the machine head moving in normal use. The machine-head top bolts also work loose with wood shrinkage and require a 10mm socket spanner to ensure a snug fit. Also beware the rear string ferrules, which are a loose fit – you don't want to lose one of those on a darkened stage.

The rosewood fingerboard would benefit from a little lemon oil. Whilst you have the tools out it's worth tightening the output jack retainer. This tends to work loose, causing crackles and intermittent output. This guitar has the traditional push-fit type, which is best left alone when firmly in place! If it does come loose then solutions include Blu-Tack or a thin

Specific routine maintenance

First check the neck relief with your feeler gauges. The neck should be fairly flat – perhaps .015 relief at the seventh fret given .012in at the first fret first string. Another pro option is to use a relief gauge. Interestingly this specific neck registers zero relief at present, and as you'd expect the guitar exhibits a fair amount of fret buzz. This is probably down to the wood responding to the climate change from sunny Corona to a record damp summer in Oakley Vale. This can be easily corrected along with the nut work to produce a great action.

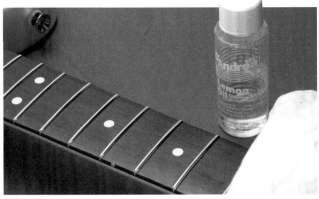

layer of electricians' tape, sufficient to engineer a snug fit. Generally, however, the modern version of this type stays in place quite well.

The guitar is supplied with the three-ply scratchplate first tried in 1959.

The strap 'buttons' are worth checking for secure fitting. If a '1' point Phillips screwdriver can't secure the screw then consider an improvised rawlplug made from a spent matchstick and a little superglue.

The frets are nicely polished and feel good as supplied. If they ever need a polish then a simple cardboard template and some light abrasive such as 'Planet Waves' fret polishing paper will do the trick.

If the neck does need adjustment, the American Standard requires a $^{1}/_{8}$in Allen or hex. Follow the Telecaster set-up guide (*page 36*) for any bridge height and intonation adjustments.

The strings on this guitar are .009–042 – a good working compromise. When changing strings, it's worth checking the machine-head fixing screws, which tend to work loose. This requires a 5mm straight-slot driver. Do not over-tighten them – just

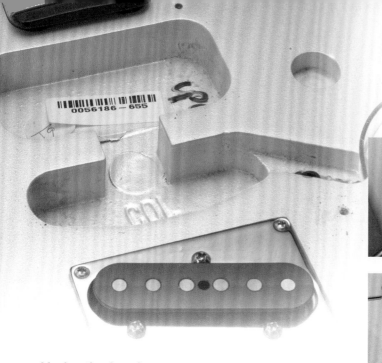

■ The three-way switch needs a '2' point Phillips for tightening and replacement.

■ The neck pickup requires a '1' point Phillips screwdriver for adjusting the height in relation to the strings. Note also the pickup is now mounted to the pickguard Strat-style, *not* the body as in '50s Teles. The rubber grommets also hark back to the '50s Strat.

Under the hood

Removing the scratchplate using the usual '1' point Phillips screwdriver reveals a very modern 'humbucker and middle pickup ready' rout (the 'Nashville' Standard is supplied with a Strat pickup in this middle slot).

During these inspections an aerosol lid can make a useful 'screw keep', avoiding accidental losses.

■ The wiring is very clean, with two small high quality CTS 250K pots, the tone with a 'straight-through' détente and one .022mF capacitor routed to a three-way switch. All the wiring is PVC.

■ The bridge pickup is accessed via a little nifty choreography of the 'new' Strat-type saddles and a '3' point Phillips and two '1' point Phillips screws. The pickup height adjustment is now via three '2' point roundhead Phillips, also suspended with rubber grommets.

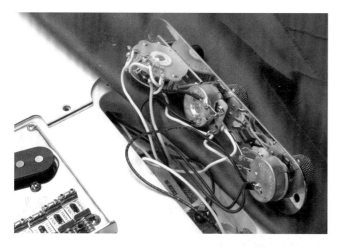

■ If loose, the volume and tone pots require a 2.5mm straight-slot screwdriver to safely remove the grub-screwed knob, and then a 0.5in socket spanner for removal or adjustment of the pot itself.

Signed off

This guitar does require a little setting up. The nut could be filed a bit lower and the neck needs a little relief to allow the strings to 'sing'. In fact the neck is currently convex, but this *should* be easily solved as the American Standard comes with a Bi-Flex truss rod which works as well on convex as concave problems. See 'Truss rod adjustment', on pages 80 and 123.

All in all, however, a good example of a classic slightly re-engineered for the 21st century. Potentially a great working instrument.

Chinese-made Squier 'Affinity'

Manufactured in 2007, this guitar represents Fender's laudable aim to make an affordable Tele that bears some 'Affinity' to the classic guitar. It does, however, feature several notable departures from the classic template.

General description

■ I admire this guitar for its 'back to basics' approach. Costing less than £120 ($75) at the time of writing, in the 21st century it offers much of what Leo Fender had in mind in the middle of the 20th century – a working musician's guitar, no frills but a great sound and playability. The cosmetic differences will offend the purist, but none of these get in the way of straight-ahead functionality. The finish is translucent dark butterscotch polyurethane that shows off the grain of the alder and agathis amalgam. The neck is a traditional maple with a satin finish.

■ The volume and tone knobs are similar to the vintage types found on '50s Fenders. These are knurled and have a flat top.

Condition on arrival

This new guitar arrives perfectly usable for the beginner market that it's clearly aimed at. That's to say, it tunes up OK and is very playable straight out of the box. But with a little setting up the guitar could also make a respectable spare guitar for a professional gig. To achieve this it would need some work on the saddle intonation and bridge radius

■ The patented three-way switch has the 1956 'Daka Ware' large black oval 'top hat' knob. All three positions operate through the master volume and tone controls. The three positions are forward or neck pickup, middle for the two pickups together, and back for the classic bridge pickup alone.

■ The integral relationship with the bridge-enclosed pickup is an important part of this guitar's sound and seems surprisingly little affected by the lack of through-stringing.

■ This new guitar was never conceived as having a traditional 'ashtray' bridge cover.

■ The new alder and agathis polyurethane-coated body of the guitar is a surprisingly heavy 8lb, given that it's approximately 1½in thick at the edge – a good ½in thinner than our case study Esquire.

■ The neck profile is a slim modern ¾in 'oval'. *See Appendix 8 for more specific information on neck profiles.*

■ The bridge pickup is an echo of the early '50s type and sounds just like a Tele. Note the vintage correct un-staggered pre-1952 pole-pieces, designed to replicate that eccentric unbalanced output from the six strings which Leo was then still discovering had differing magnetic responses – an important part of the eccentric Tele sound.

■ The neck pickup has six separate poles beneath the stray-capacitance absorbing chrome cover.

■ The familiar plain unbound maple fingerboard is slab-fitted to a knotty maple neck. The fingerboard radius is the expected modern 9½in, which is almost perfectly mirrored at the bridge. The frets are a modern medium 2.5mm gauge, much heavier than our case study Esquire.

■ The truss rod assembly is accessed from behind the nut and requires a 5mm Allen or hex key. The 'Righty Tighty, Lefty Loosy' principle applies – go left a bit first to check for freedom of movement!

■ The bridge has six Strat-type separate saddles adjustable for height and length. The six diecast chromed saddles are a tight fit in the allotted space and sit a little uncomfortably with a visible crush – the saddles huddle together closer at the neck end than the screw end, meaning they don't sit parallel. The sixth string saddle has an acoustic rattle, due, I think,

to having too little down pressure without through-stringing. Leo would, I suspect, have been unhappy with this engineering, and a similar arrangement tried by CBS in 1968–9 was unpopular with players.

■ The nut is a piece of white plastic. The spacing is a little uneven and the first and second strings could come down a little, but the strings are moving freely without that 'trapped' sound of a badly cut nut.

■ The machine heads are modern types and have no attribution. They work OK.

■ The headstock has a traditional Tele vibe. The one string tree is an early '50s type 'seagull'.

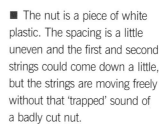

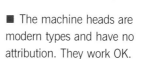

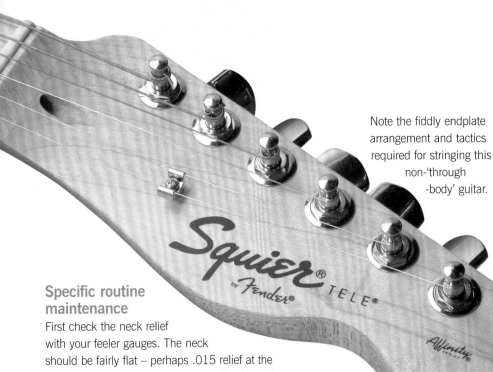

Note the fiddly endplate arrangement and tactics required for stringing this non-'through -body' guitar.

Specific routine maintenance

First check the neck relief with your feeler gauges. The neck should be fairly flat – perhaps .015 relief at the seventh fret given .012in at the first fret first string.

Follow the Telecaster set-up guide (*page 36*) for any bridge height and intonation adjustments (you will need a 1.5mm Allen or hex for the height adjustment). When adjusting the length of the string travel for intonation the spring may be inhibited by string pressure, so remember to carefully reset the saddle with a screwdriver as a lever – it may not move otherwise. The string length adjustment requires a '2' point Phillips screwdriver.

The 'top hat' knob is secure on this model.

The strings are .009–.040 gauge, a good choice for Nashville 'Chicken pickin'.

When changing strings, it's worth checking the machine-head fixing screws. They require a '1' point Phillips screwdriver. Do not over-tighten them. The front securing nut requires a 10mm socket. Tighten the string tree at the same time with a '1' point Phillips.

Whilst you have the tools out it's worth tightening the 'modern'-type output jack retainer. This still tends to work loose, causing crackles and intermittent output. Tightening entails removing the chromed jack socket fitment and getting a grip on the jack socket itself as you tighten the exterior nut with a 12mm socket spanner.

The guitar is supplied with a modern white eight-screw scratchplate.

The strap 'buttons' are worth checking for secure fitting. If a '2' point Phillips can't secure the screw then consider an improvised rawlplug made from a spent matchstick and a little superglue.

The frets are a little unfinished. A simple cardboard template and some light abrasive such as 'Planet Waves' fret polishing paper will do the trick.

The neck bolts may require a little tightening with a '2' point Phillips screwdriver.

Under the hood

Removing the plate with a '1' point Phillips reveals a very minimal modern rout with no need for Leo's original truss rod slot, and a simple hole for the pickup wiring.

■ The wiring is the 'modern' arrangement – two small 250K pots, two capacitors, the expected .047 and a 'treble bleed' .001 across the two 'hot' legs of the volume pot (to allow the higher frequencies to flow to hot as the volume is reduced, preventing the guitar sounding muddy at lower volume), all wired to an economy three-way switch. All the wiring is plastic-coated.

■ The bridge single bar magnet type pickup in its unusual housing requires a '2' point Phillips screwdriver for adjusting its height in relation to the strings. Typically this has a three-point adjustment.

■ For the best tone and intonation be sure the bridge plate is well secured, again using the '2' point Phillips.

■ The neck pickup is also a simpler bar magnet device with some height adjustment aided by two machine springs and two '1' point Phillips woodscrews. The supplied pickup height is 3mm treble, 2mm bass (fret height to pickup relationship).

■ Removing the neck bolts with a '2' point Phillips driver reveals an indecipherable neck code. The neck is a brilliant snug fit with no need of shims to achieve a good angle.

■ If loose, the volume and tone pots require a 2mm Allen or hex to remove the grub-screwed knob, and then an 11mm socket spanner for removal or adjustment of the pot itself.

■ The three-way switch needs a '1' point Phillips driver for tightening and replacement of its steel bolts.

Signed off

This guitar needs a set-up and ideally should be converted to through-body stringing. It will never be a collector's item, but that was not Leo Fender's intention with any of his guitars. Wound up to 11 through a 5W valve amp I played *Got To Hurry*, the Eric Clapton Telecaster boogie of 1966, and it was in the pocket!

The back pickup has the snarl and ching that made the Tele unmistakable. Leo Fender would have loved this guitar – but then he would certainly have set about 'improving' it!

Brilliant value for money.

USA-made Custom Shop Clarence White B-Bender

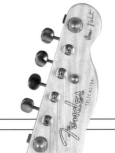

Serial No. CN402562

Made at the Custom Shop in July 1995, in some ways this is a very similar guitar to the Jerry Donahue model discussed on page 138. However, it also has some quite unique extras.

General description

The Parsons/White B-Bender installed in this guitar enables a glissandi pitch shift of a tone or semitone on the B string whilst the player's hands are otherwise occupied with regular fretted playing. The Rolling Stones used a B-Bender, as did The Eagles, notably on *Peaceful Easy Feeling*, and The Byrds, on *Chestnut Mare* (played there by co-inventor Clarence White). For the other type of B-Bender available from Fender – the Parsons/Green – see the section on *'B-Bender maintenance'*, *page 76*.

We will focus here on the key points that set this guitar apart.

■ The B-Bender mechanism. Access is via the rear Perspex panel removed with a '1' point Phillips.

Condition on arrival

This well set-up guitar has beautifully polished frets and a slightly squeaky B-Bender.

■ The strap lever. This attaches to a regular guitar strap and given a practised 'shoulder pull' raises the pitch of the B string by a preset interval (usually a tone or semitone).

■ The internal arm of the strap lever and 90° pivot.

■ The 'return to pitch' spring and rear view of the B string lever.

■ Front view. Note the B string emerging and taking a path through the specially notched bridge plate.

■ The Scruggs Banjo preset tuners. These are another unique feature of this guitar. Originally designed for banjo players, these strange tuners enable swift onstage retuning and have preset locking pitches. In this case the E on both first and sixth strings is one preset, with the other preset being a D, giving a very swift retune to DADGBD if required.

■ The pickups are interesting, combining a traditional Tele arrangement (Clarence's original was a '54) for the staggered pole bridge pickup, with a '54 Strat pickup at the neck.

■ The other side of the B-Bender 'wheel', showing the string entry point.

■ The 'pitch preset' screw. This limits the movement of the B-Bender mechanism to your desired 'bend' (tone/semitone etc).

■ The volume and tone knobs are the flat-top vintage style and the three-way switch has a version of the round 'top hat'.

The prototype

The original prototype Clarence White guitar is now owned by Marty Stuart and features a 1954 Strat pickup and *two* Tele bodies glued together to house the rather cumbersome original mechanism.

'I don't know if Gene [Parsons] did it intentionally, but the pull on this one is longer, not as snappy as the new ones, and I think that's part of the magic. If you listen to *It's All Over Now Baby Blue* (Ballad of Easy Rider), that really shows you the effect. It really has a unique sound – the lows and mids really speak, and the highs have a roundness that I just don't hear out of any other Tele.'

Marty Stuart

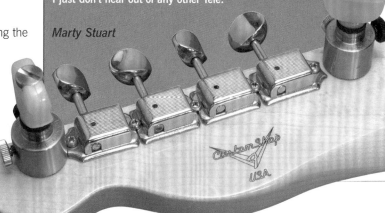

131

■ The fingerboard is beautiful integral birdseye maple with a wonderful rolled edge, and the neck profile is a comfortable 'V' type. The fingerboard radius is a bender-friendly 9½in, which is mirrored at the bridge. The frets are 2.4mm gauge.

■ The guitar is heavy at 8.5lb but considerably lighter than the two-bodied original.

■ The ash body is approximately 1¾in thick at the edge – considerably thinner than the original.

■ The bridge is unusual, combining two brass non-grooved vintage saddles with one later steel grooved type facilitating guidance for the B-Bender. Note the notched bridge plate.

■ The truss rod is accessed vintage-style at the neck butt.

■ The nut is a piece of artificial bone which needs no setting up – the strings move beautifully, especially the B. Note the extra depth to the headstock break angle! This gives a little more nut pressure for the banjo tuners, which sit higher than a conventional Fender peg.

■ The middle four machine heads are '60s vintage-type replacement '50s Kluson lookalikes.

Specific routine maintenance

First check the neck relief with your feeler gauges. The neck should be fairly flat – perhaps .015 relief at the seventh fret given .012in at the first fret first string. If the neck does need adjustment, the Clarence guitar requires a 9.5mm straight-slot screwdriver. The 'Righty Tighty, Lefty Loosy' principle applies – go left a bit first to check for freedom of movement! Note the slightly more convenient access to the truss rod.

Follow the Vintage Telecaster set-up guide (*page 32*) for any bridge height and intonation adjustments. The Clarence requires a 2.5mm straight-slot screwdriver for height adjustment and 4mm S/T for string length. Remember you may need to reset the saddle with a screwdriver as a lever – it may not move under spring tension alone.

It's worth checking the machine-head fixing screws, which tend to work loose. This requires a '1' point Phillips. Do not over-tighten them – just enough to stop the machine head moving in normal use. Securing the banjo tuners requires a ½in socket spanner and a 9mm straight-slot for re-tensioning the peg itself. Note the single ferrule-type 'string tree'.

When restringing the B string a capo holding the string in place on the bender provides a useful 'third hand'.

Whilst you have the tools out it's worth tightening the output jack retainer. This tends to work loose, causing crackles and intermittent output. Tightening entails

132

removing the outer ferrule and getting a grip on the jack socket itself as you tighten the exterior nut with a ½in socket spanner. If the vintage type is functioning OK then it's best left alone. If it does need work, *see 'Repairing or replacing a jack socket', page 64.*

The guitar is supplied with an interesting '70s-style red flecked three-ply scratchplate.

The strap 'buttons' are worth checking for secure fitting. If a '1' point Phillips screwdriver can't secure the screw then consider an improvised rawlplug made from a spent matchstick and a little superglue.

The frets are nicely polished and feel good as supplied. If they ever need a polish then a simple cardboard template and some light abrasive such as 'Planet Waves' fret polishing paper will do the trick.

For more detailed B-Bender maintenance notes – especially regarding the Parsons/Green model – *see the section on 'B-Bender maintenance', page 76.*

Under the hood

Removing the scratchplate using the usual '1' point Phillips screwdriver reveals a very clean rout and some well-screened pickup cavities. The Strat pickup housing is unusual for a Tele, as it's attached to the pickguard Strat-style.

During these inspections an aerosol lid can make a useful 'screw keep', avoiding accidental losses.

■ Removing the control panel with a '1' point Phillips reveals traditional cloth wiring with two small 250K pots and one old-style .02mF capacitor routed to a three-way switch.

■ If loose, the volume and tone pots require a 2.5mm straight-slot screwdriver to safely remove the grub-screwed knob, and then a 0.5in socket spanner for removal or adjustment of the pot itself.

■ The three-way switch needs a '1' point Phillips for tightening and replacement – this particular switch was fairly loose.

■ The neck pickup in its Strat-style housing requires a '1' point Phillips screwdriver for adjusting its height in relation to the strings. Springing is achieved by two old-style poly plastic grommets.

■ The bridge pickup has the same grommet suspension and is wax string wound to protect the coils.

Signed off

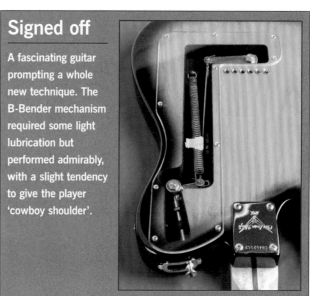

A fascinating guitar prompting a whole new technique. The B-Bender mechanism required some light lubrication but performed admirably, with a slight tendency to give the player 'cowboy shoulder'.

Japanese-made Bigsby-equipped '60s Custom Telecaster

Serial No. T004444

Made under licence in Japan for over 20 years, Japanese Fenders have a well-deserved reputation for quality. This guitar represents some interesting nods to Tele history, notably a fully bound body and the addition of a factory-fitted, Fender-branded 'Bigsby' vibrato.

General description

■ The volume and tone knob layout is the post-'53 vintage type with a three-way switch 'top hat' reflecting the '56 model.

■ The bridge pickup has early '50s non-staggered pole-pieces and is still integrated with the bridge, though naturally without the benefit of through-stringing.

Condition on arrival

This new guitar is well made and reasonably finished. With a little setting up it will make a good working professional guitar.

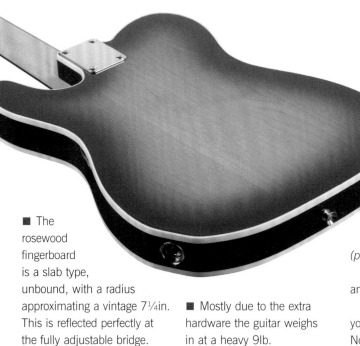

■ The rosewood fingerboard is a slab type, unbound, with a radius approximating a vintage 7¼in. This is reflected perfectly at the fully adjustable bridge.

■ Mostly due to the extra hardware the guitar weighs in at a heavy 9lb.

Specific routine maintenance

First check the neck relief with your feeler gauges. The neck should be fairly flat – perhaps .015 relief at the seventh fret given .012in at the first fret first string. If the neck does need adjustment, the '60s Custom requires a straight-slot screwdriver and a certain amount of patience! See the Vintage Telecaster set-up guide (page 32) for more on this.

Also follow the Telecaster set-up guide for any bridge height and intonation adjustments.

Due to the Bigsby obstructing the normal screwdriver path you'll need an angled '1' point Phillips to set the string lengths. None of the proprietary angled screwdrivers I could locate fitted

the gap, so in this case I bought a very cheap (soft metal) '1' point Phillips from the local 'pound store' and created a custom tool for the job. Every guitar tech and luthier I've ever met has a small armoury of self-made tools for very specific jobs, so this is not unusual. However, www.stewmac.com are contemplating making a proprietary tool for the job.

■ The bridge and Bigsby follow a 1967 factory blueprint. The bridge itself nods towards the Jazzmaster design with individual height and length adjustment and many potential string grooves provided by the threaded bridge pieces.

■ The fully bound body is approximately 1¾in thick at the edge and is constructed from three pieces of alder, all nicely grained.

■ The maple neck profile is a 'C' shape with a gloss polyurethane finish.

■ The nut is a piece of white plastic that needs a little adjustment, but nothing drastic.

■ The machine heads are '60s vintage-type Kluson lookalikes.

■ The headstock has a classic profile and a single post-less string tree. For the Bigsby to work without causing intonation problems the tree will require some lubrication.

The Bigsby itself merits special attention, especially when changing strings. For more on the Bigsby vibrato, see page 40.

When changing strings, it's worth checking the machine-head fixing screws, which tend to work loose. This requires a '1' point Phillips. Do not over-tighten them – just enough to stop the machine head moving in normal use.

Whilst you have the tools out it's also worth checking the traditional '50s-type output jack retainer. This tends to work loose, causing crackles and intermittent output. On this guitar all is well and therefore best left alone.

If the jack socket is causing trouble (as shown on this '51 Precision example – all the case study Teles were OK), first protect the surrounding

lacquer with some electrical tape and gently remove the whole assembly with some pliers. Tightening then entails getting a grip on the jack socket itself as you tighten the exterior nut with a 12mm socket spanner. Getting the vintage jack assembly to stay in place is a bit of a black art – I use a mixture of 'Plumbers Mate' cellulose sealant applied around the ferrule and gentle taps with a rubber hammer, but *see page 64* for the special tool now available for this task.

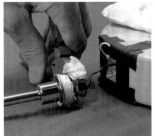

Under the hood

Removing the scratchplate using the usual '1' point Phillips screwdriver reveals a very clean and minimal rout.

During these inspections an aerosol lid can make a useful 'screw keep', avoiding accidental losses. Also, if the strings remain on the guitar pop them in a bubble-wrap bag to avoid any accidental scratches to the guitar body.

NB: A few cautions need to be noted specific to this guitar. Be aware that the bridge assembly is secured by string tension alone, so when removing the strings remove the bridge as well before it pops out and does any damage. The same also applies to the Bigsby spring and cushion washer.

The guitar is supplied with a white three-ply eight-screw scratchplate, the norm for this guitar in the '60s.

The strap 'buttons' are worth checking for secure fitting. If a '2' point Phillips screwdriver can't secure the screw then consider an improvised rawlplug made from a spent matchstick and superglue.

The frets are 2mm gauge and nicely polished. If they ever need a polish then a simple cardboard template and some light abrasive such as 'Planet Waves' fret polishing paper will do the trick.

■ The truss rod is accessed in appropriate '60s style at the neck butt. The neck itself is first removed by undoing the four '2' point Phillips neck bolts. Be careful when you do this to note the position of any shims used to set the neck angle.

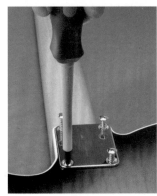

■ The truss rod requires a 9mm straight-slot screwdriver for any adjustment. The 'Righty Tighty, Lefty Loosy' principle applies – go left a bit first to check for freedom of movement! *See Appendix 8 for more specific information on neck profiles.*

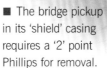

■ The bridge pickup in its 'shield' casing requires a '2' point Phillips for removal.

■ The overall pickup height adjustment is effected by the usual Telecaster '1' point Phillips arrangement. Springing is achieved by three substantial springs.

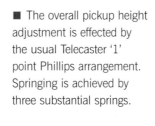

■ The bridge pickup is undesignated, very heavy, and the coil is well protected with waxed string.

■ The neck pickup is the standard 'sprung' Tele arrangement, requiring a '0' point Phillips for height adjustment.

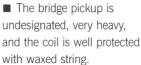

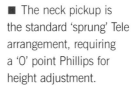

■ The wiring is very clean with two tiny 250K pots and one .02mF capacitor routed to a three-way switch. All the wiring is modern plastic-coated and the three-way switch is a fairly robust nylon enclosed type.

■ If loose, the volume and tone pots require a 2.5mm straight-slot screwdriver to safely remove the grub-screwed knob, and then a 10mm socket spanner for removal or adjustment of the pot itself.

■ The three-way switch needs a '1' point Phillips for tightening and replacement.

Signed off

This guitar presents an interesting twist on the classic Tele. It does require a little setting up, but nothing drastic.

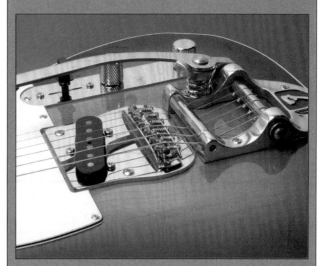

USA-made Jerry Donahue 'Signature' Telecaster

Registered at the Corona Custom Shop in October 1994, this guitar represents the best of the Fender Signature JD guitars. Other JD guitars have been made in the Far East, and Jerry himself now often plays a 'Tele-like' Peavey.

Serial No. JD0189

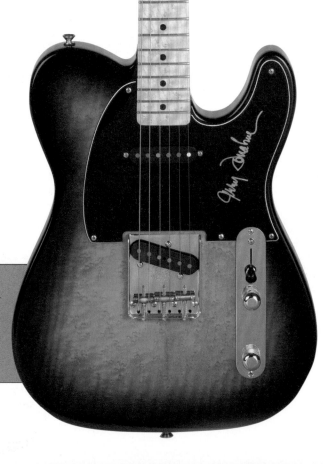

General description

■ The volume and tone knobs are a vintage domed type, 'gold'-plated as is all the hardware.

■ The unusual *five*-way switch has the round '50s-type 'top hat'.

Condition on arrival

This guitar currently belongs to player and collector Darryl West and was personally signed by Jerry at the 2008 Cropredy Festival, where Jerry headlined with Fairport Convention. The guitar is 'as new' and beautifully set up.

■ The fingerboard radius is a bend friendly, but fairly conservative 9½in, which is mirrored at the bridge, apart from the sixth string which often needs a little more excursion space and consequently sits a little high.

■ The pickups are special Seymour Duncan customs, one a Strat type and the bridge a slightly staggered late '50s Tele type.

■ The fingerboard is a triple-ply five-screw type.

■ The guitar is a relatively light 7¼lb.

■ The bridge is the traditional three non-grooved brass saddle type preferred by Jerry for the good reasons explained in his contribution on *page 37*. It's 'gold'-plated and has a serial number engraved in the usual 'Patent applied for' position.

■ The truss rod is accessed traditionally at the neck butt,. The truss rod requires a 9mm straight-slot screwdriver for any adjustment. The 'Righty Tighty, Lefty Loosy' principle applies – go left a bit first to check for freedom of movement! The frets are 2.6mm gauge.

■ The neck date is 4 July 1994 and assembly 23 September 1994.

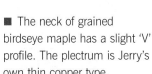

■ The nut is a finely cut piece of artificial bone. The signed headstock has the distinctive Tele profile and one frugal but 'gold'-plated grommet string tree. The headstock has the steeper break angle (10.5mm as apposed to the American Standard 8.8mm) also seen on the Clarence White Tele, giving more downward pressure at the nut for better tone.

■ The body is basswood with birdseye top and back and a sunburst finish, approximately 1¾in thick.

■ The neck of grained birdseye maple has a slight 'V' profile. The plectrum is Jerry's own thin copper type.

■ The machine heads are '50s vintage 'undesignated' Kluson lookalikes with a modern gearing ratio and nylon bushes.

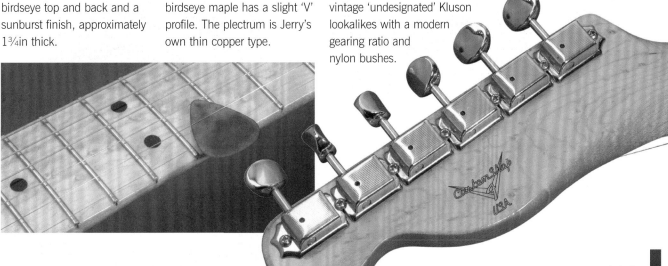

Specific routine maintenance

First check the neck relief with your feeler gauges. The neck should be fairly flat – perhaps .015 relief at the seventh fret given .012in at the first fret first string. If the neck does need adjustment, the Donahue requires a straight-slot 9mm screwdriver.

Follow the Vintage Telecaster set-up guide (*page 32*) for any bridge height and intonation adjustments. The Donahue requires a 3mm straight-slot screwdriver for the height and a beefy 5.5mm straight-slot for the string length. These adjustments need to be performed height first, as the height can affect the length.

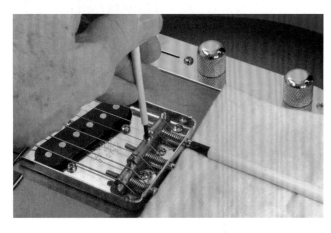

It's worth checking the machine-head fixing screws, which tend to work loose. This requires a '1' point Phillips. Do not over-tighten them – just enough to stop the machine head moving in normal use.

Whilst you have the tools out it's worth tightening the output jack retainer. This tends to work loose, causing crackles and intermittent output.

The strap 'buttons' are also worth checking for secure fitting. If a '1' point Phillips screwdriver can't secure the screw then consider an improvised rawlplug made from a spent matchstick and a little superglue.

The frets are beautifully polished and feel good as supplied. If they ever need a polish then a simple cardboard template and some light abrasive such as 'Planet Waves' fret polishing paper should do the trick.

Under the hood

Removing the scratchplate using the usual '1' point Phillips screwdriver reveals a very clean rout with some screening paint in the fairly minimal cavities. Removing the plate also gives access to the truss rod via a convenient channel. The rod requires a 9mm straight-slot driver. During these inspections an aerosol lid can make a useful 'screw keep', avoiding accidental losses.

■ Note that unlike most Teles the Strat-type pickup is attached to the pickguard and is 'sprung' with traditional poly rubber grommets. The Strat pickup is designated 2E1.

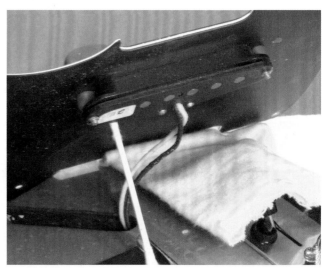

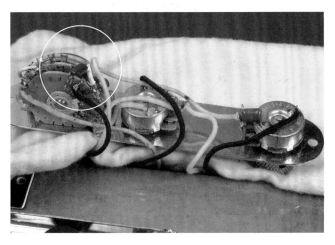

■ Replacing or tightening the five-way switch requires a '1' point Phillips.

■ The Strat-like neck pickup and the Tele bridge pickup are custom Seymour Duncans. They both require a '1' point Phillips screwdriver for adjusting their height in relation to the strings. *See page 101 for recommended pickup heights.*

■ The wiring is very clean, with two regular 250K pots, one .01uF capacitor and two 6.2K resistors routed across the double-layered five-way switch. The treble bypass on the volume pot is 1200pF in parallel with a 390K resistor. All the wiring is cloth-covered push-back type.

■ If loose the volume and tone pots require a 2mm Allen wrench to safely remove the grub-screwed knob, and then a 0.5in socket spanner for removal or adjustment of the pot itself.

■ The bridge pickup is designated Seymour Duncan 3B. The screening paint extends to an overlap on the guitar body, ensuring a good ground/earth connection when the bridge plate is in place.

■ The five-way switch provides what is probably the most versatile Tele switching arrangement. This is Jerry's own description of his preferred wiring:

Position 1: The bridge pickup, which gives a true-to-life 1952 vintage sound.

Position 2: The bridge pickup and the neck in a controlled degree of out-of-phase. Here is that unique Strat 'quack' sound (found in the same position), as it puts a Tele pickup and the Vintage Strat pickup in this slightly tilted phase mode.

Position 3: The bridge pickup and the neck pickup in parallel, creating that sweet full sound, typically found on Teles in this position (middle).

Position 4: The neck pickup, which gives a true-to-life '57 vintage Strat sound running through the tone control.

Position 5: The neck pickup completely bypassing the tone control for the full punch of this vintage pickup. If you have the neck tone rolled off a little on position 4, and then choose to jump into a more powerful lead solo, just flip the switch!

Signed off

This is a very special Tele befitting a very special player. Jerry's quest for perfection has most recently sent him of to Peavey for the Omniac guitar, but *this* is the guitar that launched a thousand Telecasting licks.

USA-made Custom Shop 'Limited Release'

In 1968, long before the Fender Custom Shop existed, Fender decided to introduce a luxury Telecaster with a rosewood body and to send one to George Harrison.

With The Beatles at the zenith of their fame, George was perhaps the most famous lead guitarist in the world. Two prototype Rosewood Teles were made by Philip Kubicki of the Fender R&D department. Serial number 235594 arrived at Apple in December 1969 and George used this extensively for The Beatles' *Let it Be* album and their last public appearance – playing *Get Back* on the rooftop of Apple headquarters in Savile Row, London. That guitar sold at auction at Heritage Galleries (Lot 29) on 13 September 2003 for $434,750.

Some production guitars of this type were then made but remain a rarity.

This Limited Release replica guitar was completed on 25 October 2007 at the Fender Custom Shop, Corona, California.

Condition on arrival

This guitar is designated a 'Closet Classic', built as if it was bought new in its respective model year, played maybe a few times per year and then stored. It has a few 'dings', a mildly 'checked' finish, lightly oxidised hardware, and the plastics show some apparent ageing.

General description

- The volume and tone knobs are an example of one of the vintage types found on late '60s Fenders. These are knurled and have a flat top.

- The patented three-way switch has the '60s-type oval knob. The switching is the rationalised arrangement – forward for the neck pickup, middle for both, and back for the bridge.

- The 'through-body' stringing is an important part of the Tele sound. Note the protruding string ferrules.

- The neck is also rosewood with a very slim '60s profile – George's original had a two-piece neck, but most production guitars have one-piece.

- The pickups are a Vintage '63 Tele single-coil for the neck and a Vintage '67 Tele single-coil pickup for the bridge. The integral bridge pickup has the 'correct' staggered and bevelled pole-pieces – a nice touch.

- The Vintage-style bridge has three threaded steel saddles.

- Originally many '60s Teles had a chrome 'ashtray' cover over the bridge. This made good cosmetic and even electrical screening sense, but prevents the player from palm muting and

'playing on the bridge', both of which techniques are key to the classic Tele sound. Consequently most 'ashtrays' are 'missing in action'. George, however, often left his in place and one is supplied.

- The plain unbound integral fingerboard is naturally rosewood and the radius is the expected 7¼in, which is perfectly mirrored at the bridge. The position marker dots are tastefully aged. The frets are a medium 2.6mm gauge.

- The truss rod is accessed traditionally at the neck butt. Any adjustment requires a straight-slot 8mm screwdriver. The 'Righty Tighty, Lefty Loosy' principle applies – go left a bit first to check for freedom of movement!

- The nut is a nicely hand-carved piece of artificial bone which is perfectly cut and slotted. The strings are moving freely without that 'trapped' sound of a badly cut nut.

- The machine heads are Fender/Gotoh late '60s Vintage style and are accurate reproductions of the much maligned Schaller CBS era type, stamped with the large Fender 'F'.

- The headstock has the distinctive Tele shape with a plain Fender logo and a single 'seagull' string tree. Note the slight artificially induced oxidisation.

- The body of the guitar is remarkably beautifully grained rosewood, book-matched front and back with four pieces of rare timber enclosing a thin wafer of maple.

- At 8¼lb the guitar is not disastrously heavy – perhaps a pound heavier than the average Tele, and still a lot lighter than a Les Paul. The finish is a pleasant slightly aged thin satin urethane.

The guitar is supplied with a black triple-ply eight-screw scratchplate, with some typical plectrum wear patterns.

The strap 'buttons' are worth checking for secure fitting. If a '1' point Phillips can't secure the screw then consider an improvised rawlplug made from a spent matchstick and a little superglue.

The frets are beautifully finished. If they ever need a polish then a simple cardboard template and some light abrasive such as 'Planet Waves' fret polishing paper will do the trick.

The neck bolts sometimes require a little tightening with a '2' point Phillips screwdriver.

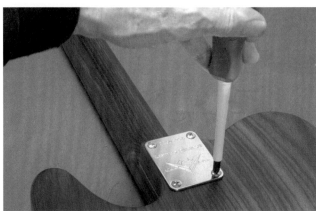

Specific routine maintenance

First check the neck relief with your feeler gauges. The neck should be almost flat – perhaps .015 relief at the seventh fret given .012in at the first fret first string. If the neck does need adjustment, the Rosewood requires a straight-slot 9.5mm screwdriver.

Follow the Vintage Telecaster set-up guide (*page 32*) for any bridge height and intonation adjustments (you will need a 3mm straight-slot screwdriver for the height adjustment). When adjusting the length of the string travel for intonation the spring may not always actually move the saddle – it may be inhibited by string pressure – so carefully reset the saddle with a screwdriver as a lever; it may not move otherwise. The string length adjustment requires a '1' point Phillips screwdriver. A little pre-lubrication with WD40 may be necessary. Take care to protect the body lacquer from any oil by using some low adhesion masking tape.

When changing strings, it's worth checking the machine-head fixing screws, which tend to work loose. This requires a '0' point Phillips screwdriver. Do not over-tighten them – just enough to stop the machine head moving in normal use.

Whilst you have the tools out it's worth tightening the infamous output jack retainer. This early countersunk design tends to work loose, causing crackles and intermittent output. Tightening entails removing the chromed jack socket fitment and getting a grip on the jack socket itself  as you tighten the exterior nut with a ½in socket spanner. In this particular case the chromed milled fitting is actually very secure and a quick tighten of the ½in nut was all that was required – otherwise leave well alone. If just the exterior nut needs tightening, try using 'Jack The Gripper' (*see page 64*).

Under the hood

Removing the plate reveals a very minimal 'let's leave all that beautiful rosewood in place' approach. However, removing the control panel reveals a different approach, with a six-inch ruler disappearing into the hollow lower bout.

During these inspections an Asian food or canapés tray can make a useful 'screw and tool keep', avoiding accidental losses.

■ The truss rod adjustment is a single straight-slot 9.5mm type. Safe access to this is best achieved with the strings removed and the neck bolts loosened.

■ The wiring differs from the early '50s arrangements – two small 250K pots remain but there are now *two* capacitors, a .022 across the volume and tone and an extra .001mF across the two 'hot' legs of the volume pot. This design is intended to prevent the guitar tone from losing too much HF as the volume is reduced. All the wiring is cloth-covered, befitting the 'vintage'.

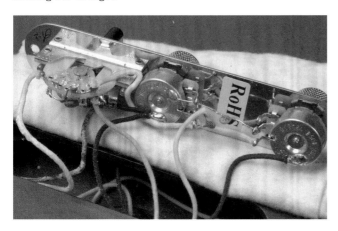

■ If loose, the volume and tone pots require a 2.5mm flat-head screwdriver to safely remove the grub-screwed knob, and then a 0.5in socket spanner for removal or adjustment of the pot itself.

■ The three-way switch needs a '1' point Phillips driver for tightening and replacement.

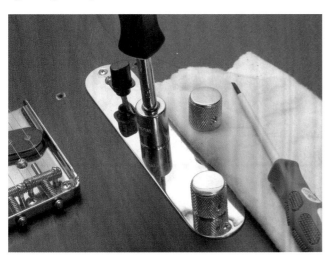

■ The bridge pickup in its patented housing requires a '1' point Phillips screwdriver for adjusting its height in relation to the strings. Typically this has a three-point adjustment. The springing is achieved with poly rubber grommets. Note the unusual earthing wire arrangement and wax string.

■ For the best tone and intonation be sure the bridge plate is well secured. This also requires a '1' point Phillips.

■ The neck pickup is a sophisticated six-pole device with some height adjustment aided by two small poly rubber grommets. Note the 'CC' accreditation in the minimal rout.

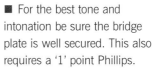

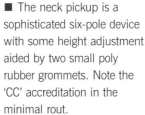

■ Removing the neck bolts with a '2' point Phillips reveals a very tidy neck pocket requiring no shims. Note also the smaller than usual 8mm screwdriver required for the truss rod, and the nicely aged position markers.

Signed off

This guitar is brilliantly Custom Shop set up and has a real character. 'Get Back! Get back to where you once belonged. *Take it away JoJo!*'

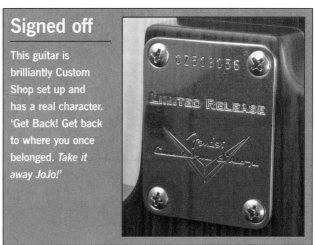

USA-made Avril Lavigne 'Signature' Squier

Serial No. ic080111906

The Telecaster has always found favour with 'ladies who rock', from Chrissie Hynde to the present. The latest adoptee, Canadian singer Avril Lavigne, has been granted an artist signature model in the Squier series of affordable guitars. Beyond the obvious style statement in the 'Pop Art' scratchplate, this guitar has some interesting features. One coil split capable humbucker replaces the Tele signature bridge pickup, and the rosewood fingerboard has 22 frets. The guitar has one control – volume.

General description

■ The volume knob is a knurled dome type first seen in 1955.

■ The three-way switch also has the '50s round 'top hat' and offers a very unusual set of options for the twin humbucker – position 1 front coil, position 2 full humbucker (both coils), position 3 rear coil.

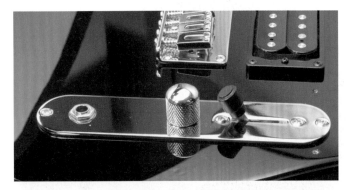

Condition on arrival

The new 'economy' guitar comes in a no frills cardboard box and, as expected at this price, needs a set-up. Unusually some of the machine heads are loose.

■ The jack socket on this minimal guitar is relocated to the control plate.

■ The pickup is an un-canned Fender humbucker with no individual pole-piece adjustment.

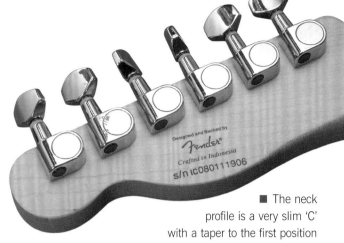

■ The neck profile is a very slim 'C' with a taper to the first position

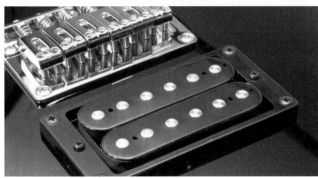

■ The unbound rosewood fingerboard has Avril's trademark graffiti 'tag' inlaid. The radius is a modern 12in (not the 9½in specified), and this is not currently mirrored at the bridge. The frets are a relatively slim 2.48mm gauge.

■ The truss rod is accessed at the headstock and requires a 4mm Allen or hex wrench for any adjustment. The 'Righty Tighty, Lefty Loosy' principle applies – go left a bit first to check for freedom of movement! *See Appendix 8 for more specific information on neck profiles.*

■ The rosewood fingerboard is unusual in having 22 frets – this requires a 'lip' overlapping the neck and body.

■ The guitar is an appropriately light 7lb.

■ The nut is a crude piece of white plastic which does the job.

■ The machine heads are the modern Fender type and the headstock has a version of the distinctive Tele profile with Avril's signature.

■ The unusual stop tail bridge retains the signature through-body stringing but in every other respect is unique for a Tele, having six individual cast economy Stratocaster-type saddles.

■ The basswood body gives a whole new meaning to 'solid', with less wood removed than a '50s Esquire, but is approximately 1.65in thick at the edge – thinner than the Standard.

147

Specific routine maintenance

First check the neck relief with your feeler gauges. The neck should be fairly flat – perhaps .015 relief at the seventh fret given .012in at the first fret first string. If the neck does need adjustment, the Avril Lavigne requires a 4mm Allen or hex.

Follow the American Standard Telecaster set-up guide (*page 36*) for any bridge height and intonation adjustments.

The supplied strings on this guitar are .009–.042. If you change the gauges be aware that the intonation and relief may need adjustment.

While changing strings, it's worth checking the machine-head fixing nuts, which tend to work loose. On this specific guitar they are currently very loose! This requires a 10mm socket wrench. Do not over-tighten, just enough to stop the machine head moving in normal use.

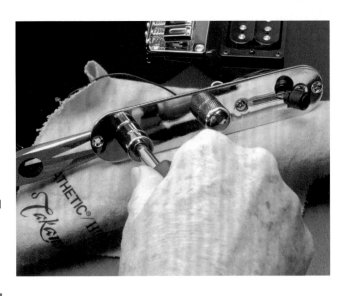

Whilst you have the tools out it's worth tightening the output jack retainer. Any looseness here can cause crackles and intermittent output. Tightening entails removing the control panel and getting a grip on the jack socket itself as you tighten the exterior nut with a 12mm socket spanner, or you could try using 'Jack The Gripper' (*see page 64*).

The strap 'buttons' are worth checking for secure fitting. If a '2' point Phillips screwdriver can't secure the screw then consider an improvised rawlplug made from a spent matchstick and a little superglue.

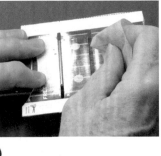

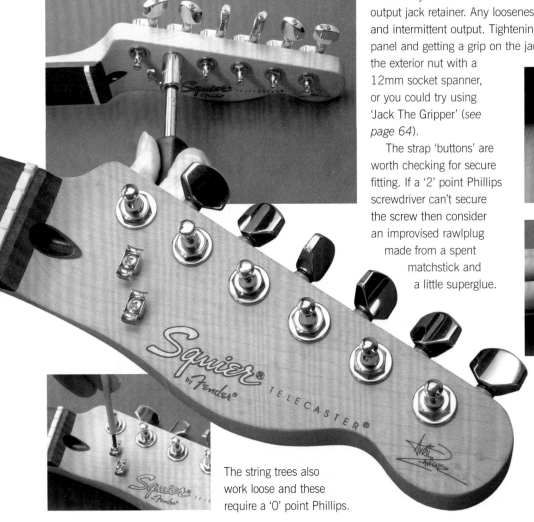

The string trees also work loose and these require a '0' point Phillips.

The frets feel a little unfinished – a simple cardboard template and some light abrasive such as 'Planet Waves' fret polishing paper will produce a smoother playing surface.

Under the hood

Removing the scratchplate using the usual '1' point Phillips screwdriver reveals a very minimal rout.

During these inspections an aerosol lid can make a useful 'screw keep', avoiding accidental losses.

■ The wiring is very minimal, with one tiny 250K volume pot and split wiring from the humbucker routed to a three-way switch.

■ If loose, the volume knob is a push-fit and can probably be persuaded to stay on with the help of a little plumbers' tape.

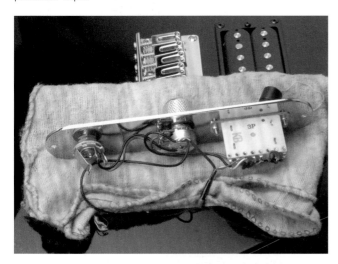

■ The three-way switch is tightened with a '2' point Phillips. As stock the guitar has a budget switch that's easily replaced with a more robust professional type.

■ The unusual pickup is attached by four '1' point Phillips and the overall pickup height adjustment is also effected by two spring-loaded Phillips. There is no provision for individual pole-piece adjustment.

Signed off

This guitar does require a little setting up. The nut could be filed a little lower and the saddles could be adjusted to mirror the fingerboard radius, but these factors are expected in a budget guitar.

This is an interesting guitar – many guitarists have upgraded their Teles with the addition of a humbucker but as an *addition* to the classic bridge pickup sound – the sound the Telecaster is famous for. This guitar sacrifices the pickup/bridge combination but offers something new – so what's the verdict?

For me the single coil (split) at the bridge position provides something like a Strat bridge pickup lacking the sting of a traditional Tele, the humbucker sounds like a humbucker on a piece of pine, and the other split single coil sounds almost like a Strat middle pickup. All in all, an OK rhythm guitar...

USA-made James Burton 'Signature' Telecaster

Serial No. N4944300

This 2008 guitar hails from the Corona, California, factory (assembled 23 June) and is the most recent version of the James Burton 'Signature' guitar. It differs from the paisley finish associated with James's '70s Elvis Presley appearances in that the finish is more 'flamed' and less floral than the hippy-inspired original. It isn't easy to confuse this guitar with The James Burton 'Standard', as that has two Texas special pickups in a more conventional alder Tele.

General description

■ The volume and tone knobs are 'gold'-plated Vintage type with the usual one master volume one master tone. The volume control has a switch built into the top dome which performs several functions in conjunction with the 5 way switch, these are outlined below.

Condition on arrival

The new guitar has an unusual Strat-like pickup arrangement and a shaved heel for better 'dusty end' access. It lacks a traditional Tele bridge, which is interesting! The guitar is strung with Nashville bender-friendly .009–.042s.

■ At 8½lb the basswood guitar is a pound heavier than an ash Tele. The body is approximately 1¾in thick. A small chamfer at the neck heel makes for better fret access.

■ The back of the guitar is as elaborate as the front and features raised gold 'through- string' ferrules.

Basswood

Basswood seems an unusual choice, but this is an environmentally friendly timber that's replacing some traditional tone woods. It's derived from the Tilia genus of trees, native throughout the northern hemisphere and known in the UK and USA as lime or linden but referred to in the trade as basswood, particularly in North America. This name originates from the inner bark of the tree, known as bast, which has many uses in its own right.

These trees grows fast and straight, so there are very few knots in the timber, and being a hardwood it's very durable, especially when it has been kiln-dried. However, in its 'green' state it's soft enough to be easily milled and sawn.

The paleness of the natural timber makes it extremely accepting of stains and colourings. In combination with having very little grain, this results in it being possible to produce stained wood that resembles an extremely wide range of other timbers. This is important, as many types of tree are now endangered or even protected due to over-logging and should not be used. Basswood is easily managed due to the speed that it grows, which means that there's very little environmental impact.

■ The pickup selector switch is a five-position type with extra options via the built-in S-1 switching giving:

Position 1: The bridge pickup.
Position 2: Bridge and middle pickup in parallel (series w/S-1 DOWN).
Position 3: Bridge and neck pickup in parallel (middle pickup only w/S-1 DOWN).
Position 4: Middle and neck pickup in parallel (series w/S-1 DOWN).
Position 5: Neck pickup.

■ The unusual Strat-like pickup arrangements are:
James Burton neck 'blade' pickup.
James Burton mid 'blade' pickup.
James Burton bridge 'blade' pickup.

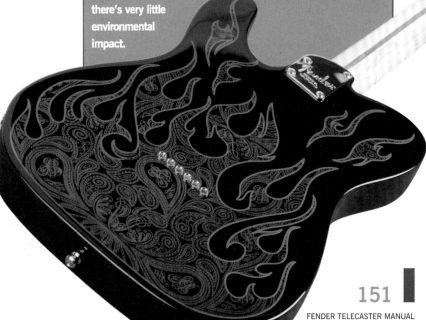

■ The fingerboard is integral to the maple neck and has a '60s U-shape in satin urethane finish. The fingerboard radius is 9½in (241mm), which is accurately mirrored at the bridge. Extra access to the higher frets is afforded by the rounded heel.

■ The substantial bridge of 'gold'-plated steel has six cast 'gold'-plated saddles but does *not* have an integral pickup – most unusual for a Tele.

■ The truss rod is accessed traditionally at the neck butt and, given the pickup arrangement, will naturally require part-unbolting of the neck for any adjustment. You'll need a '2' point Phillips. The truss rod itself requires a 9.5mm straight-slot for any adjustment. The 'Righty Tighty, Lefty Loosy' principle applies – go left a bit first to check for freedom of movement! *See Appendix 8 for more specific information on neck profiles*. The frets are a slim 2.37mm. The neck date is 4 January 2008.

■ The 1.65in (42mm) nut is a piece of nicely cut artificial bone.

■ The machine heads are unusual 'gold'-plated Fender/Schaller Deluxe cast/sealed with pearl buttons.

■ The headstock has the distinctive Tele shape with a traditional but 'gold'-plated string tree. It has James's signature.

Specific routine maintenance

First check the neck relief with your feeler gauges or a relief gauge. The neck should be fairly flat – perhaps .015 relief at the seventh fret given .012in at the first fret first string. If the neck does need adjustment this is easiest to do *without* strings. Given the .009 stringing, setting the neck 'flat' without strings should result in the required relief when restrung. The Burton requires a 9.5mm straight-slot screwdriver (though a '2' point Phillips does the job). Sometimes a 'string action gauge' can provide a useful guide.

Follow the American Standard Telecaster set-up guide (*page 36*) for any bridge height and intonation adjustments. The James

Burton requires a .050in Allen for the saddle height grub screws and a '1' point Phillips for string intonation.

The strings on this guitar are slinky .009–.042 'Nashville stringing' without the pain of locating a banjo string for first! When changing strings, it's worth checking the machine-head fixing screws, which tend to work loose. This requires a '1' point Phillips. Do not over-tighten them – just enough to stop the machine head moving in normal use. The locking nuts also repay a little attention, and these require a 10mm socket spanner.

It's also worth tightening the output jack retainer. This tends to work loose, causing crackles and intermittent output. The Burton has a traditional Tele jack socket, which is best left alone if it's stable.

The strap 'buttons' are worth checking for secure fitting. If a '1' point Phillips screwdriver can't secure the screw then consider an improvised rawlplug made from a spent matchstick and a little superglue. The Burton comes supplied with James's choice of 'gold'-plated 'Straplock' Schallers.

Under the hood

The Burton guitar, in common with some Thinlines, has no scratchplate, leaving the very clean rout exposed. Removing the control panel using a '1' point Phillips screwdriver reveals the usual resistive capacitor arrangement combined with a very complex set of wiring between the five-way switch and the S1 push-button. All the wiring is modern vinyl – which is just as well, as cloth wiring would make a very tight squeeze in the limited space. During these inspections an aerosol lid can make a useful 'screw keep', avoiding accidental losses.

■ The wiring is very clean, with one 250K pot incorporating the S1 and the other a conventional pot. One .022mF capacitor is connected late '50s style, between the volume and tone controls.

■ If loose the volume and tone pots require a 2.5mm straight-slot screwdriver to safely remove the grub-screwed knob and then a 0.5in socket spanner for removal or adjustment of the pot itself.
NB: The S1 pot doesn't come off even with the grub-screw loosened – however, it lifts *enough* to carefully tighten the retaining nut with some long-nosed pliers.

■ The three-way switch requires a '1' point Phillips for tightening and replacement.

■ The special design James Burton 'blade' pickups are mounted directly to the timber using '1' point Phillips screws. The recommended pickup distance from the open strings is ³/₈in – enough to avoid any magnetic interference with the string excursion. Springing is achieved by two rubber grommets on each screw.

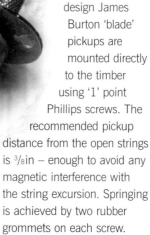

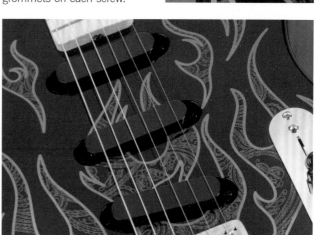

Signed off

The James Burton guitar produces a range of interesting sounds – some Strat-like tones, a biting but refined Tele tone, and some very convincing mellow humbucker sounds through use of the S1 switching. A very versatile guitar.

Mexican-assembled Thinline 'Partscaster'

The semi-acoustic Thinline Telecaster first appeared in 1968. This may have been a response to the then rising popularity of semi-solid guitars. At that time The Beatles were playing Epiphone Casinos, The Byrds Rickenbacker 360-12s, and BB King had entered the mainstream with a Gibson 355. In the charts *solid* guitars were temporarily out of fashion, despite the emergence of Jimi Hendrix and the re-emergence of the blues favourite Les Paul guitar.

Serial No. MZ3004298

This particular guitar echoes the '68 model in having single-coil pickups – later Thinlines have humbuckers of various types, but this Warmoth example differs in abandoning the scratchplate to better show the impressive flame top.

Assembled from custom parts, this guitar represents a trend for making your own personal guitar from a smorgasbord of available Internet options. This particular instrument blends a Warmoth body with a Fender neck and Fender Custom Shop pickups.

Condition on arrival

This guitar turned up at auction as a pre-owned guitar but appears to have been little used. It's in good condition apart from some localised cracking in the polyurethane, probably attributable to a heavy knock. All the metal parts are luxuriously 'gold'-plated. The guitar arrived in a recent Fender hard ABS case.

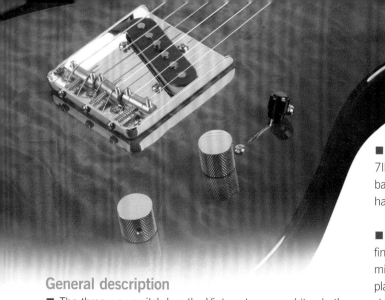

■ Being semi-hollow and rear-routed the guitar is a relatively light 7lb. The unbound hollow body is the expected 1¾in thick. The back appears to be mahogany with a maple quilt top. The guitar has a solid wood centre section to which the neck attaches.

■ The unbound rosewood fingerboard is nicely edged and the fingerboard radius is a traditional 7¼in, which is *not* currently mirrored at the bridge. This simple adjustment will improve playability tremendously. Some frets are protruding due to wood shrinkage – this is dealt with in this manual in the section *A little fretwork, page 74*.

General description

■ The three-way switch has the Vintage-type round 'top hat'.

■ The volume and tone knobs are a vintage knurled metal type but very flat topped. The semi-solid approach means the guitar controls are all flush-mounted – unusual for a Tele.

■ The neck profile is a fairly slim oval profile slightly tapered to the headstock. This is one gloss-finished piece of maple.

■ The pickups are also traditional Tele types from the Fender Custom Shop. The bridge is conventionally mounted and the neck carefully routed. Note the traditional truss rod adjustment at the neck heel.

■ The bridge is also traditional, with three brass saddles 'un-grooved' as per our '51 but with compensated angles to aid intonation. Danny Gatton used this solution on his signature Tele.

■ The neck is a snug fit requiring a '2' point Phillips for removal and has one slim paper shim. The neck is designated MOO279568 and the body pocket has an interesting Warmoth cartoon.

■ The truss rod requires a 9.5mm straight-slot screwdriver at the neck butt for any adjustment. The 'Righty Tighty, Lefty Loosy' principle applies – go left a bit first to check for freedom of movement! *See Appendix 8 for more specific information on neck profiles.* The frets are a narrow 2.1mm gauge.

■ The nut is a piece of white bone substitute which needs a little adjustment – the strings are binding slightly in the slots, causing the intonation to drift. We tried a graphite substitute in the chapter on nut adjustment (*see page 82*).

■ The machine heads are '60s vintage-type replacement Kluson lookalikes designated 'DELUXE'.

■ The headstock has the distinctive Tele shape with a very modern low-friction string tree.

Specific routine maintenance

First check the neck relief with your feeler gauges. The neck should be fairly flat – perhaps .015 relief at the seventh fret given .012in at the first fret first string. See below for adjustments.

Follow the Vintage Telecaster set up guide (*page 32*) for any bridge height and intonation adjustments. This model requires a 3.5mm straight-slot for the saddle grub screws and a '1' point Phillips for string length adjustment. Remember to reset the saddle with a screwdriver as a lever – it may not move otherwise.

The strings on this guitar are .009–.042, a good choice for slinky Tele work. When changing strings, it's worth checking the machine-head fixing screws, which tend to work loose. This requires a '1' point Phillips. Do not over-tighten them – just enough to stop the machine head moving in normal use (go careful with the 'gold' plating).

Whilst you have the tools out it's worth tightening the output jack retainer. This tends to work loose, causing crackles and intermittent output. This guitar has an interesting variant on the traditional Tele socket which is held in place with two '0' point Phillips (an Electro-socket – *see page 64*). Tightening entails removing the two screws and getting a grip on the jack socket itself as you tighten the exterior threaded rim. The quality of the screws used on this US guitar is much higher than usual and this makes maintenance much easier.

The strap 'buttons' are worth checking for secure fitting. If a '1' point Phillips screwdriver can't secure the screw then consider an improvised rawlplug made from a spent matchstick and a little superglue.

The frets are a little rough – a simple cardboard template and some light abrasive such as 'Planet Waves' fret polishing paper will enable smoother string bends. Some proud frets will need more extensive attention.

Under the hood

Removing the unusual Warmoth rear access port using a '1' point Phillips screwdriver reveals a very clean rout – but no screening. See *'Earthing and RF induction issues', page 68*.

During these inspections an aerosol lid can make a useful 'screw keep', avoiding accidental losses.

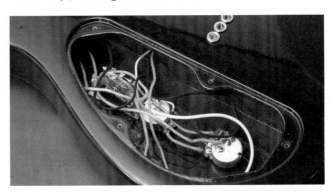

■ The wiring is very conventional, with two small 250K pots and one .022mF capacitor routed to a three-way switch. All the wiring is cloth push-back type and the pots are mounted directly to the wood. The ruler indicates the extent of the Thinline hollow – the centre of the body is solid.

■ If loose, the volume and tone pots require a 2mm Allen or hex to safely remove the knob and then an 11mm socket spanner for removal or adjustment of the pot itself.

■ The three-way
switch requires a '2'
point Phillips for tightening
and replacement.

■ The bridge pickup
in its familiar housing
requires a '2' point Phillips
screwdriver for adjusting
the overall height in
relation to the strings.
Springing is achieved by
three shock-absorbing
rubber grommets.

■ The bridge pickup is
designated 'Fender Custom
Shop' and has the traditional
waxed string protecting the
coil wire. It is very loud
and country brash!

■ The neck pickup is
wood-screwed directly into the
mahogany and requires a 4mm straight-slot
screwdriver for height adjustment, the positioning
aided by a couple of light machine springs. The
pickup itself is a classic six-pole Tele type.

Signed off

This 'parts' guitar does require a little setting up. The nut could
be filed a little lower or replaced, and the saddles should be
adjusted to mirror the fingerboard radius. For some reason the
neck is less stable than on solid guitars. The neck also needs
a shim. A small sliver of
wood veneer does the job.
However, this is a fine
guitar and through a clean
Fender amp delivers that
defining country twang. It
was the loudest guitar in
our level checks.

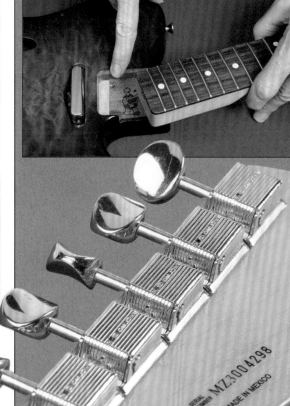

Mexican-assembled 'Special Edition' Deluxe

The '70s era Deluxe has some significant features which set it apart from the standard Tele – most significantly the 'Wide Range' humbucker pickups designed by non other than Seth Lover.

Serial No. MZ7017860

In the 1970s the inventor of the humbucker had been lured into the Fender fold with a brief to make a Fender Humbucker very like the Gibson PAF. However, Seth preferred to improve his design rather than go over old ground. Cosmetically the only difference may seem to be the larger size and offset pole-pieces, but the 'Wide Range' (as it became known) is in fact a radically different pickup. The single alnico bar magnet of the PAF is replaced with six individual

Condition on arrival

The humbucker Tele is riding a sudden wave of popularity. It's easy to see why with this versatile and unusual-looking guitar.

magnets made of cunife (copper/nickel/iron). The idea was to not just buck the hum but to retain something of the Telecaster's characteristically bright sound.

The pickup selection is also wired 'Gibson style' with each pickup having its own volume and tone control, each selected by a 'Gibson-located' and unusually orientated toggle switch.

Other distinctive features include:

■ A contoured Strat-like alder body.

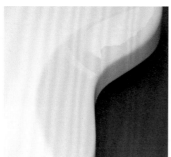

■ A C-shaped maple neck with a bend-friendly 12in fingerboard radius.

■ A 'bullet' truss rod which requires a .13in Allen wrench.

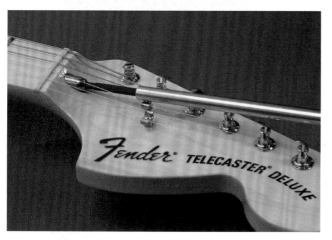

■ '70s vintage 'hard tail' string-through Strat bridge.

■ Three-bolt Micro-Tilt neckplate which requires a 2.5mm Allen wrench.

■ A '70s Strat headstock with two string trees.

Under the bonnet

Removing the many screws with a '1' point Phillips reveals a necessarily large rout. The substantial humbuckers and indeed all the electrics are attached to the pickguard in true Fender tradition. The series wiring of the individual coils is unusually seen at the rear of the pickups – presumably Fender had in mind optional configurations being readily available. The pots are traditional Fender 250Ks.

Signed off

Roy Buchanan famously remarked that 'putting humbuckers on a Tele was like painting a moustache on the Mona Lisa'. I know what he meant, but this is still a cracking guitar. It has the familiar bright Tele sound as well as the power and tone of humbuckers – all on one guitar. Nicely set up straight out of the box.

Japanese-made left-handed Thinline '72-type Deluxe

Serial No. R049817

So far in this series I have concentrated on right-handed guitars, but the lefties now get a look in at last! This excellent guitar has a smorgasbord of features, some 'classic', some '70s, some downright individual.

General description

■ The hollow Thinline had been originally intended to make the Telecaster lighter, as addressed in the 'Partscaster' case study above. The beautiful ash of this model even *looks* lightweight.

■ The 'Wide Range' pickups are identical to those found on our other Deluxe, just 'upside down'.

Condition on arrival

A very nice Tele, beautifully finished. Good to see the 'lefties' getting a rare treat.

■ The headstock has the unusual hybrid of a 1951 Nocaster-like headstock with '50s-type Kluson lookalikes, two string trees and a '70s 'bullet' truss rod. This requires a 4mm Allen wrench.

■ The neck itself has a C profile and features the '70s Micro-Tilt adjustment requiring a 2.5mm Allen. **NB:** *Slacken the neck bolts before making any adjustment.*

■ The bridge is a six 'cast' saddle 'hard tail' Strat type with through-stringing.

■ The maple fingerboard has a vintage 7¼in radius – a contrast to our other Deluxe with it's modern 12in radius.

■ The unusual pearloid scratchplate has an integrated control panel and an oval 'top hat' pickup selector.

Signed off

The guitar sounds great – even if I can only manage three chords upside down. Present owner John Catlin makes it sing!

SPEEDY WEST and JIMMY BRYANT
2 GUITARS COUNTRY STYLE

SERENADE TO A FROG

GEORGIA STEEL GUITAR

BRYANT'S BOUNCE

MIDNIGHT RAMBLE

HOP, SKIP AND JUMP

BLUE BONNET RAG

LOW MAN ON A
TOTEM POLE

OLD JOE CLARK

COUNTRY CAPERS

THIS IS SOUTHLAND

SWINGIN' ON THE STRINGS

ARKANSAS TRAVELER

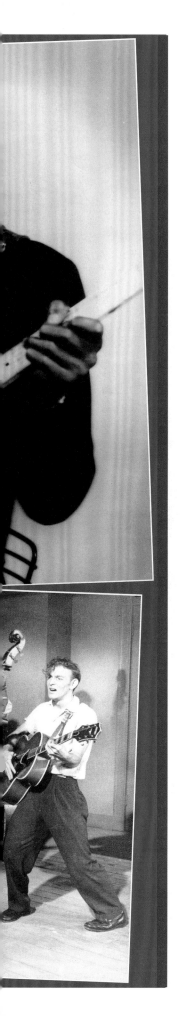

Key Tele players and their guitars

The Telecaster – a radical departure as the world's first 'production' electric guitar – was for Leo Fender a natural development of his popular Lap Steel guitars and a solution to the problems of 'Spanish' guitars being heard in a western swing band.

But Leo could never have predicted the astonishing rise of this then minority instrument. Creative players soon found a range of applications from the commercial rise of rock'n'roll, to blues, jazz and blues rock variants yet to be named.

LEFT Some early 'pioneers'. Clockwise from top left: Paul Burlison with Johnny Burnette and Dorsey Burnette, circa 1956; Clarence Gatemouth Brown, 1950s; Gene Vincent and Russell Willaford, 1956; Jimmy Bryant, circa 1953.

RIGHT Circa 1957 Esquire.

> Leo Fender's invention would be a key moment in the rise of what has become the most popular instrument in the history of the world.

The early pioneers who took the prototype to the dance band stage included Roy Watkins and Bill Carson, who used it 'as designed' for western swing, a music incorporating elements of country and popular dance music with a 'swing' nod to '30s 'hot jazz'. Jimmy Bryant soon saddled up his Telecaster with Bigsby steel guitar ace Speedy West and produced a virtuosic danceable jazz that still retained country roots. The agile fast-necked Tele gave Jimmy the edge to keep up with Speedy's slide.

For Clarence Gatemouth Brown the Tele gave a biting sting to early electric blues, encouraging Muddy Waters to amplify his bottleneck wail.

Rockabilly players like Paul Burlison were soon giving acoustic guitars and stand-up bassists a challenge and early rock'n'roll adopters can be heard and seen in the 1956 film *The Girl Can't Help It*, where the same Esquire seems to be shared by the bands of Little Richard and Gene Vincent.

In the late '60s the Tele even had a hand in the birth of Heavy Metal, as it was used by all the Yardbirds' guitarists – Eric Clapton with *Got To Hurry*, Jeff Beck with *Shapes of Things*, and finally the radical Jimmy Page, who even kept his Tele for Led Zeppelin and the acclaimed *Stairway to Heaven* solo.

We must never forget the important role of the Telecaster as a rhythmic powerhouse, as much a percussion instrument in its muted off-beats as harmonic underpinning. In 1956 Luther Perkins with Johnny Cash *Walked The Line*, and subsequent rhythm players such as Bruce Springsteen, Bob Dylan and Chrissie Hynde made the guitar a rock icon, epitomised in the poster for Martin Scorcese's film *The Last Waltz*.

Danny Gatton continued the exploration of what can be had from a once denigrated 'canoe paddle'.

In the next few pages I have tried to give some insight into the sounds and techniques of the crucial second wave of Tele giants who all carved a place in history for the Tele. And in the 21st century a third wave – including Jonny Buckland from Coldplay and Alex Kapranos from Franz Ferdinand – have found new ways to spank a Tele.

This guitar will live forever.

> The Telecaster has two sounds, a good one and a bad one.
>
> *Jimi Hendrix*

James Burton

By appointment to the King

Paisley '70s Tele and 'James Burton' Signature

Born in Dubberly, Louisiana, on 21 August 1939, James Burton grew up in Shreveport. His parents purchased his 'beginners' guitar, but one day in the J&S Music store he saw a '52 Fender Telecaster and knew that this was the guitar for him. His parents had the foresight to realise this radical new invention would be their son's perfect musical complement.

At 14 he turned professional, working local club gigs and private parties, skipping school to play guitar. This led in the same year to an invite to join the staff band of the prestigious Louisiana Hayride.

His first hit record came in 1957, when Burton recorded *Susie Q* with Dale Hawkins. Burton wrote the lick and Hawkins provided the lyric.

While working in Hollywood Ricky Nelson heard him rehearse and shortly afterwards James got a telegram, asking him and bass player James Kirkland to meet. They were offered the 'Ozzie and Harriet' show as Nelson's backing band. Before Burton knew it, he was living with the Nelsons. He lived there for about two years before eventually finding his own place.

During his time with Ricky Nelson, James performed at 'Town Hall Party' together with Bob Luman. Their live recording of *My Baby Walks All Over Me* and *Milk Cow Blues* can be found on the *Rockin' at Town Hall* album. Burton's first *recording* with Nelson was *Waiting in School/Stood Up*. Joe Maphis played lead and James played rhythm. After this, Burton took over from Maphis and played on every record until 1967. *Believe What You Say* was his Nelson debut as lead guitar.

James's unique right-hand style utilises a straight pick and his middle finger. Significantly, for the Nelson records James

replaced his first four strings with banjo strings and moved the A and D strings up to D and E. This facilitated expressive string bends and his legendary chickin' pickin' was born. He later gauged his strings: .009, .010, .012, .024, .032 and .038.

In 1968 James got the call from Elvis Presley to be on his Comeback television special, but at the time he was working with Frank Sinatra and had to decline. James was delighted, however, to hear how Elvis watched the Ozzie and Harriet show just to see him play.

When Elvis called James again in 1969 to play his Las Vegas engagement, it was a very tough decision for Burton, since his studio career was very busy and very lucrative. Burton had already turned down an offer from Bob Dylan. However, the King was very persuasive and James took the gig.

In August the same year James got the call from Fender, telling him they had a guitar especially for him. On seeing the flamboyant paisley guitar James was at first a little hesitant – he thought it too bright. But the band pushed him and Elvis loved it. Burton would remain with Elvis until his death in 1977. The paisley Tele was his main instrument until late 1989, when after five years of co-development Fender issued his signature 'flame' model.

Burton has since performed thousands of guest sessions, including work for Emmylou Harris, Joni Mitchell and Rodney Crowell. He also toured with John Denver for 15 years.

In 2001 James was inducted into the 'Rock and Roll Hall of Fame' by Keith Richards. The Rolling Stones guitarist and long-time Burton fan remarked: 'I never bought a Ricky Nelson album, *I bought a James Burton album*!'

Friday 7 November 2008, Pacific Road, Merseyside

I met James in 2008 as a fellow performer at The International Guitar Festival Of Great Britain. He was 'the cool dude at the circus'. At the soundcheck, whilst all and sundry fussed about with the PA and tweaked the lights, James quietly practised his scales – lost in music.

The famous 'flame' guitar sat on his hip like it belonged, its Strat-like tones the perfect match for his two Fender twins and a Boss stereo chorus. At the ensuing gig he was restrained and tasteful, using dynamics as only a true musician would. A very cool, sophisticated player, subtly laid back and leaving lots of space. *Mystery Train* was his only solo – no pyrotechnics, just a great groove, flashy only when it didn't detract from the song. I could see why Presley gave him the call. 'You must come to Louisiana!' he said. I may just do that.

Roy Buchanan

'The Messiah'

'Nancy' – a 1953 Telecaster serial no 2324

Leroy Buchanan was born Ozark, Arkansas, on 23 September 1939 and was brought up there and in Pixley, California, a farming area near Bakersfield. His father Bill was a sharecropper in Arkansas and a farm labourer in California.

Roy's first musical influence seems to have been hearing local black Gospel singers, and given Roy's later fluid legato style, his first instrument, at age nine, was significantly a Rickenbacker Lap Steel. He had three years of lessons but disregarded all musical notation and picked everything up by ear.

'If I can't *feel* the music, I can't play,' he said. 'My teacher Mrs Presher was really into that. She would say, "Roy, if you don't play with feeling, don't play it at all."'

Starting Spanish guitar on a Gibson acoustic, he soon heard the Telecasters of Buck Owens and traded up to what would became his signature guitar.

Roy's pro career starts around 1957, when he played in The Dale Hawkins band and provided guitar work for rockabilly and blues records on the Checker label (a subsidiary of Chess). In 1958 he made his recording debut, still with Hawkins.

With his lap steel background Roy would often bend strings to the required pitch, rather than starting on the desired note. He could play sweet blues or authentic country, making the guitar 'cry' by striking a note, bending it, and swelling the volume knob with the little finger of his right hand. Using his little finger on the volume control and his ring finger on the tone control would give him a wah-wah effect. He often used hybrid picking, a mix of plectrum and right-hand fingers.

> **Probably the reason I never made it big is because I never cared whether I made it big or not. All I wanted to do was learn to play the guitar for myself … You'll feel it in your heart, whether you've succeeded or not.**
>
> *Roy Buchanan*

Holding his thumb at a certain angle, he was able to hit the string and then partially mute it, suppressing lower overtones and exposing the harmonics, a technique that has become known as 'pinch harmonics'.

His favourite amp was a Fender Vibrolux, often pointed toward the back of the stage – he felt that turning the amp backward softened his sound for a small room. Late in his career he used his only stomp box, a Boss DD-2 Delay Pedal. Curiously he used lemon Pledge on the neck and strings of his guitar for lubrication!

The 'sound' of Roy Buchanan is essentially the '53 Telecaster straight into an overdriven Fender amp wound up to ten, though he also used some '54 and '55 Teles and a Goldtop Les Paul.

British guitar legend Jeff Beck dedicated his performance of *Cause We've Ended As Lovers* on his 1975 landmark album *Blow by Blow* to Buchanan.

Roy died in jail on 14/15 August 1988. He may have taken his own life.

Chrissie Hynde

'Rhythm with attitude'

'Blackguard' Tele

Seen over the years with a range of Telecasters old and new, Chrissie epitomises the guitarist who just needs something loud and brash to stomp out a few well-placed chords and drive the song along. Whilst many female songwriters have chosen the sensuality of a Martin acoustic to gently caress, Chrissie has stood out as the woman with attitude, and like so many guys has discovered the Tele is the perfect tool for the job.

Chrissie Hynde was born Christine Ellen Hynde on 7 September 1951 in Akron, Ohio, and played in several bands before moving to London in 1973. With some training in art she landed a job in an architectural firm but left after eight months. It was then that she met rock journalist Nick Kent and eventually landed a writing position at *The New Musical Express*. However, when this didn't work out Chrissie found herself working at Malcolm McLaren and Vivienne Westwood's then unknown clothing store, SEX, from where she was unfortunately fired following a fight with a customer in which Hynde was hit with a bell! She moved to France and started a band before going back to Cleveland in 1975.

Returning to England in 1978 she formed The Pretenders, the band's name being inspired by The Platters' song *The Great Pretender*. Many hits followed, all punctuated by her own and fellow guitarist James Honeyman-Scott's stabbing, angular Teles.

In March 1981 she became the first woman to grace the cover of *Guitar World* with her metallic blue Tele.

'I don't know anything about guitars, really. A guitar is just a thing, a tool. I just know what I think sounds good. I don't have the talent or natural ability to be a great guitarist. I'm not trying to be self-effacing, it's just that I know myself, and I'm lazy. I never fiddle around trying to get a good sound, and I write songs around my style of playing and singing. I always use Telecasters because they feel so good.'

The trick is, of course, picking the *right* tool for the job. Personally I feel this wouldn't be a Tele book without her.

> I always use Telecasters because they feel so good. I'm just used to it. It's a guitar I picked up a long time ago and that's it.
>
> *Chrissie Hynde*

Steve Cropper

■

'Chopping the backbeat'

'63 Tele. Rosewood board.

Often seen with a classic '63 Telecaster with 'vintage' 12th fret dot markers spacing and a single-ply eight-hole pickguard. Before this Steve had a Blonde '59 Esquire given to him by the great Stax bass player Duck Dunn. This guitar is the one he used on his classic *Green Onions* and many other pre-1963 recordings. It's also the one used for *Minnie the Moocher* in the first *Blues Brothers* movie!

As well as being a great songwriter – he wrote *Midnight Hour* with Wilson Pickett, *Sittin' On the Dock of the Bay* with Otis Redding, and *Knock On Wood* with Eddie Floyd – Steve Cropper is the man that defined the Stax backbeat with a classic Tele rhythm sound.

If you need to cut through a section of horns and a mighty Hammond with a driving offbeat the Tele is the perfect guitar and Steve Cropper was the first to really show this side of this most versatile instrument. Listen to any of the Stax record hits and there he is, soaring through the mix with a precision that nails the 'pocket' or groove.

Born on 21 October 1941 on a farm near Dora, Missouri, Steve Cropper moved to Memphis at the age of nine. In Missouri he had been exposed to a wealth of country music. In Memphis he heard Gospel, R&B and the early rock'n'roll that blazed over the local black and white Memphis radio. Suitably inspired, he acquired his first mail-order Sears Robuck guitar at the age of 14 for $17.95.

After stints with local bands he was quickly recognised as a major talent and soon became the Stax company's A&R man, sharing engineering duties with the company CEO Jim Stewart. He was a founding member of Booker T. & the MGs, the Stax house band, with Booker T. Jones on organ and piano, bassist Dunn, and drummer Al Jackson Jr. Together they went on to record many hits, and as house guitarist Steve played on hundreds of other artists' records.

On his early recordings, such as *Green Onions* and *Hip-Hug-Her*, Cropper used an unusual Fender Harvard amp. This 'Tweed' 10W amp, only produced between 1956–61, had an 8in and later 10in speaker and 6ATX, 12AX7, 2 x 6V6 or 5Y3 tubes.

These days he plays a Fender 'Twin' live – usually the red-knob version. Steve finds they distort too much if you turn them up, and their volume and tone controls are totally different from those on other Fenders, but if you back the bass off and turn the treble up you get a really good clean sound.

> For recording I mostly use a Victoria Twin-style amp – although, on the new album, I got all the tones on the songs with vocals using an ART SGX2000 that Jon Tiven ran me through. It's clean, but it has a bit of an amp edge to it, along with a little more sustain. To get the crunchier tones on the two instrumentals I cranked up an old Peavey Classic 30.

Steve Cropper

For pedals he uses a Voodoo Lab Tremolo.

'I'm mainly just a clean rhythm Tele guy, and when I play a solo I usually just bear down and play a little grittier. I turn the volume and tone controls all the way up. I tend to favour the neck pickup on my main guitar, and I've always used a combination of both pickups on the others, going back to my Teles in the '60s. I almost never use the bridge pickup by itself.

'I've been using these laminated Gibson strings, gauged .010–.046, that never hit the market. In the old days I used Gibson nickel-plated Sonomatics, and I don't think they even listed the gauges. The sixth string had to be at least a .050 something – it was monstrous!

'I tuned to open E for Otis Redding. I did it for Otis because that's the way he played, and that's the way we wrote some of those songs. I had two Telecasters, one tuned to an E chord, and the other in standard tuning. *Old Man Trouble*, for example, is in open-E tuning.

'If you want magic, we've got to go back to the Otis Redding days, when it was live-to-mono with no overdubs. After a take, the guys couldn't wait to go into the control room to hear back what they just played. That was magic. Al Jackson would listen to the take and say, "Boys, all that needs is out."'

Albert Collins

'The Iceman'

Blonde '66. Maple neck.

Albert relied on two main Telecaster guitars, a '59 and a '61 modified with a Gibson PAF humbucker in the neck position. He is also seen with a Blonde maple-neck 1966 Telecaster, this also fitted with a Gibson humbucking pickup in the neck position.

Born in Leona Texas on 1 October 1932, Albert would come to epitomise a hard-driving 'Texas blues' style, though unmistakably he had his own voice: 'I always put the volume up to ten, treble on ten and the bass "off" with the reverb set to four.'

Albert was probably the first prominent player to realise that putting a humbucker on a Tele gave you the best of both worlds – the bite of a Fender bridge and the warm guts of a Gibson humbucker at the neck.

For amplification he favoured a '70s 100W Fender Quad Reverb with four 12in speakers, three 7025s, two 12AT7s, a 12AX7A and four 6L6GCs – a veritable monster designed, perhaps, to give Marshall something to chew on.

Albert would retune his .010, .013, .015, .026, .032 and .038 Fender strings into some strange tunings, usually the Fm triad on the open strings F, C, F, Ab, C, F (think open E minor up a semitone!). He also used a capo at the ninth, fifth or seventh fret which contributed to a distinctive high sound.

Before taking to the guitar he had been a serious keyboard player, which contributed to his unconventional style – in his approach to chords he was more like a Hammond organ player, using 'stabs' not strums!

He also played with his right-hand fingers, no picks.

Collins famously performed at 'Live Aid' at the JFK Stadium in 1985, playing *The Sky is Crying* and *Madison Blues* – significantly the only black blues artist to feature at this world-shattering music event.

The Fender Custom Shop have created an accurate replica of the 'Iceman's' '66 Custom Telecaster. This guitar features a double-bound swamp ash body and a custom-shaped maple neck sporting a separate laminated maple fingerboard with 21 vintage frets. It has a custom-wound Seymour Duncan '59 humbucker in the neck position and a Fender Texas Special Tele single-coil in the bridge.

Albert Died on 24 November 1993 but will be remembered every time someone really 'digs in' and makes a Tele 'sting'.

Keith Richards

'Hot Licks'

'54 Blonde 'Malcolm'

Keith Richards of The Rolling Stones has used Teles extensively throughout his career, usually rare 1950s guitars variously modified for his unconventional rhythm technique. The best known is 'Micawber', a 1953 'Blonde', named after the Charles Dickens character. Keith has used this guitar since the album *Exile On Main Street*.

As with many of Keith's guitars, 'Micawber' is kept in Open G tuning (G, D, G, B, D) low to high and has the famous five strings, with the sixth string absent, as do all his open G tuned guitars. The nut is spaced for five strings, but not conventionally spaced, allowing extra space for the top E which is further than usual from the fingerboard edge. The strings are .011, .015, .018, .030, .042. It has replacement tuners and a brass replacement bridge with five individual saddles. It also has a Gibson PAF humbucker in the neck position and an original Tele pickup in the bridge position.

This guitar is still used live on signature Rolling Stones songs such as *Brown Sugar* and *Honky Tonk Women*.

Other Keith Richards Teles include 'Malcolm', a 1954 Fender Telecaster that usually has a Shub capo at the fourth fret and is used for *Tumbling Dice*, *Happy* and *Jumping Jack Flash*. 'Sonny' is a 1966 Telecaster Sunburst, and Keith also often uses a 1975 black Telecaster Custom. All are tuned in open G.

Keith has long been a fan of vintage Fender Twins, and though his guitar tech Pierre de Beauport encourages experiment the twins seem to come back like a bad penny! Famously Keith owns the twin serial number 00003, therefore possibly the third ever made – a *real* 'relic' with stories to tell.

In fact the very concept of Relic guitars may even be Keith's gift to the guitar world. It was apparently his request that new Fenders 'might be better if they were "played in"' that inspired Fender and others to produce the now production run 'rigour of the road' custom 'distressed' Relic and 'Road Worn' guitars.

> **Volume is the least important thing; it's tone that counts.**
>
> *Keith Richards*

Albert Lee

'Country Boy at Heart' and 'Mr Telecaster'

Unusual 'bound' Partscaster.

Albert was raised in Blackheath, London. His father was a musician, and Albert himself initially played piano, but he soon picked up on Buddy Holly and took up guitar in 1958. After borrowing a few guitars he ended up with a Victorian parlour guitar with a £3 10s Höfner pickup.

Obviously showing early promise his parents spent all their Christmas savings on a second-hand Höfner President, which he soon traded in for a Czechoslovakian Grazioso, similar to George Harrison's (this was the forerunner of the Futurama and another Fender lookalike). He really wanted Buddy Holly's Fender!

Albert left school at the age of 16, to work full-time as a guitarist. His first success came as the lead guitarist with Chris Farlowe and The Thunderbirds. He enjoyed playing their Stax material, but he really wanted to play country music. Consequently he left the band in 1968.

Founding Heads Hands & Feet, Lee became a 'guitar hero', playing his first Fender Telecaster at breakneck speed. Heads Hands & Feet became a very popular live band in the UK, making appearances on BBC 2's *Old Grey Whistle Test* and in Europe, where they appeared on the legendary German music programme *Beat-Club*.

Lee left for Los Angeles, California, in 1974 and joined the Crickets, who also included Sonny Curtis and Jerry Allison. The band cut three albums together including *A Long Way From Lubbock*. He also did lots of session work. In 1976 he was asked to join Emmylou Harris's Hot Band, replacing his hero James Burton.

Starting in 1978, Lee worked for five years with Eric Clapton, playing and singing for a live concert recording at the Budokan in Japan. He was also a regular player with the Everly Brothers for over 20 years and was responsible for their 1983 reunion concert, for which he was musical director.

In 1987 he fronted Hogan's Heroes, a band renowned for attracting celebrities to their gigs. Stars such as Eric Clapton, Tommy Emmanuel, Lonnie Donegan, Dave Edmunds, Marty Wilde, Willie Nelson, Nanci Griffith, Don Everly, Emmylou Harris and Rodney Crowell have jammed with the band at one time or another. Albert has played on several Rodney Crowell albums, which are definitely worth checking out.

In 2002 he was one of many guitar heroes who paid tribute at the 'Concert for George'. In the same year he received a

> ‘Albert Lee is the greatest guitarist in the world.
>
> *Eric Clapton*

Grammy for 'Best Country Instrumental Performance' for *Foggy Mountain Breakdown* on the CD *Earl Scruggs and Friends*.

He continues to work in the studio, and tours on a regular basis with Bill Wyman's Rhythm Kings.

He frequently mimics the sound of a pedal steel guitar with his Music Man and Telecaster guitars, which are often equipped with B-Benders. Despite his recent switch of allegiance Albert is still often referred to as 'Mr Telecaster' and owns a '52, a '53 and a 1960. For strings he uses Ernie Ball gauges 10p, 13p, 16p, 26w, 36w, 46w.

‘I'm still using my old HD 130 Music Man amps but have been very happy with a Fender Tone Master and a Rivera. Music Man amps were built like tanks – they're very loud and clean, and I also add a little compression using a Korg A-3.'

> ‘A brilliant guitar player. His sound is unmistakable, often emulated, never equalled
>
> *Emmylou Harris*

Andy Summers

'Classical Pop'

Heavily Modified '61 'Custom' Maple neck, three-colour sunburst

Andy's original Police Tele is a '61 acquired in 1972 for $200, from one of his students. This guitar had already been heavily modified. 'When I start to play it, something stirs within me ... it shakes me ... I find that I can't stop playing it. This guitar sparks something in me and I have to have it.'

Andy discovered early that the Tele's lack of a middle pickup provided the ideal picking area for a 'classical' guitarist, and he has made a signature sound out of his J.S. Bach-influenced arpeggio style, usually coupled to a phase/chorus effect and multiple delay.

The '61 Tele is a testament to the 1970s period of experimentation when players first started to ask about how the electric guitar worked and what else could be had from the very basic electronics built into standard '50s designs. Much of the electronics had already been changed and Andy simply installed the Schaller machines, as the Klusons were 'getting funky'.

Many hits were recorded and performed on the '61 – *Roxanne*, *So Lonely*, *Walking On the Moon*, *Message in a Bottle*, *Don't Stand So Close to Me*, *Every Little Thing She Does is Magic*, *Every Breath You Take*, *Wrapped Around Your Finger*, *Synchronicity II* and *King of Pain*.

Fender have recently issued a limited edition replica of this Tele, the 'Andy Summers Tribute', and the prototype, built by Fender Custom Shop Master Builder Dennis Galuszka, is currently in use by Andy. The guitar features the same 'eccentric' modifications as the original, most of which were in place throughout the Police years.

The guitar breaks down like this:

- A very hot (originally Gibson) humbucking neck pickup. In the reissue this is a Seymour Duncan SH-1N '59, a classic late '50s PAF type with plain enamel wire but with more scooped mid-response than a Seth Lover, and wax potted to avoid acoustic feedback.

- A Tele bridge pickup mounted in the body rather than in the broken brass bridge plate. The replica has a Fender Custom '63 Tele single-coil pickup (bridge). The through-body stringing employs a six-saddle brass bridge with a resonant crack in the pickup mounting hole – which pings at a definite pitch!

- The control plate has a mini-toggle phase switch that puts the bridge and neck in opposite phase, giving some fascinating tones, as per *Every Breath*.

- The guitar also has a body-mounted preamp with an on/off mini-toggle switch and a gain control mounted directly to the body. The original PP3 powered preamp died, and the Fender Custom Shop have recreated the Police-era electrics.

- The original has Schaller tuners and the replicas Fender/Gotoh Vintage Style.

- The body is two-piece select alder and the neck quarter-sawn maple with a traditional 7¼in radius and a tinted nitrocellulose lacquer finish.

- The strings are Fender Super 250R, nickel-plated steel, gauges .010, .013, .017, .026, .036, .046.

- The switching includes the conventional three-position blade alongside the two-position mini-toggle phase switch:
  Position 1: Bridge pickup.
  Position 2: Bridge and neck pickups.
  Position 3: Neck pickup.
There is also a body-mounted two-position mini-toggle preamp on/off switch.

Summers played number one of the 250 replicas when the Police once again electrified the music world by reuniting on 11 February 2007 to open the 49th annual Grammy Awards ceremony in Los Angeles. Summers also played the replica during the momentous 2007 30th anniversary worldwide Police reunion tour.

As already mentioned, Andy's unique style incorporates elements of his classical guitar background, especially the wide-ranging arpeggios and the artificial 'index finger right-hand' harmonics. His unique approach blends these with chopping upstrokes borrowed from Steve Cropper and full-on 'crunch' distortion typical of his musical roots in 1960s Britain.

Effects and amplification naturally play a big part in the Summers sound with very tasteful use of a compressor, chorus, and echo and flanger effects.

The Police 'sound' is also attributed to the use of a Maestro Echoplex tape-delay machine, which pre-dated digital delay for a warmer analogue sound.

Andy's original pedalboard was custom-made by effects guru Peter Cornish. He favoured an Electro Harmonix 'Electric Mistress' flanger, and an MXR 'Phase 90'. He played through the same effects both in the studio and on stage. This allowed him to duplicate his tone for a particular song anywhere. He used two Marshall JMP and Plexi amp heads and two 4 x 12 speaker cabinets, wired for stereo.

Jerry Donahue

Telecastin'

Telecaster Signature and Omniac guitars

I caught up with Jerry at the Cropredy Festival where we were both guests of legendary band Fairport Convention. For many musicians Jerry epitomises the Telecaster sound and he has even issued an album named after the guitar. However, it wasn't his first guitar:

'Well, it's really funny, it was not my first choice. Growing up I knew I wanted a Fender and being a fan of the Ventures, on *Walk Don't Run* the lead guitar player played a Jazzmaster, so that's what I wanted. I had to work hard, I was still in school – it was more expensive, top of the line. I loved the look of the Strat, but there was something really cool about the shape of the Jazzmaster, its sort of off-set shape and everything, and I thought "Well, I've got to have that!"

'What I got for Christmas instead was a Goya classical guitar … my parents said "If you show significant progress on this, next year we'll buy you the Fender." And I got it! – the Jazzmaster. My Dad also bought me the amp, a Fender Bandmaster, when they came out with the piggyback series. I do wish I still had it!

'Shortly after all that I moved to the UK and I quickly became a fan of the Shadows. I did an audition for Johnny Saville and the Clichés and I got the job. I was by far the youngest musician – I was 14. We worked in pubs but I passed for 17! That was as bass player on a Fender Precision.

'About three years later I started working in Selmers in Charing Cross Road and when it was quiet we used to take the

guitars down off the wall and doodle around on them. I was never really drawn to the shape of the Telecaster so I'd never really picked one up before, also it didn't have a tremolo. But when I heard the superior sound that you got in the bridge position neither the Jazzmaster or the Strat could touch it. The strength of the Strat is the combination of the neck pickup with the middle pickup or any combination of any of the pickups, but the weakness was the bridge pickup on its own. I mean most of the people that would use that pickup always engaged it with the middle in order to get that "quack" tone that everyone loved – and I still love, you know. Anyway, when I heard that bridge pickup on the Tele I thought "Man, I have to have one!"

'My first Tele would have been a '60s, but I soon managed to get hold of a '52. The body was very badly damaged and Dick Knight, a very famous luthier of the time, had all this birdseye maple. The neck I had was a birdseye, which was very rare at the time, and I had Dick make a body in the birdseye, and I still have that guitar. It's on a lot of records. I used it with Fotheringay and Sandy Denny.

'Because I'd been playing a Strat, one of the sounds I missed most was the neck pickup. I loved the Tele bridge pickup, and I liked the centre sound that the neck and the bridge got together, but the neck on its own was very limited. The time it was designed was in the late '40s, for release in 1950, during which time the two most popular sounds in America were jazz and country – rock'n'roll hadn't come out yet, so when the Telecaster was designed Leo was trying to appeal to the jazz player. So I got somebody to wind me some neck pickups in a Strat configuration, which meant routing out a little more of the Telecaster body to accommodate it.

'I think Jimmy Bryant used mostly the bridge pickup, he was very fast, a jazzy country – probably used the neck pickup as well. Leo was trying to appeal to session musicians and even bass players. Basically what he was trying to do was to get the mellow sound to emulate the fuller-bodied Gibsons. It was pretty successful and the guitar of its time – the bridge pickup for the country, the neck pickup for the jazz. But as music evolved and R&R came our tonal requirements became much broader, more demanding, and people favoured the Strat neck pickup because you could get a broader range of sounds. You could always pull back the tone control for the mellow jazz sound but when the tone was fully open you could get that nice bright majestic sound that Hendrix and Stevie Ray Vaughan used to get.

'I think the neck pickup on the Strat and the bridge pickup on the Tele are probably the most compatible sounds in terms of the way they complement one another. That's what Fender did for me, on the Jerry Donahue model. Usually, on a Strat, the neck and the middle sound great, but if you go to the bridge, unlike the Tele where attention was paid to the fact that there's very little string movement, and no harmonics – it's very thin and shrill – Leo just left all three pickups the same. But for the bridge pickup to sound good you have to build it up. A typical Strat pickup has a DC resistance between 5 and 6K and some of the early Teles were 7, 8K and even beyond that, and that's what made it sound so good. Plus you have that metal surround in the bridge, which mitigates the shrillness by having the pickups so close to the bridge [ie absorbing stray capacitance].'

An advocate of three-saddle 'vintage' bridges

'The thing about the three-saddle arrangement is *it sounds better*! Like every guitarist in the '70s I tried six saddles thinking that was the solution to intonation issues, but it isn't; but staying with the sound aspect, two strings pulling on a saddle naturally provides a better anchor, so that's part of the story, but also the old brass saddles are denser, heavier and also non-ferrous. A steel saddle is a backward step and single one per string saddles are just not anchored well enough to sustain.

'My switch to the Peavey Omniac guitar is about the constant quest for improvement. I wanted to make the pickup selector even more versatile and also improve the neck shape. Fender couldn't accommodate that quickly enough so I had to find an alternative.

'The Omniac is still a Tele-like guitar in many ways but offers three distinct improvements. Firstly position four on the five-way switch offers a real "humbucker on an L5" mellow sound which can be very useful. The neck is modelled on a brilliant '56 Mary Kaye Strat that I was lucky enough to borrow and this is anchored with five bolts, giving a more rigid neck join – good for sustain.'

(For more on three-saddle intonation see *Saddle up your Telecaster, page 37*.)

Amplification

Jerry's first amp was the Fender Bandmaster, but on coming to England in the early '60s he used AC 30s after seeing Hank Marvin. For the Fotheringay sessions he used Fender Super Reverb – a Blackface with a silver surround – a wonderful amp. He is currently (2008) using a Peavey Delta Blues equipped with *one* 15in speaker. Jerry likes the uniform phase of a single speaker over the 'drifting phase' effect of two trying to operate in tandem. The tweed Delta Blues has three 12AX7 preamp tubes and four EL84 power tubes.

Jeff Beck

'Shapes of Things'

'54 Esquire with '56 neck and heavily 'modified' ash body

Jeff Beck is now closely identified with the Fender Stratocaster and even has his own Signature guitar. However, his first serious pro instrument was the Telecaster. He had his own '59 rosewood board model in early band The Tridents, but lost that in Paris on a bill with The Beatles. He then leased another unusual red Tele from The Yardbirds following the departure of Eric Clapton, who had previously used the same guitar for their *Got To Hurry*.

Nobody ever seemed very happy with that guitar and Jeff coveted a maple-necked black guard Tele – 'the Classic early '50s type'.

Whilst touring with The Walker Brothers in April 1965 Jeff noticed John Mauss playing a battered Esquire and was smitten enough to pay £75 for it (you could get a '62 Strat for £60 in those days, so he was obviously keen).

When Jeff acquired the '54 Esquire it had already been body-contoured like a Strat, the rough hewn timber left bare, but retaining a white late '50s-type pickguard. Jeff wanted the early '50s vibe so fitted a black guard.

'Shapes of Things' – Vox sought the future in outlandish design – Jeff Beck saw the future in a '50s 'Relic'.

> **I thought it was the original one. It's spooky. Until I opened the lid it didn't really hit me. I thought "Oh, this is my original one back".**
>
> *Jeff Beck on seeing the*
> ***Custom Shop Tribute Esquire***

Seymour Duncan says: 'Jeff replaced the white guard with a black Esquire pickguard (no slot for rhythm pickup) with a five-hole pattern and two distinctive chips on the top edge and lower neck slot. Jeff liked the contrast and it looked like the Teles made just a year earlier. The '54 steel bridge saddles were completely rusted and were replaced with '52 Telecaster brass saddles from another Telecaster belonging to Jeff. The rhythm pickup cavity is routed for a neck pickup but was not drilled to hold one. The body is well worn with nicks and gouges and the nitrocellulose lacquer blonde finish has turned various shades of yellow and orange.

'Jeff could manipulate the volume and tone controls, giving it a wah-wah effect as in *Train Kept A Rollin'* or *Still I'm Sad*. The lever switch would give full treble in the bridge position, variable tone control in the centre and full bass in the front position. The bridge pickup has slightly staggered poles. The body was made in 1954 and the neck (the original was broken) was replaced with one made in 1955. The guitar weighs 5lb 10oz. This is a very light instrument and would weigh a little more if there were no cutaways or contours.'

Jeff settled into The Yardbirds very quickly and they were the perfect foil for his experimental 'no holds barred' approach to the guitar. For Jeff the blues was just a rootsy jumping off point to free-form 'rave ups' that heralded psychedelic rock and inspired everybody from The Beatles to Jimi Hendrix. Jeff's groundbreaking *Shapes of Things* established a new road for the guitar. The long sustained 'edge of feedback' guitar sounds we now take for granted were pioneered by Jeff Beck in 1966.

His amplification also evolved, from the ubiquitous '60s AC 30s to Marshalls with 4X12s and a Tone Bender Fuzz Box – all the better to imitate sitars for many of The Yardbirds' wild pop experiments. According to Jeff the Esquire featured on *Shapes*, *Over Under Sideways Down* and *I'm a Man*. By the time The Yardbirds recorded the band's eponymous album nicknamed 'Roger The Engineer' Jeff had also acquired the guitar inspired by his first hero, Les Paul. But a Fender was never far away and he is seen with one on the cover of pioneering magazine *Beat Instrumental* as late as 1967.

In 1974 Jeff finally gave this guitar as a gift to pickup designer Seymour Duncan, who wisely preserved the instrument as found. The guitar is an invaluable relic of rock archaeology – perhaps the first true 'rock' guitar?

In its honour Fender recently decided that it would build a total of just 150 Limited Edition replicas. With the original as a model, every single nick, scratch, stain, and cigarette burn has been duplicated down to the smallest detail, and the end result is an affordable piece of history that Jeff is happy to be seen with.

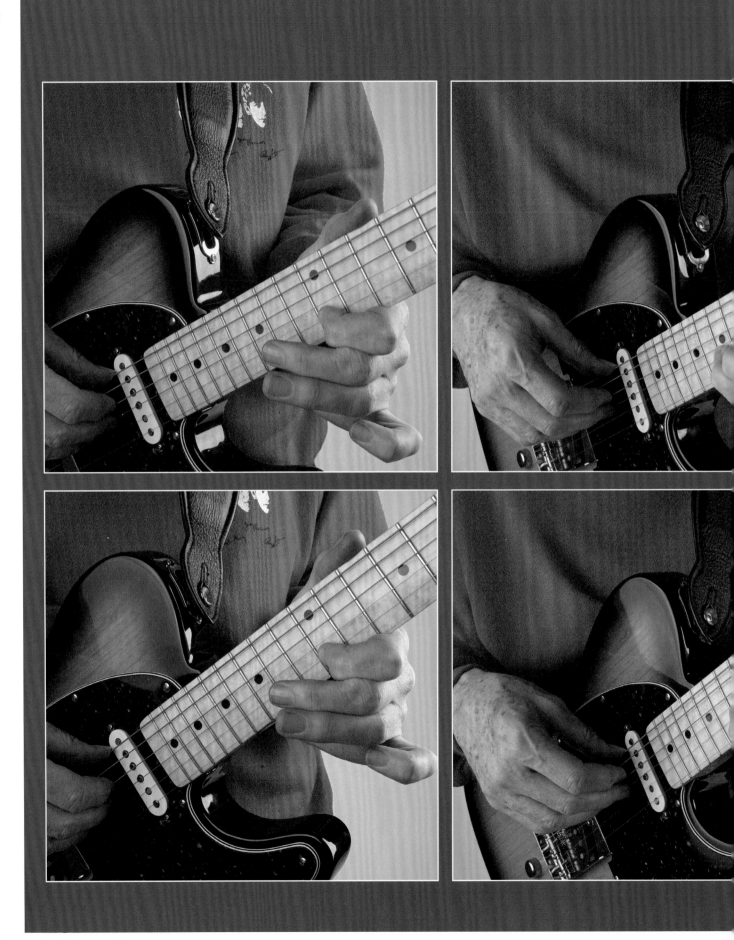

Appendices, glossary and contacts

LEFT B-Bending delight.

RIGHT Avril Lavigne Squier.

B-Bender

For more information about the B-Bender, instructional videos, tech tips, new and classic recordings featuring String Benders, workshops and other events, visit www.stringbender.com, or contact:

Stringbender Inc
44201 Caspar Orchard Road Box 76
Caspar, California 95420, USA
Tel 707-964-9538; *Fax* 707-961-1187;
email info@stringbender.com

If you are still unable to discover the cause of a problem or manifest the cure, contact Gene Parsons via email or call him at the StringBender Custom Shop on 707-964-8146.

Bridge pickup base plate functions
(Courtesy of pickup designer Bill Lawrence)

As well as serving as the ground for the bridge pickup, this base plate has three different functions:

A. Ferromagnetic functions
B. Electro-dynamic functions
C. All metal plates provide extra shielding

Only steel base plates correspond to functions A, B, and C. Brass, copper and aluminium base plates have no ferromagnetic functions, and therefore only correspond to functions B and C. Alloys of the 300 series stainless steels have neither ferromagnetic nor electro-dynamic functions and therefore only correspond to function C.

Function A
Leo Fender used copper-plated steel base plates on the Tele bridge pickup, to stabilise and to increase the magnetic force of the relatively weaker Alnico III slugs. The ferromagnetic steel plate increases the inductance of the coil (like increasing the number of turns on the coil).

The steel base plate also transmits into the pickup some of the body vibrations from the steel bridge mount, via the steel mounting screws, resulting in that typical Tele twang. As a negative, this is also the cause of microphonic squealing at high volume levels.

Function B
Base plates made of steel, copper, brass or aluminium are the cause of eddy current interference. Eddy currents shift the resonances toward the lows, resulting in a fatter, more pleasant tone, especially in the bridge position. If you don't want to increase the inductance of the coil and the magnetic force of the magnets, aluminium and brass base plates are ideal to fine-tune the tone of single-coil pickups.

These base plates can be very effective on traditional single-coil pickups with alnico slugs, but on many different designs the result can be disastrous.

Also, the thickness of the base plate is very important – if it's too thin the effect is minimal, but if it's too thick you may end up with a muddy pickup. For excellent results, keep the thickness of the plate between $\frac{1}{32}$in and $\frac{1}{16}$in and make sure that the plate is firmly attached to the pickup.

In addition the iron back plate of a traditional Tele pickup functions as a 'keeper' which increases the stability of the magnets.

Appendix 3

Comparative pickup outputs on the case study guitars

Reference '0' level = −18dB. Pots flat out. No EQ.

NB: The three-position switch does different things on different guitars. The Avril Lavigne has one humbucker pickup but series parallel switching. The Esquire has complex EQ switching (see case study).

Three-way switch	Bridge	Middle	Neck
'56–'57 Esquire	−16dB	−20db	−26dB
Relic Nocaster	−18dB	−22db	−30dB
			(less transient)
Rosewood Tele	−16dB	−20dB	−20dB
Japanese Bigsby	−16dB	−18dB	−20dB
Thinline Partscaster	−14dB	−18dB	−18dB
Avril Lavigne	−16dB	−14dB	−14dB
Vibe '50s	−16dB	−18dB	−20dB
(standard pickups)			
Jerry Donahue	−16dB	−16dB	−16dB
(consistent in five-way options as well)			
Custom Shop B-Bender	−16dB	−18dB	−18db
American Standard	−16dB	−20dB	−20dB
James Burton	−18db all five positions		
Affinity Squier	−20dB	−20dB	−20dB
Deluxe	−14dB	−14dB	−14dB
Left-handed Thinline	−14dB	−14dB	−14dB
Parsons/Green Tele	−14 dB all settings of five-way except −16dB 'middle' position (bridge and neck pickup)		

Subjectives

The Jerry Donahue sounds like a 'super Tele' and has some Strat-like tones in the five-way position options. All the five-way options are even, which is very useful.

The Clarence White sounds very like a Strat in the neck pickup position.

The James Burton sounds 'Super Strat'-like.

The 'Delta Tone' option on the American Standard is brasher but not louder.

The Vibe '50s with its original factory pickups stands up very well next to the Nocaster – just a little less 'spit' and character in the voice.

The two Seth Lover Fender 'Wide Range' humbucker guitars still retain a Fender tone quality despite the humbuckers.

The Parsons/Green American Nashville B-Bender has a Texas Special Strat pickup in the middle position, with all the expected 'quirky phase' tones when combined with the Tele pickups.

Appendix 4

Tempered tuning

Equal temperament is the name given to a system of dividing the chromatic scale into 12 exactly equal half-steps. This is a compromise but does allow us to play reasonably in tune in all keys and to modulate between keys during a performance.

Guitarists must learn to understand and accept equal temperament. You might be interested to know that to approximate 'pure' chords in all forms would require about three dozen frets within the octave. The system of equal temperament reduces the required fret number to 12 – a workable compromise.

Many guitarists are frustrated at their attempts to tune the guitar to pure chords (free of perceived 'beats'). These players have very sensitive ears that prefer 'pure' intervals and reject the mandatory equal temperament. They tune their guitar beautifully pure on one chord only to discover that the next chord form is unacceptable. In too many instances they assume that there must be a flaw in the workmanship on the fingerboard. But the problem is not in the construction of the guitar. It is one of 'pure' or 'mean tone' tuning versus equal temperament.

A 'mean tone' fretted guitar would in fact only sound acceptably in tune in about three keys, so from the 18th century onwards we have learned to live with the compromise of 'equal temperament'. Prior to this period lutes and early guitars often had movable 'gut' frets which were 'tempered' to the key of the piece to be performed. This system works fine until the piece modulates into a different key. The modern North Indian sitar still retains movable frets and the player tempers his frets according to the raga he is about to perform. Indian music, however, never modulates.

As practical working guitarists we must accept the equal tempered compromise, because the guitar is an instrument of fixed pitch and the strings must be tuned to tempered intervals, not 'pure'.

Here is what all of this means to the guitarist:

You must not, at any time, use harmonic tones at the seventh fret as a point of reference (skilled piano tuners could use them because they know how many beats to introduce between fourth and fifth). Harmonic tones at the seventh fret are pure fifths, while in equal temperament each fifth must be lowered slightly. To tune by harmonics at the seventh fret (as occasionally ill-advised) will make the guitar sound entirely unacceptable on some chord forms.

On the other hand, all harmonics at the 12th and 5th frets, being one and two octaves above the open strings, are immediately useful as explained below. All octaves and unisons are pure on all instruments of fixed pitch. Therefore you may use harmonics at 12th and 5th as reference tones in the following tuning instructions.

Actually this discussion and the following suggestions are for those players who have been tuning to 'pure' intervals. When the steps have been followed correctly the guitar will be as perfectly tuned as it could be in the hands of a professional. Nevertheless, when you've finished your sensitive ear may notice that on each major chord form there is always one tone slightly high. If you start adjusting a particular string on a certain chord form, you only compound the problem because then the next chord form will be completely objectionable. Tune the guitar as instructed below and let it stand.

It's possible to help your ear accept equal temperament, since it's easier to face a problem if you're prepared in advance and expect it. If you're one of those people who's sensitive to 'pure' intervals, here is what you're going to notice on an absolutely perfectly tuned guitar in equal temperament. Play an open E major chord. Listen to G# on the third string and you'll most likely want to lower it very slightly. Don't do so – ignore it. Enjoy the overall beauty and resonance of the chord, just as pianists do.

That troublesome second string – play an open position A major chord. Listen to the C# on the second string and you may want to lower it slightly. Play a first position C chord and listen to the E on the first string and fourth string at two. These tones are slightly higher than your ear would like.

Now play an open position G chord. Listen to B on the second string. Yes, it would sound a little better if lowered ever so slightly. Why not try it? Slack off the second string a couple of vibrations and notice what a beautiful G chord results. Now play the C chord with that lowered second string, and you're going to dislike the rough C and E a lot more than before. Take the open B, second string, back up to equal temperament so that it will be equally acceptable on all forms. Learn to expect and accept the slight sharpness of the major third in each chord (and oppositely, the flatness of the minor third in each minor chord). Train your ear to accept tempered intervals and you'll be much happier with your guitar.

Procedure

Tuning the first and sixth strings: The E, open first string, must be in pure unison with the harmonic of the E, sixth string at the

Another option is to use a Peterson 'Stroke' tuner in 'sweetened' mode.

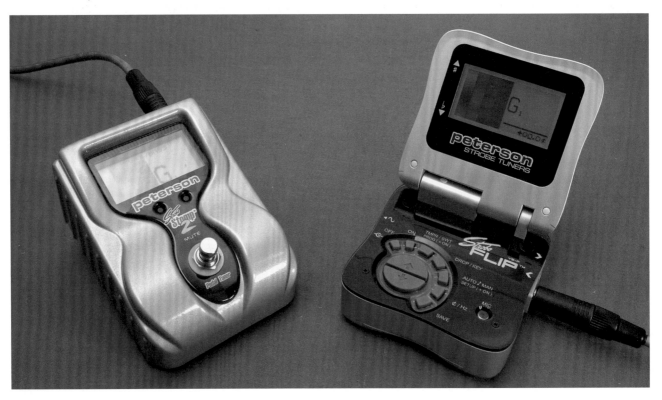

fifth fret. When these two strings have been properly tuned with each other, continue as follows.

Tuning the fourth string: Play a harmonic on the (in tune) sixth string at 12, and as this harmonic sounds, adjust the fourth string until the tone E on the second fret is in pure unison. Now you have the E, open first string, first on the fourth string at two, and E, open sixth string tuned pure (permissible because they're octaves).

Tuning the second string: Play a harmonic on the (in tune) fourth string at 12. As this sounds, adjust the second string until D at the third fret is in pure unison. As you've used two fretted tones for references and as the frets are positioned for tempered intervals, you now have the open first, second, fourth and sixth strings, in tempered tuning.

Tuning the third string: As it's easier to adjust a string while listening to a continuous reference tone, you may first try the following. Play a harmonic on the (in tune) fourth string at 12, and as this sounds adjust the third string until D at the seventh fret is in pure unison.

Double check: Now make this check to see if you've been accurate or if the instrument plays tune when fretted at seven. Play a harmonic on the (now tuned) G string at 12, and as this tone sounds play G on the first string at three. The two tones should be in pure unison. If they aren't, either you're at fault or the instrument doesn't fret tune at seven. Go back to the beginning and carefully check each step up to this point. If the tones are still faulty, then readjust the third string until the harmonic at 12 is in unison with the first at three. Do not tamper with the first and fourth strings because it's the third string you're trying to bring in tune. When you have the first, sixth, fourth, second and third strings in tune, in that order, continue with the remaining fifth string.

Tuning the fifth string: Play the tone A on the (in tune) third string, at the second fret. Listen to this pitch carefully and now adjust the fifth string until the harmonic at 12 is in pure unison. When the foregoing steps are followed correctly the strings will be tuned perfectly to equal temperament. No further tuning adjustments are permissible.

This is an edited version of The Guild of American Luthiers' data sheet 45. The Guild is a non-profit making organisation formed in 1972 to promote the art of the stringed instrument maker. This is done through its quarterly journal *American Luthiers*, conventions and exhibitions, and its data sheets, one of which you've just read. The Guild is an information-sharing organisation, and membership is not restricted to practising instrument makers. For more information on Guild publications, membership and activities write to:

The Guild of American Luthiers
8222 South Park Avenue, Tacoma, WA 98408, USA
Tel 206-472-7853

Just and equal tempered scales

	Ratio to just scale	Ratio to fundamental equal temperament
Unison	1.0000	1.0000
Minor second	25/24 = 1.0417	1.05946
Major second	9/8 = 1.1250	1.12246
Minor third	6/5 = 1.2000	1.18921
Major third	5/4 = 1.2500	1.25992
Fourth	4/3 = 1.3333	1.33483
Diminished fifth	45/32 = 1.4063	1.41421
Fifth	3/2 = 1.5000	1.49831
Minor sixth	8/5 = 1.6000	1.58740
Major sixth	5/3 = 1.6667	1.68179
Minor seventh	9/5 = 1.8000	1.78180
Major seventh	15/8 = 1.8750	1.88775
Octave	2.0000	2.0000

You will notice that the most 'pleasing' musical intervals above are those which have a frequency ratio of relatively small integers. Some authors give slightly different ratios for some of these intervals, and the 'just' scale actually defines more notes than we usually use. For example, the 'augmented fourth' and 'diminished fifth', which are assumed to be the same in the table, are actually not the same.

The set of 12 notes above (plus all notes related by octaves) form the chromatic scale. The pentatonic (five-note) scales are formed using a subset of five of these notes. The common Western scales include seven of these notes, and chords are formed using combinations of these notes.

As an example, the chart below shows the frequencies of the notes (in Hz) for C Major, starting on middle C (C4), for just and equal temperament. For the purposes of this chart it is assumed that C4 = 261.63Hz is used for both (this gives A4 = 440Hz for the equal tempered scale).

Note	Just scale	Equal temperament	Difference
C4	261.63	261.63	0
C4#	272.54	277.18	+4.64
D4	294.33	293.66	-0.67
E4b	313.96	311.13	-2.84
E4	327.03	329.63	+2.60
F4	348.83	349.23	+0.40
F4#	367.92	369.99	+2.07
G4	392.44	392.00	-0.44
A4b	418.60	415.30	-3.30
A4	436.05	440.00	+3.94
B4b	470.93	466.16	-4.77
B4	490.55	493.88	+3.33
C5	523.25	523.25	0

Since your ear can easily hear a difference of less than 1Hz for sustained notes, differences of several Hz can be quite significant!

■ **Appendix 5**
Potentiometer codes

The numbers found on many potentiometers can provide useful clues when dating guitars. However, they are not infallible, as fakers use old pots derived from radios etc – so beware!

Pot codes have the following configurations: MMMYWW or MMMYYWW. The first three digits indicate the maker of the pot. Among the most common are the following:

Code	Maker
106	Allen-Bradley Corporation
134	Centralab
137	CTS (Chicago Telephone Supply)
140	Clarostat
220	Jensen
304	Stackpole
328	Utah/Oxford
381	Bourns Networks
465	Oxford

The fourth digit in a six-digit code corresponds to the last digit of the year of manufacture. Pot makers used a six-digit code prior to 1961 and a seven-digit code from 1961 onwards. Some other companies, however, continued with a six-digit code.

The fourth and fifth digits in a seven-digit code correspond to the last two digits of the year of manufacture.

The final two digits in a six-digit code or a seven-digit code correspond to the week of the year in which the pot was made. Note: A series of numbers greater than 53 cannot be a week dating code as it would be longer than the weeks in a year.

■ **Appendix 6**
Capacitors

A basic rule for tone capacitors is that the bigger the capacitor, the darker the tone. Depending on the cap's value (capacitance) the effect can reach from 'slightly warmer', to a 'woman tone', and all the way to 'completely dark and clinically dead'. Remember, the tone cap is always part of the guitar circuit and it even influences the tone when the tone pot is fully opened.

As a basic rule you can say that every cap with a voltage rating of 0.5V or higher will work inside a passive electric guitar, with higher voltage ratings resulting in larger caps. The reason for the high-voltage tone caps that you find in guitars is easy to explain. A lot of popular caps, like the Sprague 'Orange Drops', are for tube amps with inside voltage of 600V or higher. Nevertheless, the caps sound great inside a guitar, but an 'Orange Drop' cap with a 10V rating would also sound great. A cap with a higher voltage rating does not sound different from the same cap with a lower voltage rating.

In the 'golden days' of electrical guitars, Fender and Gibson used tone caps with a very high capacitance (0.1uf/0.05uF and 0.047uF/0.022uF, depending upon the time period). The 0.022uF value is still the standard today. If you need very dark and bassy tones, this value may work for you. For most of us, however, this value is much too large and the effect is more or less useless, resulting in the aforementioned problem of the effect only taking place between ten and eight. The solution to the problem is simply a tone cap with a much smaller value. This little change will enhance the usability of your tone control dramatically, giving you a good evenness among the complete taper of the tone control without any hotspots, and every movement of the pot will result in a change of tone.

To find the perfect value for you, I suggest getting a piece of cardboard, two 10in pieces of wire, two solderable alligator clips and some cheap standard ceramic caps. The cheapest caps from a local electronic store are good enough for this, and the voltage rating is completely unimportant. Get values from 1200pF to .1uF, plus every value in between you'd like to try. One piece of each value is enough. Glue the caps side by side on a piece of cardboard, with the legs reaching over the edges.

Don't forget to note the value of each cap on the cardboard! Then solder the alligator clips to the wires (one clip per wire, soldered to one end of the wire).

Now open your guitar and de-solder and remove the existing tone cap. Solder the end of the wires opposite to the alligator clips to the points where the original tone cap was connected and close your guitar, leaving the wires hanging out. Now you can change the different caps within seconds by simply connecting with the alligator clips. Play your guitar and use the tone control to see which value works best.

Hopefully you'll be able to determine through this method what your favourite cap value is.

Try 2200pF, 3300pF, 4700pF and 6800pF and listen to how they interact with the tone and taper of the pot. Chances are good that you'll like them!

(Source: 'Auditioning tone capacitors' by Dirk Wacker, *Premier Guitar* magazine, at www.premierguitar.com/Magazine/Issue/2008/Mar/Auditioning_Tone_Capacitors.aspx)

■ Appendix 7
Plectrums

The ancient plectrum has been made from feather quills, turtle shell, ivory and wood. These days more eco-friendly options include diverse plastics, stone (hematite) and various metals. A clever hybrid plectrum combines the rhythm-friendly pliability of polygel with more rigid solo-friendly hard plastics.

Different plectrums work for different tunes so it's worth experimenting and keeping a range available – especially when recording. Bear in mind your choice of string gauges, since a lighter string usually responds better to a lighter pick, heavy picks work well with heavy acoustic strings, and so on.

■ Appendix 8
Neck profiles

The letters V, C and U are used to describe the shape and contour of the back of the neck of Fender guitars. Necks described by these letters will correspond approximately to the shape of the corresponding letter of the alphabet.

The V-shaped necks come in 'soft' (fig 2) and 'hard' (fig 4) forms. The 'soft' V shape is a bit rounded off, whereas the 'hard' V is more acute.

The letter C is used to describe two neck shapes which do not have corresponding alphabetic letters – these are the 'oval' (fig 3) and the 'flat oval' (fig 5).

The U shape is usually clubby and rounded, with high shoulders (fig 1).

All this makes perfect sense when you put your hands on the various necks and get the feel of them.

There is sometimes confusion about the use of the letters V, C and U to describe neck shapes and the use of the letters A, B, C and D between the '60s and '70s to describe Fender neck widths at the nut. These letters stamped on the butt end of the neck had no relevance to the shape or contour – they are references to nut widths. An A neck was $1\frac{1}{2}$in at the nut; B was $1\frac{5}{8}$in; C was $1\frac{3}{4}$in; and D was $1\frac{7}{8}$in.

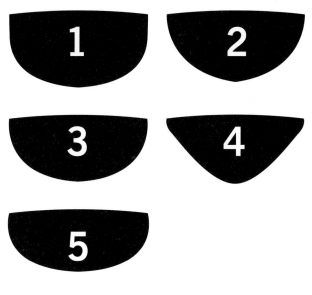

■ Appendix 9
Serial numbers

Other extremely useful serial number and corroborating dating information is available from two sources ; Werners List (elderley instruments) and 'The Blackguard' by Nacho Baños. The latter is an astonishing work documenting 33 early Blackguards in forensic detail – don't buy an early Tele, Broadcaster, or Esquire, before checking these!

Odd serial numbers

AMXN + 6 DIGITS
California Series electric guitars '97 and '98

DN + 6 DIGITS
American Deluxe series instruments, '98 and '99

FN(XXXXX)
US made guitars and basses destined for the export market. Some may have stayed in the US or found their way back.

I(XXXXXXX)
A limited number of these 'I' series guitars were made in '89 and '90. They were made for the export market and have Made in USA stamped on the heel of the neck

CN(XXXXXX), VN(XXXXXX)
Korean made Fender/Squier guitars (dating unclear)

SE(XXXXXX), SN(XXXXXX), SZ(XXXXX)
Signature Series Instruments
1988	SE8(XXXXX)
1989	SE9(XXXXX)
1990	SN0(XXXXX)
1991	SN1(XXXXX)
1992	SN2(XXXXX) etc
2000	SZ0(XXXXX)
2001	SZ1(XXXXX)
2002	SZ2(XXXXX) etc

T(XXXXXX)
Tribute series instruments

C(XXXXXX)
Collectors Series

NB: As you can see neck dates are very important and a tally between these and the serial number is a good cross check. Neck dates are usually stamped or inked on the heel of the neck.

Please see Fender's own excellent website for more on serial numbers.

Year	Serial number
1950 to 1954	Up to 6000
1954 to 1956	Up to 10,000
1955 to 1956	10,000s
1957	10,000s to 20,000s
1958	20,000s to 30,000s
1959	30,000s to 40,000s
1960	40,000s to 50,000s
1961	50,000s to 70,000s
1962	60,000s to 90,000s
1963	80,000s to 90,000s
1963	90,000s up to L10,000s
1963	L10,000s up to L20,000s
1964	L20,000s up to L50,000s
1965	L50,000s up to L90,000s
1965	100,000s
1966 to 1967	100,000s to 200,000s
1968	200,000s
1969 to 1970	200,000s to 300,000s
1971 to 1972	300,000s
1973	300,000s to 500,000s
1974 to 1975	400,000s to 500,000s
1976	500,000s to 700,000s
	76 + 5 DIGITS
	S6 + 5 DIGITS
1977	S7 + 5 DIGITS
	S8 + 5 DIGITS
1978	S7 + 5 DIGITS
	S8 + 5 DIGITS
	S9 + 5 DIGITS
1979	S9 + 5 DIGITS
	E0 + 5 DIGITS
1980	S9 + 5 DIGITS
	E0 + 5 DIGITS
	E1 + 5 DIGITS
1981	S9 + 5 DIGITS
	E0 + 5 DIGITS
	E1 + 5 DIGITS
1982*	E1 + 5 DIGITS
	E2 + 5 DIGITS
	E3 + 5 DIGITS
	V + 4, 5 or 6 DIGITS
	(US Vintage Series
	except '52 Telecaster)
1983*	E2 + 5 DIGITS
	E3 + 5 DIGITS
	V + 4, 5 or 6 DIGITS
1984*	E3 + 5 DIGITS
	E4 + 5 DIGITS
	V + 4, 5 or 6 DIGITS
1985*	E3 + 5 DIGITS
	E4 + 5 DIGITS
	V + 4, 5 or 6 DIGITS
1986*	V + 4, 5 or 6 DIGITS
1987*	E4 + 5 DIGITS
	V + 4, 5 or 6 DIGITS
1988*	E4 + 5 DIGITS
	E8 + 5 DIGITS
	V + 4, 5 or 6 DIGITS
1989*	E8 + 5 DIGITS
	E9 + 5 DIGITS
	V + 5 or 6 DIGITS

Year	Serial number
1990*	E9 + 5 DIGITS
	N9 + 5 DIGITS
	N0 + 5 DIGITS
	V + 5 or 6 DIGITS
1991	N0 + 5 DIGITS
	N1 + 5 or 6 DIGITS
	V + 5 or 6 DIGITS
1992	N1 + 5 or 6 DIGITS
	N2 + 5 or 6 DIGITS
	V + 5 or 6 DIGITS
1993	N2 + 5 or 6 DIGITS
	N3 + 5 or 6 DIGITS
	V + 5 or 6 DIGITS
1994	N3 + 5 or 6 DIGITS
	N4 + 5 or 6 DIGITS
	V + 5 or 6 DIGITS
1995	N4 + 5 or 6 DIGITS
	N5 + 5 or 6 DIGITS
	V + 5 or 6 DIGITS
1996	N5 + 5 or 6 DIGITS
	N6 + 5 or 6 DIGITS
	V + 5 or 6 DIGITS
1997	N6 + 6 or 6 DIGITS
	N7 + 5 or 6 DIGITS
	V + 5 or 6 DIGITS
1998	N7 + 5 or 6 DIGITS
	N8 + 5 or 6 DIGITS
	V + 5 or 6 DIGITS
	(American Vintage Series)
1999	N8 + 5 or 6 DIGITS
	N9 + 5 or 6 DIGITS
	V + 5 or 6 DIGITS
	(American Vintage Series)
2000	N9 + 5 or 6 DIGITS
	Z0 + 5 or 6 DIGITS
	DZ0 + 5 or 6 DIGITS
	(Am. Deluxe)
	V + 5 or 6 DIGITS
	(American Vintage Series)
2001	Z0 + 5 or 6 DIGITS
	Z1 + 5 or 6 DIGITS
	DZ1 + 5 or 6 DIGITS
	(Am. Deluxe)
	V + 5 or 6 DIGITS
	(American Vintage Series)
2002	Z1 + 5 or 6 DIGITS
	Z2 + 5 or 6 DIGITS
	DZ2 + 5 or 6 DIGITS
	(Am. Deluxe)
	V + 5 or 6 DIGITS
	(American Vintage Series)
2003	Z2 + 5 or 6 DIGITS
	Z3 + 5 or 6 DIGITS
	DZ3 + 5 or 6 DIGITS
	(American Deluxe Series)
	V + 5 or 6 DIGITS
	(American Vintage Series)
2004	Z3 + 5 or 6 DIGITS
	Z4 + 5 or 6 DIGITS
	DZ4 + 5 or 6 DIGITS
	(Am. Deluxe)
	V + 5 or 6 DIGITS
	(American Vintage Series)
	XN4 + 4 Digits
2005	Z4 + 5 or 6 DIGITS
	Z5 + 5 or 6 DIGITS
	DZ5 + 5 or 6 DIGITS

* For US Vintage Series, check neck date for specific year.

Glossary

'Ashtray' – Affectionate name for the original 1950s and '60s chrome bridge cover of a Fender Telecaster, Fender Stratocaster or Fender Precision. Often removed and lost.

Ball-end – Conventional type of guitar string securing fixture.

'Biasing' – Setting the idle current in the power output valves of an amplifier. A valve is 'biased' by setting the amount of DC current flowing through it when no signal is present at the valve's grid with respect to its cathode. Increasing the bias determines the power output and the amount of distortion.

Bigsby – A patented vibrato device developed by the late Paul Bigsby.

Bout – Curve in the side of a guitar's body – upper bout lower bout etc.

Capo – Abbreviation of 'Capodastro', originally a Spanish device. A clamp across the strings of a guitar, shortening the effective sounding length for musical transposition.

Closet Classic – A newly manufactured guitar mildly distressed to look as if it had been carefully stored away in a cupboard for several decades.

Dead spot – Spot in the machine head mechanism turn where no pitch-change is heard in the relevant string.

'Delta Tone' pots – Potentiometers that provide no resistive load in the détente position.

Earth loop (or ground loop) – A situation that arises when two pieces of equipment with earthed mains plugs are also connected by audio cables, effectively creating two paths to earth.

EQ – Equaliser.

Equal temperament – The name given to a system of dividing the chromatic scale into 12 exactly equal half-steps.

Feeler gauge – A gauge consisting of several thin blades, used to measure narrow spaces.

FX – audio effects devices.

Gotoh – Manufacturer of a bolt-on vintage-like machine head introduced in 1981.

Ground loop – See 'earth loop'.

Heat sink – A means of drawing heat away from areas adjacent to components that are being soldered, often achieved by the use of crocodile clips or similar.

Humbucker – Double-coil pickups wired in opposite phase and arranged in parallel or stacked to cancel induced low frequency hum.

Kluson – Type of machine head used on many early Telecasters.

'Nashville stringing' – Modification in which a banjo G string was substituted for a guitar's E first string, the E string subsequently used as a second string, the B string as its first unwound 'plain' third, the normal wound third as its fourth string, and so on.

N.O.S. – 'New old stock', a new guitar made as if of the model's original 'vintage' year of manufacture.

PA – Public address system.

Phase reversal – When the polarity of a DC circuit is reversed, often in the context of mixing polarities – *eg* one pickup 'in phase' the other 'reverse phase'. The ensuing phase cancellation produces interesting and unpredictable perceived equalisation effects, infinitely adjustable by volume control adjustment on the individual pickups.

Pots – Potentiometers.

Relic – New but convincingly 'worn-in' replica of a '50s or '60s classic guitar, with distressed body, rusty screws and faded pickups.

RF – Radio frequency.

'Road Worn' – A Telecaster distressed on the assembly line to a tolerable amount of wear and tear.

Schaller – Type of machine head used on some Telecasters.

Screen(ing) – Metallic shield around sensitive 'unbalanced' guitar circuits, connected to an earth potential to intercept and drain away interference.

Shimming – Adjusting the pitch of a Vintage Tele neck by inserting thin wooden shims or wedges in the neck cavity.

Wall warts – External DC power supplies.

Useful contacts

- Peter Cook's Guitars, Hanwell, London (www.petercooks.co.uk), a great source of classic guitars, amps and advice.
- Stewmac in the USA (stewmac.com), the world's best source of luthiers parts and tools.
- www.jawbonepress.com, for guitar books and music biographies.
- Draper tools, for all the general tools you'll need for guitar repair and maintenance.
- Dave Storey, Dava Company, 11521 Snowheights Blvd NE, Albuquerque, NM 87112, USA (www.davapick.com), for plectrums.
- wdmusic.co.uk, for guitar parts, including excellent Bakelite pickguards.
- Warmoth Guitar Products Inc, USA (www.warmoth.com, *tel* 253-845-0403), for Partscaster projects.
- Seymour Duncan Pickups (www.seymourduncan.com/ariauk.com).

Bibliography

Tony Bacon, *Six Decades of the Fender Telecaster* (Backbeat Books, 2005).
Nacho, Banos. *The Blackguard: A Detailed History of the Early Fender Telecaster, Years 1950–1954* (Nacho Banos, 2006).
Donald Brosnac, *Guitar Electronics for Musicians* (Omnibus Press, 1995).
A.R. Duchossoir, *The Fender Telecaster* (Hal Leonard, 1991).
Seymour Duncan, *Pickup Sourcebook* (Seymour Duncan, 2005).
Dan Erlewine, *The Guitar Player Repair Guide* (Backbeat Books, 2007).
Mo Foster, *17 Watts?* (Sanctuary, 1997).
Les Schatten, *The New Book of Standard Wiring Diagrams* (Schatten, 2008).
Richard R. Smith, *Fender – The Sound Heard Round the World* (Hal Leonard, 2003).
Jim Werner, *Werner's List* (Elderly Instruments, 1999). Useful source of dating information.

Acknowledgements

My thanks to:

The great luthier John Diggins (www.jaydeeguitars.com), who gives me the run of the workshop and puts right my errors!

Peter Cook's Guitar World, who made most of the guitars available, and particularly Paul White – who knows his guitars and makes a fine cup of tea – Richard Chong, Rob West, Rob Paddington West and Trevor Newman.

'The Keith Shrine' and 'Blue Lena' websites for Keith Richards info.

WD Music, the UK's largest online source of guitar parts.

Rob Rounds, sales manager of Warmoth Guitar Products Inc.

Wikipedia and PBS for Roy Buchanan quotes.

Gene Parsons, B-Bender inventor (www.stringbender.com), who was most generous.

Aria UK Ltd (www.ariauk.com, *tel* 01483 238720), for pickups and information.

www.myspace.com/seymourduncanuk.

Andy Summers's 2006 memoir, *One Train Later*, for information on his '61 Tele.

Guitar Player magazine for Chrissie Hynde quotes and info by Barry Cleveland on Steve Cropper.

Dirk Wacker and *Premier Guitar* magazine for information in Appendix 6.

www.iMuso.co.uk for supplying the Parsons/Green guitar.

Musik Produktiv UK Ltd, 34 Central Avenue, West Molesey, Surrey, KT8 2QZ (*tel* 0208 481 9610).

The Marty Stuart Fan Page (unofficial website) for original Clarence White guitar info.

www.riffinteractive.com and *17 Watts?* by Mo Foster (www.mofoster.com) – an invaluable source of information on early British Rock – for Albert Lee info.

Ric Sanders, 'fiddler extraordinaire', for arranging the Jerry Donahue interview, and Jerry Donahue for the interview and permission to include 'Saddle Up Your Telecaster' from his website at www.myspace.com/jerrydonahue.

Dave Storey, Dava Company, for great plectrums.

Russell North, Fender Great Britain & Ireland Marketing & AR.

Bruce Coyle, Fender GBI Service Co-ordinator, for much help and for ordering some *Haynes Stratocaster* manuals for the Fender workshop!

J K Lutherie

Ed Treat, Fender Consumer Relations, Fender Musical Instruments Corp, 8860 East Chaparral Road, Suite 100, Scottsdale, AZ 85250-2610, USA.

John Catlin for the left-handed 'Deluxe' and much enthusiasm and support.

Patrick Reed Music, Kettering, for the '56–'57 Esquire and a fine welcome!

Judy Caine for Music On Earth management.

Karl David Balmer for putting up with Daddy making a noise.

Brendan McCormack for 43 years of inspiration and endless patience. This book is dedicated to Brendan, pupil of Emilio Pujol and Barney Kessel and my unwavering mentor. I shall practice his Zen mantra as he did: 'As if you were to live forever'.

Stewmac.com for many specialist guitar tools, excellent advice and luthiery, especially Jay Hostetler, Jayme Arnett and Erick Coleman (Technical Adviser).

Basil Henriques for advice on Fender Champions and much more.

www.chanos-isgf.org/ESGForum.

Henry Froelich, Marketing Manager – Europe for Line 6 UK Ltd, 4 Sopwith Way, Drayton Fields Industrial Estates, NN11 8PB, Daventry.

Bill Lawrence, pickup designer, for bridge pickup base plate functions info in Appendix 2.

'The Vintage Guitar Gallery' for info in Appendix 5.

The Jeff Beck Fanzine for the Esquire information and Seymour Duncan quotes.

Richard Shatz for the photo of his Fender Champion steel guitars.

Credits

Author – Paul Balmer

Editor – Steve Rendle

Design – Richard Parsons and James Robertson

Copy editor – Ian Heath

Studio photography – John Colley

Technical macro photography – Paul Balmer

Library photos – Fender Musical Instruments Corporation, Getty Images, Helen Ashford, John Peden, Redfern Music Picture Library, Cache Agency

Photo research – Judy Caine

Index